Making Schools Better

MAKING SCHOOLS BETTER

How Parents and Teachers
Across the Country Are Taking
Action—And How You Can, Too

Larry Martz

INTRODUCTION BY ROBERT COLES

Library of Congress Cataloging-in-Publication Data

Martz, Larry.
  Making schools better : how parents and teachers across the country are taking action—and how you can, too / Larry Martz : introduction by Robert Coles. — 1st ed.
      p.   cm.
  Includes bibliographical references and index.
  ISBN 0-8129-1939-4
  1. Public schools—United States—Case studies. 2. Educational change—United States—Case studies. I. Title.
LA217.2.M37   1992
371'.01'0973—dc20   91-51018

BOOK DESIGN: MINA GREENSTEIN

Manufactured in the United States of America
9 8 7 6 5 4 3 2
First Edition

For Jenny-Anne and Geoffrey,
two prime learners and fine people;
with love and great pride

CONTENTS

AUTHOR'S NOTE

A book like this deals with hundreds of real people who live complex lives; it reports only small pieces of what they do, seen briefly by a writer with his own fish to fry. I have tried to be both accurate and fair, but I apologize in advance for the things I have got wrong and the nuances I have missed. These chapters have not been shown to my sources, who can't be blamed for any errors I have made.

Unless otherwise specified, I have seen all the scenes described in this book. I have changed some names to spare embarrassment, and I have said so each time a fictional name is introduced. In most cases, these are young people whose detailed problems are of legitimate interest, but whose privacy should be respected. I have used a tape recorder and a notepad interchangeably, and in quoting people I have smoothed out ragged bits of spoken conversation. Thus my quotations are not always literal transcriptions, but I have tried to retain the flavor of each person's speech and convey accurately the sense and substance of what was said. All the anecdotes and case histories are factual, with one exception: The story of "Clarissa" in chapter 5 is a composite, assembled from three separate cases that were in various stages during my visit to Moorhead High School. Apart from its compressed time frame, however, it is meant to be a realistic case study of how the program works.

INTRODUCTION
by Robert Coles

"Schools, those factories of despair." It was half a century ago that the
poet and physician William Carlos Williams wrote that line in his
novel *White Mule*, putting it in the mouth of a wise children's doctor
who was a stand-in for himself. But similar lamentations can still be
heard across America. A whole industry of cultural and educational
criticism portrays the schoolroom as a warehouse, a combat zone, a
place where the hearts, minds and souls of children are stifled or
destroyed.

That picture is not entirely wrong. Without question there are
schools galore, entire school systems, that have earned all the censure
they have received, and then some. Yet as I have talked with parents
and children of varying social and racial backgrounds across the country, I have often heard another side of the story. It is a point of view
given strong and eloquent support by this important book.

A few years ago, a black mother in Cambridge, Massachusetts, told
me, "I pray for our school"—and I braced for yet another searing litany
of woes, ranging from a decaying building in an unsafe neighborhood
to outdated textbooks, a misguided curriculum and uncaring teachers.
What I heard instead was quite another story: a mother's great, thankful

pleasure at what had been happening in the lives of her son, her two daughters and even herself. "I get down on my knees every morning and thank the good Lord for that school," she said. "It's the best place you could want for your kids." She gave credit mainly to the principal—a man who could preach better than a minister, who instilled confidence in the teachers and in the kids, and who told the children that their lives were their own to shape, for better or worse. "He's saying that if you're out to kill yourself, then no one can stop you," she said. "And if you're out to ruin yourself for life, and end up in some gutter or even lower than that, then all right, no one can stop you there, either. *But,* he says, *but*—if you want *life*—then that's another matter!"

What she had discovered was that one determined person can make a big difference in life, no matter the carelessness (or worse) of others. And her story kept coming to mind as I traveled through this book with Larry Martz, a wise, thoughtful observer and a clear and down-to-earth writer. Seeing through his eyes schools that work, I heard through his ears voices like hers and her children's.

As the reader will learn, to improve a school is not necessarily to give it more funds or a proud new curriculum. To be sure, many of our schools are hard pressed financially and in great need of intellectual energy. But the issue is not only bricks and mortar, or even the techniques that our educational theorists urge upon us. The critical issue for many of our children (and for the rest of us, too) is purpose. Beyond the factual information a child stores up and disgorges for a test, education must provide a sense of meaning—a conviction that what others are saying to us, asking of us, really matters in our lives.

"Making schools better" comes down to reaching deep within the community that is a school. It involves giving both the adults and the children in a building a sense of hope, a faith that the daily rhythms in their classrooms really will amount to something important—helping to shape life itself and make it better as well. Tremendous energy becomes available to young and old alike when such a vision is accepted. It is that "secret," known to so many parents in their hearts, that a school can use to become transformed.

In the schools we get to know in this book, it was *someone* who set things going, a person or a group of people whose hopes, worries and disappointments prompted a search for new and better ways of working with children—not only reaching them with facts and figures but touching them, inspiring them and giving them the vision of what could come of all this work. In many cases, as in that lucky mother's school in Cambridge, it was the principal who supplied the vision. In other schools, readers will see the energy coming from individual teachers, parents, even citizens unconnected with the schools. The result is an abiding conviction: This school, we who make it up, are headed someplace; and as a consequence, work that might have been meaningless or futile becomes profoundly worthwhile.

Among his vocations, William Carlos Williams was a school doctor for many years. Many of the children he saw would be described today as culturally deprived, and they agreed with him that the schools they attended were indeed "factories of despair." They told him so. But sometimes there were exceptions, and I recall the old Doctor Williams remembering them. "You'd find a teacher or a principal who'd figured out a way of getting to those kids," he told me, "and by God, they stopped and took notice. The next thing, they'd have some light in their eyes—and were inspired to work!" That's all very imprecise, indirect and suggestive, but I suspect it's also to the point of this book: that schools as institutions can make a turn for the better just as individuals can, often under difficult and adverse circumstances. For schools are, in the end, human beings assembled together day after day in a shared pursuit, and they can control their own destiny. So it ought to be, and so it can be. Here's the proof.

PREFACE

There's good news in this book: We *can* make our schools better for our kids. We don't have to wait for the President, the Department of Education or Congress to act. We don't have to stand by while "experts" in ivory towers squabble over cures for the epidemic of mediocrity that is sapping our children's minds and threatening our country's future. We can simply take action to make the schools better places for teaching kids. Not perfect, but better. Maybe a lot better.

But that puts the ball in your court: If there's something you can do, you ought to be doing it. Our children's future is at stake, and one of the many things we haven't taught them is that they have a terrible grievance against us. Not only have we burdened them with our debts, our toxic wastes and all of our social ills, but we are sending them off to deal with these problems without giving them the tools for the job. That's like throwing raw recruits into battle—and it puts our country at risk, too. If our people are decently educated, America can and will thrive. But if we go on with our academic child abuse, we will sink giggling in a sea of self-indulgence and reckless ignorance. The challenge to you is hardly new, but it grows more urgent with each day's news from the educational front. If you don't take it on, who do you think is going to volunteer?

There's no lack of ideas. The twelve programs in this book barely scratch the surface of the proven ways to make schools better. And you needn't be an expert or a genius to do it. Most of these programs were conceived and carried out by ordinary teachers, parents, principals and school board members—fine people, dedicated, a pleasure to meet and to know, but no smarter or better qualified than you or I.

Do you have something more important to do?

Making Schools Better

1.
Revolution in Small Bites

When nearly everybody agrees on something, it probably isn't so.

Nearly everybody agrees: It's going to take a revolution to fix America's public schools. George Bush, the self-proclaimed Education President, set the tone early in 1991 when he announced his "America 2000" program: "There will be no renaissance without revolution. For the sake of the future, of our children and our nation, we must transform America's schools. The days of the status quo are over." He got surprisingly little argument. From the great national think tanks to the neighborhood PTA, from corporate boardrooms to union halls, the call to the barricades is being trumpeted. Louis V. Gerstner Jr., head of RJR Nabisco and one of the business leaders in education reform, proclaims the Noah Principle: "No more prizes for predicting rain. Prizes only for building arks." Education Secretary Lamar Alexander agrees. So does Albert Shanker, head of the American Federation of Teachers. "Because the crisis is so great," says Marian Wright Edelman, founder and head of the Children's Defense Fund, "we don't have a lot more time for the small-scale, innovative and demonstration programs. We've got to change whole schools, and the whole school system."

But it isn't so; most of that is just rhetoric. In the first place, nobody really wants any revolution. Revolution brings terror, chaos, the unknown. Revolution would mean junking the whole present structure overnight and inventing a new one from scratch, in the giddy conviction that anything must be an improvement—no matter what it costs in terms of untaught kids, wrecked careers and doomed experiments. What these folks really want isn't revolution but major reform, changing the system radically but in an orderly fashion. The changes are supposed to be tested in large-scale pilot programs—Gerstner's "arks"—and then installed nationally. But even that is just a distant gleam in the eye, and a dubious proposition too. There's nothing like a consensus even on designing those arks, let alone where they are supposed to come to ground. And anyone who has watched radical reforms in the real world has to be wary of them: Invariably, they take a long time and cost a great deal, and even so they fail more often than they succeed. In organizations as in organisms, evolution works best a step at a time. The best and most natural changes come not in wholesale gulps, but in small bites.

What the big-think reformers fail to acknowledge is that schools all over the country are changing all the time. It's precisely those "small-scale, innovative and demonstration programs" that are doing the job, in literally thousands of schools. Some of these efforts are only partly successful; some fail; some work small miracles. The important thing is that local schools aren't waiting for a revolution, or for gurus to decree the new model classroom from sea to shining sea. They are working out their own problems and making their own schools better. And anyone—teachers, parents, principals, school board members— anyone who cares enough and works hard enough can do the same.

Americans love the big fix. We have a national impatience with slow tinkering of any kind. If there's something wrong with the carburetor, throw it away and get a new one; better yet, throw out the whole idea of a carburetor and invent the fuel injector. We crave magic bullets that will solve the whole problem, whatever it is, letting us dust our hands briskly and move on to the next subject. Education is a prime case in point.

Cynthia Parsons remembers the crusade for the New Math with

rueful good humor. A dedicated teacher and the longtime education editor of the *Christian Science Monitor,* she was one of those who toured the country with her pamphlets and Cuisenaire rods—little kits of colored sticks, designed to make such mathematical concepts as sets and fractions perfectly clear to everybody—trying to get across this revolutionary idea to the arithmetic teachers who were going to have to tell the kids about it. The New Math was a brilliant rethinking of the subject, an effort to start with fundamental concepts and teach by understanding rather than by rote. But somehow, she says, it always boiled down to one moment of bafflement, usually when she got to the problem of what is one-half of one-third.

"I'm standing there in some school in the Carolinas on a hot night," she says, "and I can hear it hit. These teachers start mumbling to each other. 'Half of a third? Well, "of" means "times," I know that. But do you multiply the numerator by the denominator, or straight across?' So I get out the little rods and try to show them that two sixths fit into one third. But I don't get through. They don't see that as anything to do with the problem." Too many teachers were stuck in the jargon and procedures they had learned by rote; they had never taken in the basic idea of manipulating fractions as parts of a whole, and they saw the New Math and the Cuisenaire rods as just another kind of mumbo jumbo that they would make the kids memorize, as soon as they learned the new terms themselves. For all practical purposes, the New Math was laid to rest in that Carolina classroom. Yet another magic bullet had ricocheted off the target.

So it has gone. Ever since *McGuffey's Reader,* our educational system has been a history of sweeping reforms, often followed fairly closely by counterreforms. Many of them, like tax-supported schools and the basic concept of universal public education, were good ideas that worked. Others—consolidated school districts, for instance—may well have done more harm than good. And some good ideas (the New Math among them) have gone aground because the system wasn't ready for them, or they weren't adequately thought out, or they needed too much time and money. But every reform has its passionate advocates. With this one stroke, they promise, all the children, like the kids in Garrison Keillor's mythical Lake Wobegon, are going to be above average. Somehow that never happens.

Even when major reforms are successful, as kindergartens and separate middle schools were, they aren't magic bullets that will solve every problem in sight. At most they are effective ammunition in an arsenal that still needs all the other elements of education: a good curriculum, adequate funding and above all dedicated and talented teachers and administrators. And all too often, when people get the reforms they want, the promised results simply don't show up. For decades, teachers have been saying they could be more effective in smaller classes; and sure enough, class sizes have been declining. Forty years ago there were twenty-eight students for every teacher. In 1988 the ratio was 17.6 to one. Is the teaching more effective? Similarly, open classrooms and the New Math have come and gone, leaving no miracles behind. Just ten years ago, computers were going to revolutionize education. Now there are 2.7 million of them in the nation's classrooms—more computers than teachers—and hardly anything seems to have changed.

This history of futility doesn't stop the quest for magic bullets. Many people think parental choice of schools could solve all the big problems. Others argue for empowering teachers by giving them a voice in educational decisions, or for a whole new kind of school that's more user-friendly for children. Some reformers argue that longer classes, or longer school years, would magically turn the system around. Others call for national minimum standards of what kids should know, with tests to measure it. There are radical solutions for particular problems: all-male classes taught by black men, for instance, to provide role models for inner-city boys. Some ideas never quite die. Even rote learning finds new respectability in the theories of behavior analysts. These psychologists argue that the entire educational establishment conspires, for ideological reasons, to ignore a true magic bullet that was uncovered more than a decade ago in the federal research project Follow Through. It found that a technique called "direct instruction" clearly proved more effective than any other method of teaching children. But since direct instruction at first sight resembles rote learning crossed with brainwashing, the fact that it works has been irrelevant.

At this writing, the trendiest idea in education is choice. From the liberal Brookings Institution to the conservative American Enterprise

Institute, the line is that all would be well if only parents could shop around for schools for their children. Then schools would have to compete for students, administrators would crack down on incompetent teachers, and parents could have more or less "structure" or "creativity" in the curriculum, depending on their view of what their children need. At the logical extreme of the choice proposals, parents would be given vouchers representing the public money available to be spent on their child, and would pass the vouchers on to the school of their choice—public or private—to be cashed in for real money. The general level of schooling would almost magically improve, since a school that didn't measure up would literally have no customers and go out of business.

Or so the reformers believe. Skeptics argue that the choice system would be just another way of separating sheep from permanent goats, since parents who cared enough to shop would flock to good schools while the hapless children of the underclass would be left behind, to be neglected by dispirited rejects in decaying hulks that would get just enough students to stay alive. The danger is real. But in pragmatic truth, that fear probably overstates the real-world effects of choice. In places where parents have been given a choice, academic excellence is far down the list of reasons they give for the schools they choose. Far more often, they pick a school because it is close to home, or it has pleasant facilities, or their child's friends go there.

Reform built around choice is tailored to appeal to market-oriented conservatives, and it's not surprising that George Bush's reform proposals endorse the basic idea. Another hot new ticket, site-based decision making, speaks to educational "progressives" as well. The idea here is to free schools from their bureaucratic shackles, giving principals more power to govern themselves and letting teachers have more say in what happens in their classrooms.

This kind of empowerment is a central feature of the reforms being pushed by James Comer, the Yale educator whose ideas are being tried in more than one hundred schools in eight states, and in the Coalition of Essential Schools formed by Brown University's Theodore Sizer. Both aim to restructure schools and entire systems to deal with students in a more child-centered way. Sizer stresses smaller and more intensive classes, using teachers as coaches rather than lecturers, while Comer's approach emphasizes dealing with the whole child, not simply as a student who must be filled with a given set of facts and theories. One Comer school, for instance, found that one of its students was living in a hopeless wreck of a home with an uncaring mother and her drug-abusing boyfriend. The school found an uncle who would take an interest in the boy and a foster family to care for him. Both Comer and Sizer grant local schools considerable discretion and initiative, and both have shown promising results, in measurable test scores and in less tangible subjective reactions. Sizer says his students "stand tall and look you in the eye."

There's nothing fundamentally wrong with any of these ideas, as such; if they don't turn out to be magic bullets, they may well be useful. Prototypes of national tests have already been administered in states across the country, and experiments with longer school years are under way. In Chicago, New York, Miami Beach and Minneapolis, experimental schools feature varying degrees of choice and autonomy within the public system. The cities of Miami and Rochester are trying dramatic experiments in teacher empowerment and site-based decision making. Comer's model is being installed in all forty-two public schools in New Haven. Eleven states have adopted versions of parental choice programs.

But major reforms can cost more than they're worth. As with any other innovation, it turns out that each major change in schools involves a lot of problems (and even more money) on the way from pilot project to full-scale operation:

• There is always resistance to change. The system has 45 million children and their parents, 2.5 million teachers, 110,000 principals and 92,000 school board members, all of them with minds that must come to some rough consensus on solving problems that haven't yet been properly defined. Administrators, teachers and their unions must be coaxed through demonstration projects, then elaborately educated by pamphlets and seminars and reassured that each new deal won't invade their turf or cost them anything. In New York City, everybody's candidate for educational hell, even the janitors can veto curriculum reforms.

• The new techniques must be refined and codified, and teachers and administrators have to be trained to use them. School boards must provide seminars and workshops, extra pay for teachers who attend them, and new supervisors to stand by during the first few years of the new program. Complications multiply. Everything takes longer and costs more than planned.

• Objectives multiply, and perfectionism creeps in. The argument, spoken or not, is that if something can't be all but perfect, it isn't worth having. The best becomes the enemy of the good. Schedules stretch out, and costs spiral out of control.

• Inevitably, there will be teachers and administrators who can't or won't learn the new approach. What will be done with them?

• The bigger the reform, the bigger the risk involved. If a major change turns out on balance to be a mistake, reversing course can be difficult or even impossible. Large numbers of children are damaged by the failure. Teachers are demoralized and parents antagonized. Perhaps worst of all, the failure of a major reform makes it harder to try another change. People are discouraged, frightened, bruised. The tolerance for risk of any kind is gone, and from then on the status quo reigns unchallenged.

If the reforms actually work after all this, the price will still be high, both in money and time. Even if one of the current big ideas turns out to be effective, it can't be simply plugged in and switched on all over the country. There will be years or decades of trouble-shooting. And before that's done, the next big change must be introduced into the system in the same laborious way. Children who are now in the schools will have graduated or dropped out, and their parents will be grandparents, before the reforms are all in place. Today's teachers will have gone through a whole generation of students and finished their own careers. Even if the reform process is relatively painless and generally successful, most people now involved with the schools will get few of its benefits and all of its disruptions.

In all such radical reforms, the assumption is that there is a right way to run schools, better than all the others. But a truth that the big-thinkers tend to overlook is that there's no one good formula. Almost every educational method has been, and can be, good enough to convey information to children and help them use it. Scandinavian children get progressive, creative teaching methods; Japanese kids memorize vast amounts of material; German students get tightly structured lessons. All of them learn—or enough of them to give Americans competitive fits. By the same token, any method of teaching can be abused or misapplied, and no formula is absolutely foolproof. The basic point is still true: A reasonably good teacher can make practically any method effective.

That brings up the knottiest problem of all. Everyone who has ever had a good teacher knows that good teaching solves all the other problems. The movie *Stand and Deliver*, the real-life story of Jaime Escalante teaching calculus to inner-city kids in Los Angeles, merely underlines the lesson. The dirty secret about educational reform is that if more of our teachers were top guns, we wouldn't need any magic bullets. Putting it baldly, the secret we keep trying to find is a formula that will make kids learn no matter how dumb their teachers are. Take it as given: It doesn't exist. The best we can hope for is to work out methods of teaching and administration that will inspire enthusiasm and help mediocre teachers get better results.

Can we improve the teachers? In the long run, that's probably the most useful question anyone can ask. But it's not a question that can be answered in a hurry, or an issue that today's parents and educators can do much about in the time they have. Our society has never valued teaching highly, and the call to teach still doesn't reach many students in the top quarter of the college class. Status and salaries for teachers have recently been on the rise, and some say the quality of young people going into education is improving, but that's a long, slow business. There are 2.5 million public school teachers in the country. It's safe to say that most of them are not going to change overnight, and that the next generation's teachers will be much like the ones working now.

There's one common judgment that is indeed true: Our schools are in crisis. The state of American education is very nearly as dreary as we all think it is.

But the first step in solving any problem is to see it clearly, and we haven't yet done that. For most people, the symbol of educational failure is an inner-city high school with guards at the doors, bars on the windows, graffiti on the walls and drug peddlers roaming the corridors. In reality, there are only a few such hellholes. Most of the schools in this country are serious enterprises, pleasant enough to visit, full of people working hard at the business of education. The real national problem is that hard as they try, few of them do the job brilliantly and most don't do it very well. Our schools are fortresses not of violence and despair, but of mediocrity. They wither the juicy apple of learning into a dry nubbin of boredom and resentment, turning out kids who don't know enough to live in their own world. It's been nearly a decade since the national policy report *A Nation at Risk* warned bluntly: "If an unfriendly foreign power had attempted to impose on America the mediocre educational performance that exists, we might well have viewed it as an act of war." The problem has become a crisis because hardly anything has really changed.

We have all heard the horror stories—the high school students who can't place the Civil War in the right half century, the four out of five young adults who can't decipher a bus timetable. But beyond the anecdotes, the cost of educational failure is eroding the nation. Citing facts almost at random:

• Every eight seconds of the school day, says the Children's Defense Fund, a student drops out. Every sixty-seven seconds, a teenager has a baby. These are not just symptoms of the problem. They are guarantees that it will be permanent, and probably will get worse.

• Among minority students, who are sent disproportionately to the worst schools and often drop out, illiteracy approaches 40 percent. In another decade, minority students will be a majority of the public school population in ten states.

• In 1988, there were 3.8 million Americans who were eighteen years old. Of these, according to the Department of Education, 700,000 had dropped out of high school. Another 700,000 had stayed in, but they were really interior dropouts: they couldn't read their own high school diplomas. And the nation has had to adjust to its new work force. At McDonald's, the cash registers no longer have numbers on the keys, but little pictographs—a burger, a Coke, a container of fries.

• The most talented kids are also losing ground. Scores on the college-entrance Scholastic Aptitude Tests test, a flawed but telling measure, have crept upward in the past decade, but they are still well below the levels of 1970. And the top students aren't scoring as high as the cream of the crop in the 1960s. When the schools go sour, the cream curdles too.

All that is bad, of course. On the most obvious level, it's bad because it hurts the bottom line: If Americans aren't smart and well educated, they won't be able to compete with the tough foreigners. Already, the nation is losing the international competition. In international tests, American students regularly score near the bottom of the list in math and science.

Kids have always failed and dropped out of school. As recently as 1950, half the students who started high school never graduated. But the country can no longer afford that solution, because the high-tech economy doesn't have jobs for dropouts any more. A kid can't make a living with a shovel. His uncle can't take him down to the union hall and get him signed up as an apprentice. And his girlfriend isn't going to marry him and spend the rest of her life keeping house; she'll have to find a job, too. If they want a real future, they'll get not just high school diplomas but college degrees. If they drop out, they could wind up dishing burgers or even homeless. And every city now has its packs of aimless, empty-eyed young people—white, black and Hispanic—with nothing to do, nowhere to go and no future.

But that dead end is only part of the damage—the pragmatic, utilitarian part. The larger society pays a price, too. As the schools go bad, parents who have a choice pull their kids out of the system. Lacking middle-class support, the schools lose political clout and financial resources, and their problems get worse. The children of the poor lose touch with the values and the sense of possibilities of the middle class; they know the trap they're in, and they resent the wealth and ease they see only from afar. Meanwhile, privileged kids lose all contact with the majority of their fellow citizens. Class and race tensions rise. The common educational experience that has been the basic glue of democracy no longer exists.

Even worse, people without education live shrunken lives. Americans tend to see diplomas as a kind of meal ticket, priced in dollars and cents: the average college graduate earns $46,000 a year; high school dropouts get only $13,900. That's true, give or take a few bucks, but there's a spiritual price, too. It isn't only intellectuals who can take pleasure in learning things, or in dealing with a full deck of information at home, on the job and in the world. It enhances lives and improves the country when people understand basic economics, know the rudiments of history, see the world around them as more interesting than TV game shows and can talk to each other about something besides Bart Simpson. The play of minds is what proves our humanity—and it's a lot more fun than most people's sex lives. What we don't know not only hurts us, it makes us less human.

But this isn't a counsel of despair. It's also true that schools can be made better, in a time frame that will help this generation of kids.

Defining a good school is as elusive as Potter Stewart's perplex on pornography: We can't tell what it is, but we know it when we see it. In a good school, whatever its methods, children learn; parents are involved and interested; teachers are cheerful and work hard; the children and the teachers like each other. And a good school can take almost any form. It can be the classic one-room schoolhouse, with a stern and dedicated teacher, or a free-form collection of open classrooms verging on chaos. It can be an urban miracle, an island of order and hope sprouting in the roughest slum. It can even be the deluxe suburban high school, with platoons of teacher's aides trying experimental techniques, batteries of extracurricular activities and 90 percent of its graduates going to college. But any of these paradigms can also be a bad school. The key to the difference is not the school's model or its method of teaching, but the spirit of the place.

The most important factor in a school's spirit is its principal. Parents and teachers have known this for years, and now educational theory recognizes it too: good schools almost always have good principals— men and women who care about education, who genuinely like kids and who will fight hard enough for their ideas to make them work. Good principals attract good teachers, fire up the mediocrities and get the maximum possible from their staff. They get what they need from the school board, and chalk up high average test scores. A good principal takes it for granted that children will learn, and helps both students and teachers overcome their limitations. Teachers know the tricks of finding good principals, and parents are beginning to learn them, too. These days, most systems allow parents to shop around at least a little to choose a school. A good principal is interested in working with parents, and may help cut the red tape if she thinks a parent will be an asset. Getting into a good principal's school is worth a lot of trouble.

There are also bad principals: time-servers, political hacks, mediocrities and outright stupid or malevolent men and women who have no business anywhere near children. Parents and teachers alike should do everything they can to retire such people, and meanwhile avoid their schools. A school with a really bad principal can't get better, because the principal won't let it happen. But if the principal is good, or somewhere in the midrange—weak but willing, say, or smart enough but not politically gifted—good schools can be made better, mediocre schools can be bootstrapped into good ones and even bad schools can be turned around.

Good schools begin with a sense of excitement, a kind of electricity. Interesting things are happening there; parents, children and teachers have become involved with the school and with each other. If a school is to be improved, this is the kind of atmosphere it has to have. Which brings us to the Hawthorne effect.

Back in 1927, at the Hawthorne Works of the Western Electric Company in Cicero, Illinois, Professor Elton Mayo of the Harvard Business School began a series of experiments on how working conditions affect productivity. It was a highly focused, intensive project; just five women workers, assembling relay units, were to be studied for five years. One at a time, Mayo changed conditions: the group's wage incentives, hours of work and rest periods, levels of lighting and ventilation and all the other variables he could imagine. The results fluctuated, but production per woman-hour generally improved. Finally in 1932, with the experiments over, everything reverted to the 1927 conditions. Then somebody noticed a curious thing. Productivity didn't revert. It remained 25 percent higher than it had been at the starting point.

It turned out that there had been an unsuspected factor in the mix: the experiment itself. The workers had become a social group, set apart from the other workers and friendly among themselves. They had an informal relationship with their supervisor, who discussed proposed changes before they were made. The women were aware that their activity was important; they were being studied and fussed over, and their lives were being changed every so often in ways that were usually interesting, or at least not boring. Just as patients given a sugar pill often feel better, the workers responded to almost any change with a new burst of energy.

The intangible factor became famous as the "Hawthorne effect." The study became the foundation for the human relations school of management, and it is still being recycled in industrial relations, most lately as the theoretical basis for trendy quality circles and team management structures. In some academic circles, however, the study became a kind of cautionary tale about researchers who miss the real point, and it's a byword among some social scientists. Educators have used Hawthorne for years to put down their rivals' proposals for reform. Oh, sure, they say, the pilot study looks good—but pilots always look good; you know that's just the Hawthorne effect. It doesn't prove that there's anything in your idea.

That putdown misses a real point. Within reason, the Hawthorne effect is important for its own sake. It's beneficial to have experiments going, to get people involved, to make them feel that they matter and that exciting things are happening. It's just as true in schools as anywhere else. And while major reforms can produce a Hawthorne effect, it can also come—at considerably less risk—from small-bite programs of much more modest scope.

The point is to make the school feel special. Kids in special schools begin to act as if they were special too, and the same thing is true of parents, teachers and administrators. People are motivated by the feeling that they have a choice in what happens to them, that they matter, that they "own" what they are doing. They get that feeling when they say something and the system responds—and the response doesn't have to be a major convulsion. A modest change in a school's curriculum or a new mentoring program probably won't work a miracle, but making the effort will change the people involved, raise the level of their interest, perhaps even prompt them to make other creative contributions. What's most important is to go for the Hawthorne effect. A school should always have one or two programs going on that promise something interesting and different.

That's what this book is about. The chapters that follow will report on a dozen small-bite programs around the country in considerable detail, from the first "what if" through all the struggles to make things happen. This isn't an uncritical exercise in boosterism: Some ideas work better than others, and it's necessary to see what's lacking, and why, as well as what's effective. It's just as important to see that programs needn't be perfect to be effective—that ordinary people, with flaws and shortcomings like yours and mine, can have an idea, bring a program to life and, for all its imperfections, make a school better.

The projects range from preschool through high school, from dropout prevention and drug education to college preparation and executive mentoring. They focus varyingly on children, teachers and parents, on methods of administration and techniques of teaching, on efforts to motivate kids and to teach values and to mobilize community support. Some are relatively expensive, others cost almost nothing. But all of them can be done—have been done—by teachers, parents and administrators in ordinary schools of all kinds. Whether a school is in the inner city or lush suburbia, in an Appalachian hollow or a small Western city, at least eight of the twelve ideas detailed here ought to work there. But since every school has its own distinctive character, each of the programs can be tailored to fit, and new ones can be devised to meet specific needs.

The best news is that there's no shortage of ideas. Through the years, literally hundreds of projects have made schools better across the country. They're no secret; there are several published catalogues with capsule descriptions of such programs. The Department of Education (DOE) has a booklet, *What Works*, summing up current research about teaching and learning, and an annual catalogue called *Educational Programs That Work*—440 of them at last count. The National School Boards Association lists eighty-eight programs, some of them duplicating the DOE list, in a pamphlet called *The Learning Bank*. There are specialized catalogues of programs for minority students and handicapped students, and subdivisions dealing with math, language arts, parental involvement, substance abuse, motivation and self-esteem, among others. Some small-bite programs have been nationally publicized and widely copied. Some have died after the pilot project stage, from lack of funding or follow-through or simply because somebody lost interest. There are some really effective ideas that attract no attention just because they aren't grandiose, or they don't fit any neat ideological agenda.

These programs make their changes on a human scale, a step at a time. It's an approach that may lack drama and scope, but has real advantages. If it's less sweeping than wholesale reform, it's also less costly; if it gets smaller results, they come sooner. And change in small bites must be led by people in local communities, not presidential commissions and cabinet secretaries and platoons of bureaucrats fueled with federal tax dollars. Small bites are genuinely democratic with a small *d*, untidy and idiosyncratic as a New England town meeting. They fit no national mold or universal doctrine. Nevertheless, a nonexpert visiting these programs can pick out a set of general principles underlying them. The principles add up to a kind of credo for successful innovators, equal parts idealism and hardheaded practicality. These are the main points:

• **All children can learn.** This sounds like a truism, and it should be; as any parent knows, children are learning machines. Many schools seem almost to try to make learning painful and unpleasant—to stifle curiosity, demand rote memorization, punish wonder; to make even sex education a bore—but they still can't keep kids from learning. A dropout who can barely write his own name and can't find his country on a globe understands every balletic nuance of Michael Jordan's drive to the basket, recites endless lyrics of rap songs and knows how to operate in complex criminal enterprises where mere survival takes courage, diplomacy and arcane lore. Yet far too many teachers tell themselves and each other that many children are unteachable, that it is somehow acceptable that kids get through high school without achieving functional literacy. Good schools know that some children learn more quickly than others, and some must work harder than others to succeed, but they never give up on any child. When Parkway North High School outside of St. Louis started applying that principle to its slow learners, good things started happening in the whole school (see chapter 2).

• **Set expectations high.**   As the Department of Education puts it in *What Works,* "Students tend to learn as little—or as much—as their teachers expect." If a teacher accepts low achievement, a student will assume that's all that's needed, and perhaps all that can be done. Low expectations are a signal that a teacher doesn't respect her students, and they can easily become a self-fulfilling prophecy. A good teacher can understand a child's limitations, but still demand that she perform up to her full ability, whatever it may be. And when expectations are raised and students are rewarded for meeting them, the general standard rises too. In Woodson High School in Washington, D.C., a mentoring program called Futures 500 shows the way by demanding achievement—and providing real help on the road to a better life (see chapter 3). Good schools hold teachers accountable for teaching, and children accountable for learning.

But standards also imply measurements. Obviously, tests aren't the object of education and a grade point average isn't the measure of a child, but good schools know that both tests and reports are necessary to find out what's being learned and let all concerned know it. And standards can't be eroded or abandoned in a misguided effort to nourish self-esteem. Educators believe, rightly, that self-image is important, especially for deprived children, who tend to think that they simply can't perform well and therefore stop trying. But higher self-esteem can't mean merely an inflated ego; it must always be grounded in genuine achievement. The prototype national math test in 1991 turned up a classic example of pathetically misguided pride: Students in the Virgin Islands and the District of Columbia scored lowest in the nation on the test. Yet when asked whether they were good at math, those same students ranked highest in the country in self-appraisals. Good teachers don't have to delude kids to persuade them that they are capable of learning.

• **Education is done with children, not to them.**   Learning is an active process of questioning, exploring and understanding; a child is not a receptacle to be filled up with lectures and memorized facts. Yet far too many schools try to do just that, filling the day with talking teachers, tests, worksheets, assignments to be copied from the chalkboard and passive learning in general. In a recent study in 162 middle schools across the country, the National Association of Secondary School Principals followed individual eighth-graders through the day to see what they actually did. The result was a dismaying record of apathy, tedium and boredom, with a minimum of active participation or critical thinking by the students. Good schools are communities, with the children at the center and teachers functioning as coaches, discussion leaders and provocateurs.

A corollary: The most neglected assets in all of our schools are the students, and good programs tend to make maximum use of them. In educational jargon, the term is "ownership": when people have a stake in anything, they tend to feel more interested in it. If students have real responsibility for what they're doing, they become passionately involved in it. In San Antonio, the Valued Youth Partnership persuades low achievers not to drop out of school—by making them tutors of younger children (see chapter 4). Both the tutors and their small charges benefit from the arrangement. Similarly, the peer helper program in Moorhead, Minnesota, trains students to spot problems, to see a friend poised for drug trouble or some other personal crisis and quietly offer to call for help (see chapter 5).

• **It takes only one person to make a difference.** One person with an idea can be a powerful force in a community, and the examples are legion. In Hamilton, Indiana, Becky Norris had a notion about parents getting kids ready for school that led to a whole new preschool program (see chapter 6). In city after city, the vision and dedication of individual principals, teachers and parents has been crucial to a program's success. It's even possible for a single teacher to make a powerful impact on his students and his community without much support from his principal or the school system—as Al Haskvitz has proved (see chapter 7) out in Walnut, California.

• **Educators can use help.** If students are the most neglected asset in the schools, the second most ignored is the local community. Many good programs reach outside the school to enlist parents, local business, local government facilities and any available volunteers. In Vermont, Cynthia Parsons got the governor's blessing to organize community service programs and now has every high school in the state taking part (see chapter 8). All too often, however, schools merely pay lip service to the idea of getting parents and the community involved in education. Parents are welcome to raise money and do gofer work, but any real ideas and suggestions are greeted like a child's mud pie, with a condescending smile. Good schools really welcome parental involvement, as the Indianapolis system has proved with its ambitious Parents in Touch program (see chapter 9).

• **Professionals have to carry the ball.** Parents can and should make suggestions, take an active interest, seek out lively teachers, encourage their ideas, volunteer help and provide political support. There are even times when parents must organize to fight the system, with a political battle to reverse a bad policy or get rid of incompetent principals or school boards. But there's a limit to what parents can contribute. They have their own lives and careers, they don't have educational expertise and they can't operate inside the system. In the end, educators must take responsibility for running things—and sometimes they have to call on other professionals for help.

Local educators in Helena, Montana, found a way to combine professional help and new technology with community volunteers to create something approaching a new kind of school system. Using a computerized remedial program called HOSTS, teachers in Helena are learning a new role. They can be executives, planning and supervising, while kids get individually tailored, one-on-one lessons from the volunteers (see chapter 10).

• **Aim high, but be realistic.** Children have a deep sense of justice, and teachers tend to share it; like Al Haskvitz, Cynthia Parsons and dozens of others in this book, they respond idealistically to a project designed to make the world better, whether it's conserving water, saving whales or raising voter turnout. Thus a good program always has an idealistic goal: to help deprived children overcome their handicaps, to fight drugs and crime, to perform community service, to raise the number of graduates going to college. A Harvard educator, Lawrence Kohlberg, set up programs to teach ethics in a dozen high schools, with "just communities" of students and teachers making and enforcing rules for themselves. There's even one such community in the inner-city Roosevelt High, a rough corner of New York City's South Bronx (see chapter 11).

But programs operate in the real world of money and politics, and a touch of Machiavelli is also necessary. Noble objectives must always be measured against costs, both financial and political. Any program, no matter how righteous, can be defeated if it costs too much or offends a powerful constituency. In reality, as all these stories demonstrate, a good program is politically defensible and begins with a sense of (a) how much it will cost and (b) where the money will come from. School boards and taxpayers being what they are, that usually means (a) as little as possible and (b) not from our budget.

• **Good programs deal with real problems.** The trick is first to perceive what's really wrong, and then to identify a handle of the problem that can be grasped. Neither is always obvious. Bob Coplan, a Cleveland lawyer, was puzzled that a scholarship program for inner-city youth wasn't being used. When he asked the right questions, it turned out that the kids being targeted simply didn't think college was a choice for them. His Cleveland Scholarship Program (see chapter 12) put its own special counselors in the high schools and helped 65,000 students on to higher education.

• **Ideas are where you find them.** Good programs are seldom truly original; at most, like the Valued Youth Partnership of San Antonio, they are a bold new application of somebody's time-tested theories. Most successful innovators borrow or outright steal their ideas. Even when somebody thinks an idea is unique, as in the preschool program in Indiana, it often turns out to be already in use somewhere. If a program looks good, it should be appropriated without hesitation; if it's for sale and comes with good training, like the HOSTS remedial program, it should be bought. But even the best idea must be adapted to mesh with local conditions. A program forced into a system will be rejected like a clumsily transplanted organ.

• **Good programs blow their own horns.** Modesty has a place, but not in improving the schools. Most of these small-bite reformers know how to use publicity and active public relations to tell the community what's going on, help people find and use programs, provide rewards for the participants, reinforce political support and raise financing.

• **There's no substitute for long hours and hard work.** Systems resist change, and good programs work because the people running them have a clear goal and are truly dedicated to reaching it. Taken together, these twelve programs show that it helps to be smart and have a talent for leadership, but the indispensable quality is determination and a willingness to spend time and energy for the cause. Fortunately, this tends to be contagious. For all the cynical talk about obstructionism and foot dragging by time-serving teachers' unions, there's enough idealism and professional pride in the system that innovators can find ways to bend the work rules and get around the obstacles. Good programs make better schools, and better schools make teachers' lives more interesting and less difficult. That's a powerful incentive to cooperate.

But here, too, there's a corollary: as programs mature, they must find ways to replace their founders' energy and enthusiasm with new leaders or an institutional structure that works just as well. Many good programs die with their founders, unable to adjust to long-term existence. Those that survive and prosper, like the pioneering student advisory program in the Shoreham–Wading River Middle School on Long Island (see chapter 13), learn to run on a lower key, with incentives and rewards to keep their people going.

None of these principles comes as a major surprise; they are mostly common sense. The main point is that the people now in the education system aren't helpless pawns. Teachers, parents and principals can keep on making their own changes and improving their own schools, as some of them have been doing all along. They may well anticipate major reforms and their modest programs may help shape the national model. And the more change of this kind happens, the easier it will be to mobilize local systems for grand designs if and when the time comes. But the first goal is to make a school better, and the main tool for accomplishing that is not any particular project, but the process of change itself. The idea is to pick some modest program and make it work; once the school is actively involved, it will be time to try something more ambitious. And the process goes on from there, one program after another.

Small bites won't change the whole world, not right away. None of the programs in this book, by itself, will cure the ills of American education. But collectively they have made a real difference in a dozen systems across the country, and the success of each effort encourages new programs in its wake. This is the real world, where people with real problems grope and stumble, aim high and achieve only part of their goals. The point is, that can be enough. This is the way real change happens. And in the long run, this kind of change can be as important as any revolution.

2.
Getting Rid of "Dummy 101"

There are eight kids gathered around the big conference table outside the principal's office, explaining their special program to a visitor. These high school freshmen and sophomores came to school far behind their classmates, with an average reading score somewhere between fourth-and sixth-grade level, and in most schools, their program would be the "Dummy 101" routine, where slow students learn mainly how hopeless it is to try. But this is Parkway North High, a school with a firm commitment to the first basic principle of small-bite programs: the conviction that all students can learn. And sure enough, it is a place where former losers are learning how to win. Its remedial classes are actually returning many kids to grade level and pushing some on to the honor roll. These students had been at high risk of dropping out. But in a follow-up study covering 168 students over three years, more than 89 percent of the onetime dummies were still attending classes.

The students around the table are a rough cross section of the program: three whites, all from the Parkway North school district west of St. Louis, and five blacks, bused from the inner city in a voluntary desegregation plan. Most of them have talked to visitors before, and at first their testimony is both dutiful and predictable. Yes, they chorus, their grades are improving; they are learning to get organized; skills class is a chance to do most of your homework in school, with somebody there to help with the hard parts.

"Something can sound pretty easy in class, but when you land at home, whoo," says Darrell Cole, one of the kids from St. Louis.

"If you get home and your parents don't know algebra, you're in big trouble," agrees Kristy Lueck, from nearby Maryland Heights. "But we get to work with the teachers one on one." And the teachers don't just help with homework, she says. They teach about taking notes and budgeting time and dressing for job interviews. It gives her self-confidence, she says.

Then Mitchell Stovall speaks up. He's a big kid; Don Hugo, the Parkway North principal, says later that Mitchell arrived from St. Louis with an attitude, but is finding his way—and incidentally scoring eighteen to twenty points a game on the basketball team. "Oh, yeah, man, skills is really great," Mitchell says. There's a note of mockery in his voice, the singsong half-joking of a boy just a little afraid of being put down for brown-nosing. "My grades were really terrible, man, but they showed me how to study, and they really helped me." Then his voice slows and deepens, and the parody drops away. "The thing is," he says, "they proved to me they really cared about me. And I started to think I better care too."

Nobody laughs. There's a kind of murmur around the table. "They really do care," says Laura Rader, a student from Creve Coeur. "They don't just say, 'You can do better than that.' They show you how you can do it."

"Not saying, 'Put your mind to it,' " says Mitchell. "I hate that, 'Put your mind to it.' What's that supposed to mean?"

Now they are all warmed up. "Sometimes you can help other people in the class," says Jacquetta Peoples, black and bright-eyed. "If Mrs. Morgan is busy with somebody else and your friend has a problem, sometimes you can help."

"That feels good," says Eddie Current, another St. Louis import. "Makes you feel like a real teacher." They all laugh, delighted.

"Power," somebody says, and they laugh again. But what they mean is self-esteem. It's a room full of one-time losers who have learned they don't have to be.

Jacquetta puts it best. "When I first got there, I looked around and said to myself, 'Is this a class for stupid people?' " she says. "But after a while I came to think no, it couldn't be for stupid people. Because I'm in here!"

When Carol Kolar heard that dialogue, she misted up a little. "That's perfect," she said. "That's exactly what we're trying to do for them." It's Kolar who runs the school's Reading/Writing Center, which is built around the special program; and while the program itself has never had the kind of snappy name that gets instant recognition, what it's about is enrichment. Like most schools, Parkway North used to send underachievers to remedial classes, the classic "Dummy 101" where they would be drilled endlessly in spelling, grammar or times tables while their former classmates ran farther and farther ahead of them. No more. Instead they are kept in the mainstream, where they are expected to try to keep up. But at the same time, they are offered an elective class to go over the ground again and learn the skills they need to be able to study at all.

There are two sets of classes: English Skills, specifically for kids behind in English (about thirty each semester), and a general Skills Tutorial, for about sixty freshmen and sophomores. Some of the Tutorial students attend English Skills as well; others have been recommended for Skills Tutorial by their parents or teachers from other classes. They learn the art of managing time, for instance, or noting down assignments, or keeping legible notes and using them to study for tests. Since the skills classes aren't required, the teachers can enforce discipline by suspending or expelling students who won't do the work. And since the students tend to show dramatic gains in their class participation and grades, the classes don't have the stigma of the old "Dummy 101." There's even a bit of envy among some students who aren't included. "Some people have asked me how they can get into that," said Jacquetta Peoples.

Kolar runs the two skills classes with the help of two aides and a rotation of four regular English teachers. Among them, they deal with a total of about eighty students every two days, in groups as small as six at a time to maximize individual attention. It isn't a magic formula, she cautions: by the time they come to high school, some kids just have too long a history of frustration and anger to benefit from help. Some have problems at home too horrendous to overcome. Even for those who find a haven in skills class, who begin to like themselves and understand the hows and whys of learning, it's just a beginning. In reality, most of them won't become A students. But if improvement isn't automatic, it is at least possible—and with it, a better life.

That's what the skills program has aimed at from the beginning. The idea is a backlash against the "track" system of education. Tracking dates back at least thirty years, and on the face of it, it's a logical idea: Put the smartest students in advanced classes, the bulk of the kids in the mainstream and the slow learners in a remedial class where they can try to catch up. But some educators have argued for years that it simply doesn't work—that the mainstream shouldn't be deprived of the contributions of gifted students, and that low achievers merely fall farther behind when they are segregated. In scores of scholarly papers, these educators have labored to document an obvious point: that separating sheep from goats, and labeling the goats, will be a self-fulfilling prophecy.

"It begins with the assumption that the kid is defective," says Henry M. Levin, professor of education at Stanford University and a leader in reforming remedial teaching. When teachers, parents and fellow students alike assume that a child isn't very bright, the child tends to believe them; expectations are lowered all around, and performance gets even worse. No matter what it's called, it's the dummy track, and the euphemisms inevitably escalate: "Remedial" classes turn into "basics" classes, which in turn pick up the stigma and then become known as "skills" classes. Under any label, the student painfully drills in lessons that the mainstream class has long since mastered.

The work is boring and demeaning. Teachers don't enjoy it any more than their sulky, rebellious students, and they usually repeat the same teaching methods that the child didn't respond to the first time around. As Levin points out, even in the unlikely event that the classes succeed, the remedial student who masters the work emerges back in the mainstream even farther behind her classmates than she was when she was put on the lower track. She will never catch up; she will be a goat forever. As if to rub in the lesson, "basic" classes often devalue even the grades they give. A student who gets an A or B on the low track finds that it counts only for C or D on his official transcript. It is hard to believe that such systems are really intended to help. They seem designed to push failures into dropping out. And while that solution was arguably realistic thirty years ago, when there were still manual jobs for illiterate workers, these days there is little chance for dropouts to find a decent life.

Levin's solution was to apply the second principle of small-bite programs: Instead of lowering standards for slow learners, he raised them. He put them not in remedial classes but in accelerated groups, giving them added work so that they could catch up to their colleagues. In practice, his early experiments proved that the enrichment process did indeed help most underachievers. But they also led him to more grandiose visions. Reforming individual classes didn't work in isolation, he says; real reform required a change of attitude that "meant reforming whole schools."

To small-bite aficionados, that's a familiar fallacy: If a thing can't be all but perfect, it isn't worth having. A simple idea that could have wide application turns into a sweeping reform that demands a huge commitment of time and energy, and thus finds few takers. The best becomes the enemy of the good. These days Levin is pursuing his Accelerated Schools Project in some fifty schools in systems across the country. It requires a transformation of the entire school and the educational philosophy of its teachers, staff and directors, with a minimum turnaround time of six years. Levin's project gets generally approving reviews. But it is still in early stages, and the full cost has yet to be measured. What Parkway North has proved is that the basic idea can be applied, simply and effectively, one department at a time.

Parkway school district takes in a big chunk of the suburban sprawl west of St. Louis: 68.5 square miles of diverse communities, tract housing, pockets of small industry, the remains of farms and some wealthy exurban homes. The district has four high schools—North, Central, South and West—each with its feeder junior high and a network of elementary schools; its enrollment of 21,000 students is made up partly of 3,500 black kids from the central city, voluntarily bused each day. In turn, a tiny contingent of Parkway volunteers is bused the other way to inner-city magnet schools. Since the district is so diverse and politically fragmented, school officials have considerable autonomy.

Parkway North High is an attractive school, built two decades ago when the open-school fad was at its height. It's a good building, well designed and maintained, with clean lines and pretensions to architecture: the central office block seems to float above a glass-enclosed lobby; the classroom wings surround the open library and, one floor below, the cafeteria. Paint is clean and graffiti-free, carpets are only mildly frayed, and lighting is bright but not harsh. However, as the noise and confusion of open classrooms relentlessly bred partitions over the years, the interior of the school has become cluttered and haphazard. There are now weirdly high blank walls, narrow corridors with tacky fake paneling, unexpected and rather strange crannies and passages. It comes as a surprise to find remnants of openness in the sciences wing, where adjoining classes buzz happily on diverse subjects with only a partial partition to block the hearing lines. Outside, the grounds are spacious and well tended. There's even room for a visitor's car in the huge parking lot.

The district isn't rich: The $4,435 spent per student puts it just below the 1990 average of $4,950 for U.S. schools. But its student-to-staff ratio is less than 14 to 1. Teacher salaries in the district average $33,491, and North's buses make enough runs per day to allow a preschool study period and after-school activities in dozens of clubs, sports teams and special groups. The high school's composite mean score of 22.6 on the ACT test is comfortably above both the national and Missouri levels. Its dropout rate is only 5.6 percent, and more than half the dropouts get graduate equivalent diplomas; nearly 92 percent of the graduates go on to higher education. North is a good school.

The school has a general diversity. Though 73 percent of its 1,558 students are white, most of them from middle-income families, about a third of that number are Jewish. There are Asian and Hispanic students and a fair sprinkling of foreign-born kids, including Chinese and Russians. The 288 African-Americans bused from the central city combine with a smattering of local blacks to make up a fifth of the population. Many of the city students have been handicapped by poor schooling and family problems, but so far they haven't brought Parkway North the worst of inner-city problems: There are no heavy drugs and no gang activities. By and large, says principal Don Hugo, the city students are "pretty highly motivated," and there is a waiting list for Parkway in the inner city.

The enrichment program has a long history, none of it easy. The first experiment began in 1981, a year before the first buses arrived from St. Louis, in a junior high where a bright young teacher, Karen Helfrich, was pushing for a program to replace remedial English classes, known then as "basics." It was a case of one person with a powerful idea: she persuaded Parkway Central Junior High to try a pilot project, with ninth-grade slow learners switched from the basics class into regular English and given supplementary instruction in a skills class every other day. Problems soon became obvious. The skills class was too large for the teacher to handle effectively. The skills teacher wasn't the students' regular teacher, and thus didn't have an established relationship with the students. And since students were drawn from several regular English classes, the skills teacher couldn't know what each of the regular teachers had discussed or assigned. The next year, regular English teachers were assigned to teach their own slower learners, with skills classes limited to a maximum of six students. That cost more, but worked better.

In the 1983–84 year, however, the ninth grade was moved from junior high to Parkway Central Senior High. Helfrich's program went with it, but it died after the first year. The school's staff endorsed the idea, but there proved to be too many students who needed it and not enough commitment or flexibility on the part of the high school administration. Not long after that, Helfrich left teaching for domestic life.

But Helfrich left behind a disciple, Rosemarie Stocky, at Parkway North. As a child, Stocky recalls, she had been something of a loser herself: "In the seventh and eighth grades, I was unpopular, a loner, a nobody—yecch! And I wanted so much." She remembers brooding alone in her New Jersey bedroom, playing over and over Barbra Streisand's wistful song from *Funny Girl*: "I'm the greatest star, but no one knows it." When she came to Parkway North in 1981, young and idealistic, she was the junior member of the English staff and was automatically assigned to teach basics classes. She proved good at it; one year, she recalls, she was saddled with five of them. It was soul-killing, not because she disliked the kids but because they were so hopeless and the task seemed so futile. When she looked at Karen Helfrich's pilot program, she says, "I saw freedom."

At first, Stocky recalls, she had little theoretical foundation for her ideas and was idealistically naïve about the obstacles to reform. "I knew the four walls of my classroom and the kids I was teaching," she says. "My gut feeling was, if it's right, you should be doing it." It wasn't until the spring of 1984 that she went to her first national convention, a meeting of the International Reading Association in Philadelphia, and plugged in to the reform movement. "My eyes popped wide open," she says. "I started absorbing stuff that affirmed what I had been finding out." She became a disciple of Harold Herber, a Syracuse University teacher whose anti-dropout theories put heavy stress on self-esteem and remedial enrichment.

But she didn't get much encouragement for the enrichment program until she was relieved of some of her basics classes and the department chairman, Larry Moceri, had to teach one. A plump, acerbic and somewhat impish man, Moceri is a creative teacher, excellent with talented youngsters, who regards remedial classes as a penance for any teacher. As Stocky tells it, after the personal experience of a basics class, Moceri was much more receptive to abolishing them.

His recollection is a bit different: There was no single begetter of the idea, and no resistance to it at all. "Low tracking is just untenable," he says. "It isn't relevant to the kids, to education or anything else, and it's impossible to get most teachers to do it. There's such a stigma about it. I could put the most enthusiastic ingenue in there, and halfway through October she'd be all used up."

In any case, Moceri and the English department were committed to starting Stocky's skills program for ninth-graders in the fall of 1984. The principles learned in Karen Helfrich's pilot program would be applied. The low achievers were to be spread among the regular English classes, no more than five or six to a class, and offered a special skills course, to be taught by their own English teacher. Skills would be given every other day, alternating with a physical education elective.

Nobody would be forced to take skills; it should be a privilege, not a punishment. Students would review difficult material, get help in basic study techniques and be given an occasional preview of the next day's lesson to give them a little edge in class.

In Moceri's telling, the only real problem in starting the program was the intricate scheduling of teachers and classes. With no extra funds that year, all the English teachers had to agree to teach larger regular sessions to offset the smaller skills classes. Worse, each teacher with a skills class had to agree to teach nothing but freshmen—a fate that Moceri himself regarded with loathing. Some eccentrics actually like working with ninth-graders, Moceri maintains, but most people "certainly don't want a life sentence in freshmen. To make the program work, as chairman, I had to say some people are going to have to take four freshmen sections every day, and two skills classes a day on top of that." Even so, he says, the idea of banning basics classes was so attractive that the department voted almost unanimous support. Another small-bite principle was being borne out: when teachers saw the prospect that their work would be more interesting, they were willing to wink at technical breaches of work rules.

One major surprise could have derailed the program. Returning with Moceri from a summer program at Vassar, Stocky discovered that Parkway North had a new principal. In a quick shakeup, Don Hugo, who had been the school's vice principal and had moved on to a similar job at Central High, had come back as the new head man—and nobody had told him anything about the skills program she was about to start. It was clearly a risk for a new principal; a failure could be a permanent blot on his record. But Hugo, a relaxed and comfortable man with a gray-flecked beard, liked Stocky's ideas. He listened to her description of the plan and backed her.

There was a kind of frantic drudgery to be got through, and some unexpected pockets of resistance to be cleaned out. Rosemarie Stocky remembers making sixty-seven telephone calls from home, where her little girl was in bed with flu, to persuade parents that their children would be better off in the new class. Some of them had their doubts. The mother of a boy we'll call Darrin said it was no use trying, he was just too thick. Finally, Stocky said, "Look, would you give your child a chance?" The mother relented.

And it all worked. Moceri's teachers were persuaded that their role went far beyond baby-sitting the class dummies, and as time went on they discovered the pleasure of seeing dull eyes light up as ideas took hold. Kids who had been chronic misbehavers sensed the worth of the program, discovered a feeling of ownership in it and started getting their act together. Some of them saw their English marks improving— and with that to reinforce their self-esteem, a few had better grades in other classes, too. Some students had approached skills class with misgivings, sure that it would be just another cemetery for boneheads, but then blossomed as they found genuine help.

The next year Stocky was promised extra funding to extend the program to the tenth grade, but in the end the money got soaked up by an influx of new students. The expansion was pushed through anyway, as teachers agreed to fatten their regular English classes to as many as thirty-one students to make room for their small skills groups. Parents too were converted. By the end of Darrin's sophomore year, his mother told Stocky that she had been right. "I never thought he could do it," she said.

Each year after that brought new features and refinements. With adroit scheduling, for instance, skills classes could be set up so that each student could have his regular English teacher. And early on, it became necessary to document success. Everybody could come up with anecdotal evidence that the program worked, but what were the bottom-line figures? Parkway North won't offer classes that don't attract enough enrollment to justify them. But here were teachers devoting a full class to five or six students. Sooner or later, unless there was proof that the program was successful, that fact would be challenged. So Stocky and her successor, Carol Kolar, have done follow-up studies and surveys: Nearly 90 percent of their students haven't dropped out; 59 percent of the kids in one second-year English skills class got a C or higher in regular English, and only 9 percent failed; two-thirds of another year's class got passing grades in English, and 48 percent of them passed all their subjects. Nearly three-quarters of the skills students would recommend the class to their friends; 73 percent of their parents would rather have their kids in skills than in basics classes.

Partly because of the success of English skills, the district decided to fund a reading specialist in each of its four high schools. When Don

Hugo asked Stocky to take on the job, she agreed—but insisted she would do it only on her own terms. Reading and writing went together, she said, and she would build a center for both that would benefit all the students in the school, not just the English classes. She met no real resistance, just bureaucracy: It took two years to write all the course descriptions, enlist all the departments and work out the schedules. There still wasn't enough funding, so she applied for a $10,000 grant to buy computers for her new center. She also rounded up thirteen other computers already in the school, most of them being sparsely used for lack of software and teacher interest.

Stocky's idea was to keep the English Skills class and bolster it with a tutorial for poor students in all subjects. They would be taught what seem like elementary skills: how to use a three-ring notebook to organize work, how to keep a record of homework assignments, how to read maps, how to ask for help. Some people still think those are ridiculous things to be teaching high school students. At a parents' night, Kolar recalls, a man asked why she was wasting her time on simple common sense. "Hey," she said, "have you looked at your kid's notebook lately?" Common sense or not, these students haven't figured such things out—and when they do, their grades start improving. The teachers keep after them about skipping classes or doing their homework; if the kids keep denying they have any, the teachers consult their colleagues for verification. But there are no judgmental confrontations, just a matter-of-fact recognition that something needs fixing. "You've got to motivate them, or nothing will happen," says Kolar. The Skills Tutorial teachers give points for good behavior, the points mounting up to a pass good for one trip out of class.

How would the new tutorial be scheduled? Coincidentally, the physical education department was being reorganized, so the schedule that used to alternate a PE elective with English Skills was no longer possible. Stocky slipped the tutorial into the vacant slot, advertised the voluntary class to students and parents, and asked teachers outside the English department to refer kids who might benefit. Each day there would be three English Skills periods, each teacher working with no more than five or six of his own students at a time, and three Skills Tutorials of ten to twelve students working with Stocky and her hand-picked teacher's aide, Jackie Morgan, or the computer specialist, Jeff Woodside. Some students showed up in both classes, but some in English Skills chose not to take tutorial, and half the tutorial students weren't in English Skills.

One problem that was never satisfactorily faced was what to call the program as a whole. The educational field teems with cute names and tormented acronyms, all meant to make something stand out in the crowd. Among countless others, there are Project Adventure, Talents Unlimited, Conquest, and Success; there is MECCA (Make Every Child Capable of Achieving), NOMAD (Needs and Objectives for Migrant Advancement and Development), and IMPACT (Improve Minimal Proficiencies by Activating Critical Thinking). Stocky and Kolar tried calling their brainchild simply the English Skills Program, but then Skills Tutorial came along. They have written about it as Removing the Caste System from English Classes; they have even flirted with the acronymic SMARTIES (Study Methods And Reading Techniques In Every Subject). Fortunately, cooler heads prevailed. But the program is still wrestling with the precarious distinction between English Skills and Skills Tutorial, and searching for its own distinctive label.

Stocky's first reading/writing center was what she calls the drama pit: a room in the basement beside the stage. It was adequate, but still a symbolic cellar for low achievers. So she persevered, planting seeds with her teaching colleagues and pleading to Don Hugo that the center had to have a central location to be of real use to all the school's students. Finally she got what she wanted. The library was reorganized, expanding into some unused loft space, and what had been the periodical room was converted into Stocky's domain, two small classrooms with adjoining office space spang in the center of the school. Before long teachers were advising students that they could get help there, and entire classes were stopping by to use the computers or work on special projects. In the first quarter of the 1990–91 year, the center recorded 5,050 student visits—more than three for every kid in school.

By then, however, Rosemarie Stocky herself was gone, back to college to finish her doctorate and to move on into school administration. She's now an assistant principal at one of Parkway's junior highs.

She persuaded Hugo that the center and the program should go to her friend Carol Kolar, who had been an enthusiastic fixture in English Skills from the time she arrived at North in 1987.

That posed a major hurdle, one that comes in time to every successful program. Having survived the departure of its originator, Karen Helfrich, it now had to replace the vision and energy of the woman who had nursed it from the pilot stage to full reality. Inevitably, Kolar would change it. Such successions can also kill friendships; as a program matures and becomes identified with the new chief, the old leader can easily feel discarded and even betrayed. But there's no such problem apparent at Parkway North. The two women were kindred spirits from the start. Kolar too knows what it is to be a loser: as a child, she remembers hearing a school counselor tell her father that it would be a waste of time and money to send her to college. To this day the two can giggle over lunch like a pair of schoolgirls, Kolar's blond head bobbing close to Stocky's dark one. "Hey, I wouldn't turn this over to just anyone," Stocky says, and she hasn't been disappointed.

Buoyant, tireless and a gifted teacher, Carol Kolar has pushed the program effectively and learned the skills of bureaucratic survival. When a budget pinch came and she was asked to do without one of her two aides, she said flatly that she couldn't do the job unless both were there. And whenever she runs into reluctant teachers who would rather not adjust to skills classes, she shrugs and offers to go back to basics. "Everybody says, 'God, no,' " she says, laughing. "Once you get rid of basics, you'll never want it back." Now she is preparing the next step, an expansion of the skills project into social studies with a team-teaching feature built in.

At bottom, Kolar thinks, the skills class works through human contact. Fred Schue, one of the English skills teachers, comments dryly that this shouldn't be a big surprise; educators have known for years that one-on-one contact in small classes works. But in English Skills and Skills Tutorial, the contact is genuinely two-way. In most classes, Kolar says, teachers come to dislike the troublemaking kids for getting in the way of the lesson. In skills classes, however, "You learn to recognize their low self-esteem and you find out they're people. So when they act up, mostly because they're frustrated, you can handle it on a personal level. You take them aside and say, 'Hey, why are you

doing this to me? I'm your friend, okay?' And that's usually enough."
In return, the teachers can give students what may be their first real
edge in class by previewing a discussion. "I call it front-loading the
subject," says Kolar. "If you're going to teach, say, metaphors, you tell
a kid about it in skills class. Next day in regular class you say, 'Who
remembers what a metaphor is?' For the first time, this kid's hand goes
up. And the other kids, who haven't got a clue about metaphors, look
around and say, 'Hey, what's this?' The kid has a chance to shine.
From then on his whole attitude, his body language, starts to change."
The point is, Kolar says, that the transaction between teacher and
student is genuinely two-way: "Good things are happening on both
sides."

English Skills doesn't suit every student. Perhaps 15 percent of
those who sign up in freshman year decline the opportunity to reenlist
for the second year. But that's okay, says Kolar. Based on the record so
far, even those who refuse will probably do better in their unsupported
mainstream class than they would have done in the old basics class.
And the voluntary nature of the skills class is essential. "If they sign
up, we can expect cooperation and effort. We don't force it." Sometimes, she says, a kid who persistently misbehaves or won't work is
dropped from the class. "I'll call his parents and explain, and we keep
him out for a while until he starts missing it. Then he gets another
chance."

The telephone is an essential tool, particularly to reach parents of
the kids from St. Louis, and Kolar reports a high degree of success at
keeping in touch with parents. There are parents' nights at the school
and frequent written contacts. In the course of a year, she probably
talks to parents of all eighty children in her two skills programs. Most
parents do care, she says, but some are simply overwhelmed. They
tend to agree to whatever the teachers recommend. It's sad and unfair,
but the teachers do have to take on some of the parents' role. In Skills
Tutorial, says Jackie Morgan, "I'm a mom. I do exactly what I do with
my own kids: 'Have you done your homework? I'm gonna have to talk
to your teacher about that.' "

Skills Tutorial is a pleasant class. The room is windowless but cheerful;
posters on the wall tout the virtues of reading. There are nine kids

scattered around with two teachers, slim blonde Carol Kolar and short dark Jackie Morgan, moving quietly among them. Antoine Jones, cool and self-possessed, sits at the computer keyboard writing a composition. He likes the computer, he says, because it makes his handwriting perfect, even if he does misspell a word or two. Lisa Longhi is taking double-column notes on a social studies lesson, organizing the paper so that facts come next to subject headings and will make sense when they are reviewed. Julie Sapit is studying biology. Everybody is quiet, even Raoul Jefferson, the likable but explosive kid who seems always on the ragged edge of control. Raoul (not his real name) sometimes usurps the class, clamoring for attention no matter what else is going on, but today he is absorbed: he has a driver's education test coming up to get his license, and he's determined to pass it.

Kolar is working with Ricky Wood, a quiet youngster from St. Louis who is trying to write a descriptive essay for his English class. He has chosen to write about his bicycle, with its real neat derailleur and chrome-plated parts and stuff. "Stuff," says Kolar. "What stuff is that? Give more details." Ricky sucks his pencil. She waits, patiently.

Jackie Morgan is helping Perez Green, a large, friendly sophomore who is wrestling with algebra. The problem is converting pesos to dollars: if a dollar is worth 2,750 pesos, how many dollars will it take to buy a hat for 25,500 pesos? Perez sets up the problem, incorrectly: 1 over 2,750 equals 25,500 over X. Morgan doesn't say anything. Using a hand calculator, he multiplies 2,750 by 25,500: "Wow, seventy million." "Does that sound right?" she asks. "No it don't," he says. "So set it up the other way," she says. He does, and after more coaching, eventually gets it right.

Morgan didn't explain why Perez was wrong, and for him, the exercise was clearly an arbitrary bit of magic; he didn't get the principle of ratios and thus had no clue beyond trial and error which number should be on top or what he should do with them. That isn't ideal, but it's probably okay, Don Hugo says later. For one thing, Perez could figure out that his first answer was absurd, and that by itself was progress. If Morgan missed a chance to explain ratios, well, teachers do sometimes miss things, and there would be other days. Then too, Hugo once worked with a psychologist, and learned that about 30 percent of the patients show improvement merely because somebody is paying attention to them. "So I figure that if a kid comes in for one-on-one treatment, he's probably got a thirty percent chance of improving even if we give him bad advice," says the principal.

Most of the freshmen who enroll in the skills classes are there because their parents or teachers pushed them, and they tend to arrive sullen and resentful. For the first few days they are silent and withdrawn, or noisily rebellious. Gradually, they learn to accept help, then welcome it, then clamor for it; and most of them come back as sophomores. But the classes aren't given after sophomore year, a fact that many of the students bewail. "I wish I could have it all four years," says Raoul Jefferson. "I don't know what I'm gonna do next year without it." Parents too have learned that the program is good for their kids. In fact, says Kolar, some parents who begin by agitating for their children to be placed in honors classes are horrified when they bring home C's and D's, and start begging for a chance at skills class. The classes seem to have lost whatever stigma they may once have had. But to reinforce their prestige, Kolar is introducing the idea that they are also good for super-bright kids who may be having their own adjustment problems.

There is even beginning to be a pleasant kind of backlash over the skills program. Dan Natale, an assistant principal who helped Stocky set up the first skills classes, says he hears veiled complaints from some parents to the effect that it seems like a fine idea and it's a shame the schools aren't doing similar things for other students. Don Hugo says he has to deal with parents who ask whether it's true that the best teachers are being used for the slow learners, and if so, are their smart kids getting the leftovers? The principal assures them that all his teachers are good—and also tries to say that when low achievers do well, everybody in the school benefits: a rising tide lifts all boats. The point is a bit abstract, but it's true.

In fact, the whole program is a classic illustration of the Hawthorne effect. Hugo credits it with a good deal more than holding down the school's dropout rate. It has changed the attitude of what he calls the "inside dropouts"—those kids, a fixture in many schools, who keep coming to class but might as well not be there at all. The program has helped these students feel ownership of their own education, Hugo says, and raised the sense of self-worth that is crucial to any successful enterprise. What's more, the program's success adds to confidence and general excellence in other things the school does. As one small barometer, vandalism and petty theft have fallen to almost nil in the past five years. Not long ago, a local television station featured Parkway North as a good example in kicking off a series on education. "Everybody feels the excitement of that, and it becomes a self-fulfilling prophecy," Hugo says. "It's kind of like a good athletic program, where winning comes to be expected, a habit. Our girls' basketball team is like that, good year in and year out. We begin to think better of ourselves, and that belief system permeates the school."

What does all this cost? It's hard to say, not least because hardly anybody in the system really wants to know. In the beginning, the cost of the English skills program was soaked up in Larry Moceri's creative scheduling, with teachers willing to add to their class size to make room for the small special groups. Then the district funded Stocky's salary as reading specialist and paid for two added aides. To some extent, however, the cost of the skills program was offset as students elected it and thus reduced demand for other electives, some of which were then dropped. Creating the reading/writing center was a capital expense; keeping it supplied can be thought of as part of the library budget.

In all, by Kolar's reckoning, the skills programs are serving eighty kids each semester for a total cost equivalent to one teacher's salary. If the same eighty students were to attend all year and the teacher were paid $45,000, that would be $562 per kid per year, a true bargain. Accountants might quibble. But like any creative administrator, Don Hugo prefers to be a little vague about what things cost. "You find little ways of winning," he says airily: If you really need a teacher's aide and can't pay her enough, you may find a way to add to the job description and tack on a few more bucks. In all, he insists, the program is now an integral part of the school, and the cost factor is minimal. "We just keep milking what we've got to get the most out of it."

The skills program has naturally spread into other parts of the Parkway district, with South and West high schools introducing modified versions, and there is a related reading program in several junior highs. As word of its success has spread, Parkway has also been approached by other schools from distant parts of the country whose teachers are considering a similar approach to slow learners. From the reports coming back from those cloning experiments and the cases closer to home, Stocky and Kolar have put together a list of essential and desirable ingredients for a skills program. Some of the lessons:

• **The mind-set of the school must be prepared for a skills program.**   Parkway North has long believed that its business is mainly teaching kids,—a platitude that not all schools endorse—and that all children can learn. But some of its teachers had to be persuaded that low achievers aren't necessarily stupid, but just take longer to catch on. "The key factor is to build a climate, a culture where everybody can work together for the benefit of the kids," says Stocky. "And what we want for the kids is not that they learn a subject, but learn how to learn. That's what stays with them."

• **The program's director must have enough freedom and clout to be effective in the school.**   Over at Parkway West, says Hugo, the reading specialist has been given so many other chores that she can no longer move among classrooms, talking with teachers and helping to identify and solve real problems.

• **The program can start small, but it must eventually become part of the school's support services**—not a remedial class tucked away in the basement, but a centrally located facility that is routinely visited by high and low achievers alike. And the skills program must be run by a permanent staff. "You can't have a different teacher on duty every hour, taking turns," says Stocky. "You need continuity and a director who's a coordinator."

• **In a given subject, a student must have the same teacher in the skills class as in the regular classroom.**   "If not, it's like a doctor who doesn't know the patient's family history," says Dan Natale. "If the teacher doesn't know what has gone on in the regular class, it's no better than having a study hall teacher."

• **The stigma of "basics" classes must be avoided at all costs.**   Thus the class must be voluntary. And it's probably better to give it on alternating days rather than daily, although the program at Parkway West has worked with daily classes.

• **Skills classes in a specific subject must be small enough to**

give students individual attention. Five or six to a teacher is ideal; the maximum is probably ten to twelve. Parkway South's classes, with fifteen students, are too big.

- **Tutorial classes can be a bit larger, but not more than fifteen.** "These are kids who have been discipline problems all their lives," says Carol Kolar. "It can be scary in there sometimes. You don't want to face too many of them."

- **The right teachers are essential to the program's success.** Stocky says she spent most of a summer plowing through résumés and interviewing fully forty-five applicants to find the special blend of compassion, patience, skills, discipline and general knowledge embodied in Jackie Morgan. A certain maturity also helps: It would be unfair to give the job to someone fresh out of college, no matter how gifted.

- **Teachers must be willing to adjust their schedules to the needs of the skills classes.** In turn, teachers must be stimulated continuously and made to feel part of the program. Send them to conventions, Stocky says, and make sure they hobnob as much as possible with their principal and superintendent, so they will have a chance to earn respect and support for their ideas.

- **The skills class, like other electives, should be worth a credit toward graduation.** But it turned out to be a mistake to award grades for skills; since the first year, it has been a pass/fail course.

- **The program's director must be a diplomat, and must defend its political turf.** Keep the principal and the other teachers well informed, Stocky and Kolar advise; apply for national awards; don't hesitate to cultivate the press and professional publications. "When we got some awards, it was like, 'Maybe she's making sense,' " says Stocky. And a little visibility does wonders when budgets are being pinched. When this writer came to Parkway to see the program, the visit was the excuse for a dinner with Parkway Superintendent Don Senti and his assistant, John Borsa, over which Hugo, Moceri, Kolar and Morgan lobbied vigorously for the next year's expansion.

"We're always looking for the next step," says Don Hugo. And as he sees it, the next step for the skills program is to help integrate learning across the formal lines of the curriculum. The new pilot program was to be focused around social studies. Hugo, Moceri and Kolar saw it as an ambitious effort to integrate social studies, English, math and science through a team teaching program. Like English Skills, it would be aimed initially at underachievers. "We want to get around the typical disjointed high school experience," Hugo says. "We're creating this program to reduce the frustration level of kids who can't handle the work as it has traditionally been set up." The expansion ran into its first crisis when recession pinched the area's economy, eating into the Parkway budget by $4 million. But then came another show of small-bite spirit: The social studies teachers were so impressed by the success of the skills program that they voted to teach larger classes to make room for the pilot project, just as the English teachers had done in 1984. It was an auspicious beginning.

Parkway clearly has its sights set high, and its skills program will surely become more extensive. But the program has already forced a kind of evolution. The school's style of teaching has changed subtly, and teachers have learned to reach out to a special class of students. The teachers are experimenting with new techniques and show a new pride of ownership of the school and its programs. To Larry Moceri's pretended dismay, his staff now insists on interviewing candidates for hiring to see how they will fit into the mix. Perhaps, in the end, the Parkway system will have become what Henry Levin is trying to create from scratch: a set of totally reformed schools, built around a changed idea of how children learn. But it will have got there by degrees, taking one step at a time. The process can begin with a baby step; Rosemarie Stocky, for one, believes a skills tutorial could start in one corner of a study hall, with a single teacher offering constructive help to students who need it. "You'd get more kids coming every day," she says. "It would grow and grow as long as you kept feeding it. . . . Synergy. That's what's going to bring education back to life again. Just one thing leading to another, and more and more people getting involved."

Skills Tutorial is just breaking up when Jennifer Matthews breezes in. Jennifer is a warm, friendly girl, one of those bused to Parkway North from the inner city. She's a graduate, no longer in the class; she has learned her study skills so well that she is back on sophomore grade level. But she still drops in from time to time to hug Jackie Morgan.

Jennifer brims over with exuberant confidence: she's bright, joyous, almost bouncy. She grabs a visitor's hand and shows him the bulletin board where her name appears on two separate honor rolls, one for kids showing most improvement, the other for those getting all C's or better. "This place really helped me," she says. "They told me I had to shape up or ship out. Now I'm gonna make something of my life. I'm gonna be happy."

3.
Fannie Mae's
Great Expectations

They make an odd pair: Harriet Ivey the very model of the fast-track executive, honey-blonde, slim and thirtysomething, with just the right softly tailored suits and not-quite-feminine office decor; Lucile Christian the tough black principal, lean, sharp of eye, precise and emphatic in speech, a woman who takes nonsense from nobody. And it wasn't exactly love at first sight. From the beginning, neither wanted to be used by the other for some cheap bureaucratic maneuver or public-relations stunt. At the start, their insistence on high standards was in part a test of mutual commitment, a kind of self-protection. But in the end, everybody agrees that it was only because expectations were set high and kept there—the second major principle of small-bite programs—that the partnership has succeeded.

And succeed it did. The program, pairing the Federal National Mortgage Association (FNMA) and H. D. Woodson High School in the bleak northeast corner of Washington, is anything but cheap. In fact, it is the most luxurious effort in this book, and can be replicated only with the help of a truly generous and fully committed corporate angel. But it's worth what it costs. The program has seen 208 kids earn $225,000 in college scholarship credits, and at last count 123 of its graduates were attending classes at forty-four separate colleges and universities. It has given the school in general a new sense of achievement and a glimpse of the kind of life open to students willing to work. And its mentoring, pairing people from the company with kids from one of Washington's poorest neighborhoods, has opened flight paths to middle-class life for dozens of students and created real bonds of friendship across gulfs of class, age, race and quality of life.

The stories are legion. There was Ronald Benson-El, afflicted by senioritis, who never got around to applying to college; his mentor organized a rescue long after the deadlines had passed, and Ronald became president of his freshman class at Winston-Salem State University in North Carolina. There was the girl whose mother, hopeless and perhaps a bit envious, persuaded her that she had no chance to go to Northeastern University, and whose mentor got the company to pay her fare to Boston for the tour and interview that got her in. There was the boy who was stranded when his mother and her boyfriend, crack addicts, stole his train fare to college; his mentor drove him five hundred miles in time to matriculate. The highest expectation of all is that you don't give up.

The impetus for the program, called Futures 500, came from David Maxwell back in 1988. Maxwell was then chairman of the board of FNMA, universally known as Fannie Mae, a unique financial hybrid originally set up by Congress to rescue the housing industry in the Depression by providing federal guarantees for private mortgages. Now independent of the government, Fannie Mae has grown into the nation's sixth largest company and one of the biggest employers in the District of Columbia, and it was about to celebrate its fiftieth birthday. Maxwell was a thoughtful man who had long been troubled by Washington's tangled pathology of drugs, crime, urban decay and strained race relations, and he wanted the company to try something to help— in part to return something to the city, in part from a sense of enlightened self-interest: No company can prosper surrounded by squalor, ignorance and decay. He decided to set up a partnership with a local high school and a scholarship program for its students, modeled on a program *The Washington Post* had started the year before at the city's Eastern High.

Harriet Ivey, Maxwell's bright young vice president in charge of community relations, drew the job of making it happen. She consulted community leaders in Washington's far northeast section, one of the city's lowest-income areas, where Fannie Mae was already involved in a program to help residents buy their homes, and they sent her to Lucile Christian, the principal of Woodson High School. The courtship was cautious. On the Fannie Mae side, neither Maxwell nor Ivey wanted a superficial program to chrome-plate failures; they were willing to make a ten-year commitment of $1 million in scholarship money, but they wanted a decent school that was serious about educating kids and would commit its own time and energy to nurse the program along. But Christian wanted the same things from Fannie Mae, with assurances that the company wasn't out for a quick polishing of its image and wouldn't be hopelessly naïve about the problems it was getting into. The questions from both sides were challenging: What do you want this program to achieve? Will you assign a full-time staffer to this? Each woman soon decided the other was serious, and from that point on it went smoothly. "She was very open to ideas," Christian says. "We had a lot of very good dialogue."

Ivey's best credential was the solid ring of that figure: one million bucks. But the rest of her answers also rang true, and Christian knew that Fannie Mae had a solid record in its community service programs. From Ivey's viewpoint, what Woodson had to offer was obvious in the school itself. It had been built in 1972 as an innovation, a high-rise urban school towering unexpectedly seven stories tall amid the warehouses, small shops, dingy factories and shabby homes of the northeast side. From the start, a dedicated staff had insisted that its escalators would run, its walls would be graffiti-free and its students would show and deserve respect. It's known in the area as the Tower of Power, a source of community pride and a place where kids can get a decent start. "It doesn't appear to be an inner-city school at all," says Ivey. "It's immaculate. You could just tell there's a real feeling of care and respect. We felt the place was really under control and we could work with them."

As much as anyone at Parkway North, both women endorse the idea that all kids can learn. But this program approached that principle from the opposite side: not to help slow learners with specific subjects and study techniques, but to motivate the whole school to set higher standards and make the effort to achieve them. The scholarships were meant to raise expectations and self-esteem at Woodson by rewarding excellence, and the first standard to be raised was that there could be no exceptions: Only students with top grades would be eligible. A student who got all A's and B's for a semester would earn $500 in a special account, to be used for higher education. In theory, a Futures 500 member could earn $4,000 toward college tuition in four years at Woodson. In practice, since most Washington students stay in junior high through the ninth grade, there was a $3,000 ceiling, and some Woodson kids might not qualify before their junior or senior years. Students already in the program could remain members if their grades slipped below the threshold, but no money would be given for a below-standard semester.

Fannie Mae was willing to go for the long haul, backing up its $1 million in scholarship money with real corporate resources. There would be as many as twenty summer internships for students in the program, bringing them to Fannie Mae's campuslike headquarters cluster in northwest Washington to see the corporate life firsthand and learn how to dress, work and behave in the new environment. The company would also assign a full-time staffer to the program. That turned out to be Lonnie Edmonson, a voluble, likable former teacher; he has access to the top officials of Fannie Mae and a mandate to keep the program healthy and effective. Christian matched that commitment with a full-time coordinator at Woodson: Aona Jefferson, a warmly motherly teacher and coach who cheers, chides, exhorts and generally rides herd on her charges like a combination of Mister Chips and Henry Higgins.

In the beginning, Maxwell and Ivey hadn't envisioned any mentoring. But as the talks continued, that idea seemed more and more important. For one thing, if the program was to be more than a token gesture, there had to be contact between Fannie Mae and actual students. More important, the Woodson kids came from the bleakest of neighborhoods, many of them from broken or single-parent homes with multiple problems. They needed adult friends, and practical help in choosing colleges and applying to them. They also needed role models to give them an introduction to middle-class life. It was Christian's idea that mentors should be mandatory; as she put it to Ivey, "If you give the kids a choice, they'll say, 'I don't need that.' But they all need it. I want all of them to have that opportunity." Ivey agreed, and promised that Fannie Mae would not only seek out mentors but give them up to ten hours of company time each month so they could form more than superficial bonds with their students. "There are a lot of mentor programs around that are pretty shallow, in terms of guidance," she says. "It is much more than having lunch with your student every once in a while, patting him on the back."

By the time the two women had to go before the Fannie Mae board of directors to ask for the money, Lucile Christian knew this was something she wanted. "I serenaded them," she says with a chuckle. When a director asked whether the school would continue the program even if she weren't around as principal, "Of course my answer was yes, I was sure the district would continue it." That was at best a leap of faith, and the directors had to know it, but it was also a sign of commitment. "I guess they felt comfortable," says Christian. "The next thing I knew, we were partners."

If she had any lingering misgivings, the first Futures 500 assembly dispelled them. It had been her idea that the kickoff should be formal and ceremonious, to get the kids' attention and impress them with the program's promise. There were only thirty-three students in the school with grades good enough to qualify in October 1988, and to the rest of the 1,250 Woodson kids the program was a yawn. A few nerds were in some teacher's-pet club that had nothing to do with anybody else, and who cared?

They started getting an answer at the first sight of the auditorium. Nobody there had seen anything like it. Ivey had seen this as a chance to catch the attention not just of the kids, but the whole community, launching the program with a fanfare. For the occasion, the company had dressed up the plain room with flowers, a banner on the podium, skirts on the stage tables and decorative rubber trees eight feet high. There were visiting dignitaries, newspaper reporters, TV lights and cameras. The thirty-three lucky kids got certificates worth $500 apiece; up on the stage, they raised their right hands and took a solemn pledge to live up to the rules and standards of the Futures 500 program. The onetime nerds were celebrities, lionized and interviewed. And David Maxwell, a Philadelphia Mainline patrician from Yale and Harvard

Law, a remote and obviously powerful figure and the source of a cool million bucks, won a standing ovation when he was given a Woodson sweatshirt and, without missing a beat, stripped off his jacket and put it on.

"It was absolutely beautiful," the principal recalls. "The kids were in awe. They sat there and for the first time they realized what was happening." Not long afterward, Fannie Mae arranged to take the Futures 500 kids to a sold-out rock concert featuring Bobby Brown and New Edition, "and that kind of motivated the other kids, too," says Christian. "Some of them who had been just getting by with C's started to bombard us, wanting to know how to get in on it."

By the next semester, thirty-eight more students had raised their grades enough to qualify for the program, and parents of new students were asking about the club and whether their children could join. By the end of the second year there were forty-six graduates who had earned $84,000 in scholarship credits. And by the third year the active membership, with no grade lower than B, had risen to 10 percent of Woodson's student population. A total of 208 students had been reached by the program, earning $225,000 toward their college expenses. An outside evaluation by Coretta McKenzie, a former D.C. superintendent, concluded that Futures 500 was "a model program" that had made both school and company better places. But long before that accolade, Lucile Christian was a believer. "I know that some things cannot be measured," she told a visitor, but she could see them in the changed attitude of students and parents, the added effort and concentration and the whole atmosphere of the school. "The results might not be all that impressive stat-wise, but I can tell you that the real results, the feelings you get, have been all the way to the top of the chart."

The principal and her teachers insist that grade inflation has little or nothing to do with the rising number of kids qualifying for the program; students are simply working harder. And at Fannie Mae, where grade inflation was a worry from the start, it's no longer a serious question. The standards are being maintained, says Harriet Ivey, and at worst, "Teachers might give a kid the benefit of the doubt between a C or a B if they know he's in the program. But that's like what you factor in for attitude. I wouldn't consider it grade inflation." Lonnie

Edmonson thinks the club could grow to 25 percent of the school's population without endangering academic standards.

Critics sometimes argue that the standards are *too* high—that the great need is not to skim off the cream of the crop, who would succeed anyway, but to help kids at the bottom in danger of dropping out. Fannie Mae's answer is simply that it isn't that kind of program; as Edmonson puts it, Futures 500 is not for kids at risk, but kids at promise. They have plenty of problems as it is, all around them, but the high grade standard permits the program to be a success strategy, not social work. And Lucile Christian argues that the program really does reach beyond the high achievers, by encouraging others to try harder. "If I have a cause and sincerely want to improve, I'm going to work harder," she says, every syllable clear. "If I spend an hour at it and get a C, I can spend two hours and get a B. So we are getting to those children you might label as average. But I don't like labels. When you move their grades up to A and B, they're the same children. They were really above average all the time."

It has to be admitted that for all the talk of high standards, there is considerable room for improvement. Woodson's A's and B's come in the context of one of the nation's worst school systems, where standards as a whole are abysmally low; this is the system, after all, where the kids scored second lowest on the national math achievement test, but came in first in the nation in agreeing with the statement, "I am good at mathematics." For all their A's and B's, the Futures 500 students have yet to achieve combined SAT scores averaging 1,000 out of a possible 1,600. Some of the honor students get no better than 800, and very few go on to colleges that could be considered selective. Their SAT scores have been rising, but that is thanks partly to the Saturday Academy, an SAT preparation class run for them on weekends at Fannie Mae headquarters in northwest Washington. The hope is that the rise in scores will continue, that Woodson grades will reflect real achievement and that students from the program will gradually win admission to more selective colleges. And there's no quibbling with the club's overall success: Beyond doubt, it is nurturing achievement, sending kids to college who wouldn't have made it, and encouraging a general push for excellence at Woodson High. If that isn't perfect, it's a lot better than nothing and more than good enough.

*   *   *

In hindsight, the crucial element in the mix was the mentoring. The Fannie Mae executives could provide something that Woodson's teachers couldn't offer, and the human relationships between students and their mentors have been far more important than the scholarship money in leaping hurdles between the inner city and the college campus.

The process begins with choosing mentors. That was no problem in the first year of the program, when there were very few students and enthusiasm was high at Fannie Mae. In the second and third years, Lonnie Edmonson had to mount a modest recruiting drive, advertising openings and asking established mentors to suggest likely new members. But as the program grows, the number of people needed to run it increases, and the supply of mentors peaks out. By the third year there were about 150 people working as mentors or support staff, more than 10 percent of the total staff at Fannie Mae headquarters. Edmonson's enthusiasm for the program is contagious and his insistent tenor voice is remarkably persuasive. But given the competition from other community service organizations, that 10 percent may be the practical maximum. There are another one thousand staffers at nearby regional offices who might be tapped, but even so, Edmonson thinks he may have to start asking more mentors to take more than one student at a time—phasing in a sophomore, for instance, the year a senior is to graduate.

Putting mentors and students together is always delicate. Edmonson likes to match them by gender, though there are exceptions. It isn't feasible to match for race, even if that were desirable: All the students at Woodson are black, and roughly a third of the mentors are white.

The mentors run the gamut of Fannie Mae's staff, from secretaries to top brass. Ivey and Edmonson would like to see more corporate officers volunteering, but there are realistic limits to the time such executives can commit, and it wouldn't be fair to a student to pair her with a mentor who spends half her time on the road. Selection is also complicated by practical realities: Like other inner-city programs, Futures 500 attracts four times as many girls as boys, and that means there's an actual surplus of black male mentors. On the other hand, because Fannie Mae's female employees tend to be young and already dividing their time between family and career, there's a shortage of women mentors.

New mentors get only a brief session of formal training. "The idea is not to overtrain people," Edmonson explains. He doesn't want to encourage them to try to be psychologists or counselors, and mentors should understand that "this is a structured relationship." The mentor must initiate and control it, but without manipulation; the student shouldn't be made dependent or sent on a guilt trip. In practice, the training begins with a general orientation session and proceeds through one to four discussion periods of an hour or two each, covering adolescent development, cross-cultural sensitivity, problem solving and the pleasures and hazards of matched relationships. Then mentors are handed a fifty-page handbook and turned loose, with a promise of help when needed, to form a friendship. Goodwill is essential, but it also helps to be flexible and adaptable. "It's a teen, and it's not your child," says Ingrid Williams, a mentor who also works as a laser operations analyst. "Whatever comes along, you have to roll with it."

The first phase of the relationship is always slow and a bit stiff, a mating dance that is also a cultural collision. Edmonson begins with mixers, group events involving a basketball game or theatrical performance where students and mentors can share an experience and break the ice during intermission. After two or three such events, compatible pairs can be sorted out.

Over the years, the nature of these mixers has subtly changed. There are no more rock concerts, and fewer basketball games; the turf is shifting to the mentors' side, in museum trips and visits to the Folger Shakespeare theater, where Fannie Mae wants the students to become comfortable anyway. And these days the groups are smaller, with fewer trips involving buses. Edmonson wants to make group events more thematic and outright educational. A trip to a marine science museum, for instance, can be combined with assigned reading and a fishing and backpacking expedition, all linked in a Chesapeake Bay Studies program. But the occasion is still meant mainly to encourage casual mixing and mingling, and the beginning of real relationships.

The policy is that every Futures 500 member should have a mentor, and reluctant students feel continuing pressure from Edmonson and

Aona Jefferson at Woodson to cooperate with the program. If a relationship isn't working, assigned mentors also feel the heat. "After about two months, you either try harder or you start avoiding Lonnie Edmonson," says Donna Purchase, a mentor and secretary in the asset management department. But in practice, some students simply balk and others play at the relationship, and it's hard to know when to crack down on them. Of 104 students enrolled in the 1990–91 year, for instance, seven still hadn't submitted biographical information in February. Another twelve had been matched with mentors, but were dodging actual contact; their mentors, Edmonson says, were "anywhere from frustrated to pissed off. The other eighty-five relationships range from functional to so close I'm jealous."

No two mentor relationships are alike. On the student's side, the first awkwardness may be bridged by bringing a friend along for the first couple of visits with a mentor; the mentor in turn tries to be casual and respect a student's privacy without seeming uninterested. As the friendship grows, mentors must be flexible and avoid too much Type A executive behavior. It isn't a job that can be tackled and finished and entered on the résumé. One of the hardest things to learn, says Edmonson, is the emotional side of the relationship: to expose feelings, play roles and interact, not simply to gather facts and give sound, dispassionate advice. A good deal is left to the taste and discretion of the mentors. Most of them meet their students casually for sodas, take them to lunch and go on trips to museums, plays or out-of-town college campuses. Some develop close friendships, in and out of each other's houses; others put their family lives off limits. It can work well either way. All have been careful to avoid situations that could be sexually compromising, and so far the program has avoided any hint of scandal.

Mentors have to deal with the problems chronic to most teenagers: the students can procrastinate, forget assignments, ignore deadlines and be lazy. Mentors say they are forever reminding their kids about forms to be filled in and documents to be copied. "Take nothing for granted," says Garey Crossons, a mentor of legendary warmth and dedication and an analyst in Fannie Mae's liquidations department. "They tell you the counselor is filling out the financial aid form, but he isn't." Students may casually assume that a mentor is there to do the dirty work. Ingrid Williams recalls reviewing college applications with her student, suggesting points to be stressed in the essays. "She kept nodding," says Williams. "So later I asked, 'Did you say all that?' She said, 'Oh, didn't you write that for me?' I had to say no, that wasn't my job. She was going to have to do that for herself."

There's an added problem that seems endemic to inner-city kids, one that drives mentors crazy: a tendency to break commitments without warning. It may go with undependable lives and friends, or it may be a complex twist of low self-esteem. Whatever the cause, it's a chronic peeve for Lucile Christian. "We've had to say to them, 'You are talking about money,' " she says. " 'When you do not attend a program and Fannie Mae has paid $25 for a ticket, add that up.' And I have given them tongue-lashings. 'You are making it bad for your sisters, your cousins. The program might not be here anymore because the record shows we can't depend on the students.' " Still, most of the mentors have had at least one experience of waiting in vain for a student to show up. "We have to teach them at least, if there's a legitimate emergency, pick up the phone," says the principal. "Or have someone else call. That's just common courtesy." They learn, but not fast enough.

Nearly all the mentors describe friendships that change and deepen over time. The students often come with odd notions of what it means to work for a big company, to be a success, to have casual working relationships. "A lot of them think we're a bunch of rich folks," says Donna Purchase. "Come to find out we have the same problems as other people, just like their neighbors." Janice Daue, a mentor from the community relations department, says her first student came to her apartment expecting some sort of glitzy Brenda Starr layout and found herself instead in a typical young career woman's apartment, with a single armchair, leftovers in the refrigerator and no curtains on the windows. And if they begin with a vision of Easy Street in the corporate suites, the kids soon adjust to reality. When Natalie Thomas went from Woodson to an internship in Fannie Mae's legal department, she says, what surprised her was "the level of intensity, how competitive it is. Everybody is running around all the time doing their work and trying to get promoted. I realized I'm gonna have to be serious."

At the outset, few of the students have any real idea what the program is about. "They get into it for the money and the trips, because it looks exciting," says Ingrid Williams. "But then they start to appreciate the help they get with the SATs, the Saturday Academy, the whole relationship." Marlisa Smalls, a junior at Woodson, says her biggest payoff was a rise of fully 90 points in her SAT math score. But there was also a cookout at the home of her mentor, dinner at a good restaurant, a movie and a basketball game together; and although her mentor wasn't always available, she began to appreciate the reflected prestige in the fact that she had a mentor who was a vice president. In the beginning the corporate pecking order may be no big deal, but the students are quick to pick up the signals of status and the fact that it's earned by achievement—and Fannie Mae tries to reinforce that lesson with direct experience. Students and their mentors tour college campuses and visit a Washington they have never explored: suburban homes, corporate offices, the Folger Shakespeare theater, music that isn't rap and learning that's actually enjoyable. In one memorable outing, the Futures 500 kids got decked out in ball gowns and rented tuxedos for a dinner at the Kennedy Center honoring "living legends" of the black community. They got to meet, among others, presidential candidate Jesse Jackson and Rosa Parks, the lady whose refusal to give up her seat on a bus in 1955 launched two decades of struggles for civil rights.

The summer internships, too, are important. Edmonson hopes that some of the alumni will find careers at Fannie Mae, but there are no promises, and that isn't the main point; what matters is getting to know and function in the corporate scene. The students also get their standards raised another notch. Jacqueline Lovingood, a counselor at Woodson, observes that teachers there tend to do too much hand holding and give too many second chances, but students working at Fannie Mae "get an opportunity to see the real world and find out that it won't tolerate bad work habits." Fannie Mae executives in turn have their stereotypes stretched when it turns out that inner-city students can learn to dress conservatively, get to work on time and perform reliably, taking a real interest in their work.

As a group, the students are increasingly diverse. After that first dramatic assembly, kids who weren't traditional nerds started applying to the program; now Futures 500 includes athletes, student politicians, musicians and something like a cross section of the school. They are elite, and know it. English teacher Ken Friedman says the club members "have an air that isn't quite snobbish, but kind of says, 'I've arrived.' " But it isn't a closed group, and anyone who works hard enough can get in. Aona Jefferson underlined that after the third year with a major personal effort, plowing through the transcripts of all the students in the school to find those who missed qualifying for the program by only one or two C's. She sent them letters pointing out how close they had come and suggesting an added push, perhaps even a tutorial. That effort may pay off, or it may lie fallow for a few years, but she thinks in the long run it will make a difference. Lonnie Edmonson has been surprised by the number of double-takes he has seen: students who don't realize until the program is over what a mentor has meant to them, or kids who don't show any interest in internships until they are sophomores in college. It is a program that plants seeds.

The mentors find both frustrations and rewards in the program. For some white workers, it's their first real exposure to black folks, and they have to bridge gulfs of both race and class. After they overcome their ingrained fears and drive into shabby black neighborhoods to meet their new friends, what can they talk about? Some of the relationships founder on these differences, and some mentors, black and white alike, aren't really comfortable in the role and drop out after the first year. For others, being a mentor opens up a new world. Janice Daue's first student proved to be her first interracial friend, a rich and rewarding relationship that continues well into the college years: "She brings me her report card now. And just as I've been able to help her, she's helped me over a couple of problems, too." There are times, says corporate communications specialist Harrison Hewlett, when it's a nuisance to be mentor: you don't necessarily want to go to a basketball game or dither endlessly yet again over which college is best. But he remembers that once, when a cabbie asked him what kind of day he had just had, he surprised himself with an answer that had nothing to do with his work or his family. "I had a great day," he said. "Two kids I'm working with just got accepted to college."

None of this comes cheap—a fact that Fannie Mae has understood from the outset. When Lonnie Edmonson was first recruited to run the program, he asked Harriet Ivey, reasonably enough, how much money he could spend on each child. "I said we can't really look at it that way," she recalls; they would spend what was required. She still can't say offhand what the program has cost, "but we spend more money on supporting it than in scholarship dollars, I'm sure of that." She's right, says Edmonson. By his reckoning, in its first three years the program committed $225,000 in scholarship funds and $300,000 in direct operating costs, including everything from tuxedo rentals to time off for mentoring. In addition, Fannie Mae spent $75,000 each summer on the internship program, by no means a total loss since the kids did work for their pay. Training and development cost a total of $50,000 in staff time, and salaries for himself and his staff came to $250,000. Divided by the 208 students who benefited from the program, the outlay came to roughly $4,500 apiece. That's a little more, he says, than the cost of a good summer program for inner-city kids.

The program has also changed Fannie Mae, in ways both large and small. The experience of mentoring has brought unlikely groups together, not necessarily reflecting the corporate pecking order, and that has opened up lines of communication in the company and changed the corporate culture. This process will accelerate with Edmonson's latest shake-up. He is decentralizing the program, forming the corps of mentors into small peer groups that can take over some of the leadership he has provided. Each group leader now handles the training of new mentors, for instance, and supervises the matching of mentors with students. That will provide more time and attention for the mating dance. More important, Edmonson hopes the new group structure will encourage new ideas and approaches to problems. "When people have ownership of the program and run it themselves, they'll provide more energy," he says. In the first month of the new approach, the groups were already finding that he was right. Mentors who had never spoken out in a meeting were finding their voices.

There is a bit of nervousness about the new order: a vice president is perhaps too effusive about being a mere member of a peer group, with a lower-level executive as group leader. But the experience overall has been good for the company, in ways that go well beyond David Maxwell's original intentions. In fact, the Futures 500 program has had Hawthorne spinoffs not only at Woodson, but at Fannie Mae too. According to the McKenzie report, even staffers who hadn't joined the program were proud of working for a company "that cares about more than business itself."

Edmonson plans more improvements. He hopes to encourage more boys to get into the program, and he wants to enlist more kids at earlier stages, perhaps reaching into Woodson's feeder schools to sign up ninth-graders. He and Lucile Christian also want to use the program to fire up some Woodson teachers who seem content to coast along at the conventional D.C. speed. If Fannie Mae can offer internships to three Woodson teachers every year, they reckon, giving them summer jobs and training that qualifies them for upgraded status and pay as teachers, they will be exposed to Fannie Mae's way of doing things and will be motivated to raise their own standard of teaching.

But all these are refinements on a successful model. Futures 500 is clearly up and running, and it is a program that can be duplicated or adapted for use in other schools with other deprived populations. The first necessity is to find a corporate partner with deep pockets and a willingness to make long-term commitments. Beyond that, these are the essential ingredients:

• **Commitment.**   It must come from the top and from both partners. "You need a David Maxwell," says Lucile Christian. "And you need a me."

• **Common goals.**   The program's targets have to be thrashed out, defined and clearly understood on both sides. There are going to be problems, and they can't be solved except on a basis of shared values.

• **Leadership.**   Both school and company must designate one person, with real clout, to run the program at each end and sort out all the details. Depending on the size of the program, this may not be full-time job, but authority at each end must be delegated to a highly visible central person.

• **Coherence.**   Scholarship plans can work without mentoring, and vice versa. But the key to Futures 500 is the way the two halves reinforce each other, with the goal of college as the focus for the student, the school and the mentor.

• **Mentors.**   It isn't clear whether mentoring has to be mandatory, but it should be actively encouraged. For most students, whether they welcome it at first or not, it turns out to be a good thing. But the mentoring relationship has to be carefully nurtured and supervised, with plenty of time for the prospective partners to get to know each other.

• **Discipline.** Rules must be clear, simple and enforced without exception. If Futures 500 students get to the Saturday Academy late, they aren't given carfare; if they get a C in any course, they lose $500. It is a powerful inducement, and a clear illustration of the meaning of standards.

• **Community involvement.** Make sure the community at large knows what the kids stand to gain from the program, and welcome parental involvement. Even when homes are broken or troubled and parents have little to give, they want good things for their children.

• **Trumpets.** Provide ruffles and flourishes. It is essential to recognize and praise the successful students, and the mentors as well. Ceremonies, formal pledges, official certificates and publicity all help.

And after all that, mentors and their partners must be willing to walk whatever extra miles turn out to be needed. In the case of a kid whose real name isn't Malcolm, there were several extra miles.

The hard part was past, and Malcolm seemed to be in good shape. He had been through the program, done well in an internship at Fannie Mae and scored well on his SATs. With accumulated interest, his credit in the Futures 500 account stood at $1,566. Malcolm's mentor, business analyst Henry Cooper, had taken him on inspection rounds at several colleges, and Malcolm had been accepted in a special program in computer science and technology at a college in southern Pennsylvania. Cooper drove him up for orientation and Malcolm settled in for four years of college. Cooper figured he could back off a little now; he didn't want to be continually looking over the boy's shoulder, so he sat back and waited for Malcolm to call.

But it was Aona Jefferson who got the call, in her office at the Tower of Power. Malcolm was in trouble. "I couldn't figure out what was wrong, but I could hear the panic in his voice," she says.

The problems seemed almost trivial. Malcolm told her he had been assigned a roommate who wasn't a freshman, and said vaguely that they weren't getting along. "Yes?" she said. "And?" And he wasn't having any luck getting in touch with his official college adviser. "Yes? And?" And that was all, but it was enough: Malcolm had left school, less than three weeks after he got there. His mother had come and gotten him, and he had officially dropped out.

Cooper heard about it almost by accident, from another Fannie Mae executive who was the mentor of one of Malcolm's friends. "My mouth fell open," he says. "I went through denial and shock, and then I called his home. He was the one who answered the phone. I think that was the part that hurt me most, that he hadn't called me anywhere along the line." But now Cooper said, Well, let's have lunch and talk it over, and they did.

Cooper thought the two had a good relationship, but it had been brief; Malcolm's first mentor had left the company, and Cooper inherited him only for the senior year and the intense business of getting into college. Malcolm may simply have been too embarrassed to tell Cooper his troubles. Aona Jefferson says he's shy, wary of exposing his feelings or getting caught short; at one of the icebreaking parties, he wouldn't even try the Chinese food. In any case, he was still vague about his problems at college. Cooper never got it really straight. The roommate wasn't abusing Malcolm, but he was letting somebody else stay in the room; there were vague hints that maybe something illegal was going on. In any case, Malcolm felt somehow trapped and afraid to complain. And he was adamant: he wasn't going back.

Well, Cooper said, what *did* he want? Maybe Malcolm had made the right move in leaving, but he surely hadn't found the right way to do it. The important thing now was what he would do to retrieve the situation. "I was candid with him," Cooper says. "I told him how it would affect his application to the next school, and I told him not to expect a lot of help from the program in finding a job. I said, 'Do you want to work at Burger King for the rest of your life?' He's a sweet kid, but I don't think he realized what he had done to himself. Reality started setting in."

Malcolm decided he wanted somehow to get admitted to another college. That wouldn't be easy at this late date, Cooper told him, and Malcolm was going to have to do most of the work himself. Fannie Mae would help, and it did: Lonnie Edmonson's assistant, Lynn Williams, spent weekend time assembling records and financial aid forms for the hurry-up applications. David Maxwell, who was about to retire from the chairmanship, took an active interest in the case, and the company even cosigned a financial aid application for Malcolm. But it was Malcolm himself, with a new sense of what was at stake, who did most of the work. "We had been through this before, so he knew what had to be done," says Cooper. "When he needed something I would be there, but I was helping maybe thirty to forty percent, not seventy to eighty percent as I did the first time." Cooper's biggest intervention was to help Malcolm establish legal residence in Virginia, to qualify for lower tuition when George Mason University admitted him.

And it all worked. "He grew up really quick," says Cooper, back at his main job installing a new computerized loan system for the company. "We had given him the tools to do what needed to get done, and he had to call on those tools a little sooner than he expected, maybe. But he got it done. The nice thing about all this was that he did grow, he did learn something. I was just reinforcing his own damage control." And when they last talked, Malcolm was doing well at George Mason. "He was liking his classes, and he seemed to be on the ball," says Cooper. "He really seemed comfortable with himself. It's been a happy ending. So far."

That "so far" is a fair measure of what's needed. The highest standard of all is never giving up.

4.
Letting Those
Who Can't, Teach

Meeting Juan Gonzales and a couple of his buddies on a barrio street in San Antonio, a street-smart pedestrian might well flash red alert. Juan's hair is an eighth of an inch from his last skinhead shave, and his sneakers and T-shirt are ragged and roughly mended. At fourteen, he has crude tattoos on both arms. The fact that he reads two years behind grade level doesn't exactly show, but it wouldn't come as a surprise that he goes to something called the Southwest Enrichment Center—the latest euphemism for a school for hard cases.

The real astonishment is to watch *Mister* Gonzales, the teacher's aide, at work in the back of Kay Farmer's first-grade classroom at the Southwest Elementary School. Farmer is conducting a lesson up front, with most of the class paying close attention. Around a tiny table in the back, Juan is teaching remedial skills to three low achievers— David, with quick black eyes in his olive face; Alexis, a blond rarity in this district where 90 percent of the kids are Hispanic; and shy, pretty little Anjelica. They are all quiet and absorbed, playing an educational board game and learning to tell time. A series of clock faces marches along the winding track from Go to Finish, each face with hands set somewhere between 2:05 and 2:55. Each player turns over a card with a time printed on it and tries to find the next clock face along the track with hands telling that time. Anjelica can't find a face that reads 2:25. Juan waits, patient and quiet. Alexis counts aloud by fives—"Fifteen, twenty, twenty-five, see, Anjelica, there it is"—and Anjelica moves her plastic token six more faces toward the finish line.

Juan holds up a peppermint in a twist of cellophane: a prize for the winner. "Are you gonna try harder now?" he teases. "I'm gonna cheat," says David, matter-of-fact. The game moves on, and sure enough, David cheats. When his card says 2:50, he puts his token on a matching clock face far down the track. "Hey, David," says Juan, tapping a 2:50 face that David has blithely skipped. "Put it here, man." "Awww, Mr. Gonzales," David grumbles. But he brings the token back. Juan tousles his hair. The game goes on.

Juan Gonzales (not his real name) is an extreme example of the small-bite principle that education should be done with children, not to them, and that good programs make maximum use of the students themselves. In fact, he's giving a whole new meaning to the old canard that "those who can't, teach." Since 1984, more than 875 South Texas teenagers with severe learning problems have been put to improbable work as classroom tutors for some 2,225 elementary school pupils. It's called the Valued Youth Partnership (VYP), a program originally funded by the Coca-Cola Co. and now running with a combination of funds from Coke, the federal Department of Education and local school districts. The smaller kids, all of them behind their classmates in basic skills, have profited handsomely from the tutoring. But the biggest benefits have gone to the tutors.

The program was designed for Hispanic-American students, the nation's fastest-growing minority, who face most of the poverty problems of the black kids in Woodson High with the added disadvantage of a language barrier. Hispanics are concentrated in a few cities (New York, Miami and Los Angeles among them) and along the Mexican border, but they pose a challenge to schools across the country. All told, 38 percent of all Hispanic children drop out of school, nearly three times the rate for blacks and five times that of white children. And given their records, the Valued Youth tutors are among the likeliest to leave. If nothing were done about them, perhaps 90 percent of them would be gone by the end of the year they enter the program. But their actual dropout rate has been almost unbelievably low, between 1 percent and 6 percent. Their school attendance is up: "I have this kid depending on me," one of them explained to a reporter. They haven't become angelic, but the trouble they get into tends to be less frequent and less serious than before they joined the program. Their grades and test scores have improved. In one recent group of ninety-five, three made the honor roll and nine more came within a single grade of it. Perhaps most important, their real achievements make them think better of themselves. After two years in the program, they want to be teachers, lawyers, doctors, coaches, designers or detectives; only 10 percent of them no longer have an idea what career they want.

In the first-grade classroom, says Kay Farmer, Juan is a real help. Thanks to his tutoring, Alexis is now reading at grade level. And all the kids in the class look up to Juan, especially David. David used to be a behavior problem, but these days when he acts up, Farmer just asks him, "Do I have to speak to Mr. Gonzales about this?" He quiets right down.

The Valued Youth Partnership was created by Dr. Jose Cardenas, a longtime Texas educator who is now head of the nonprofit Intercultural Development Research Association (IDRA). In the 1970s, while he was superintendent of San Antonio's Edgewood independent school district, Cardenas experimented with a pilot program using disadvantaged youngsters to teach each other. He founded IDRA to educate the public about the inequities of the educational system for Hispanic youth and to explore ways to remedy it. And in 1983, when Coca-Cola decided to start a Hispanic education program serving five of its major markets, company executives asked leaders in each of the five cities for ideas. Henry Cisneros, San Antonio's mediagenic mayor at the time, put Cardenas together with Coke to work out a program attacking the dropout problem.

The basic idea wasn't new. During the teacher shortage caused by the baby boom generation in the 1960s, peer and cross-age tutoring came to be used almost by default: If there weren't enough teachers to go around, the kids would have to teach each other. Studying the results, however, educational researchers began finding an unexpected but oddly logical development. The tutors were learning at least as much as the people they taught.

"Of course, that shouldn't be surprising," says Cardenas. He is a brusque, stocky man in his early sixties who has a good deal of personal force: piercing eyes, a formal, professorial turn of speech, and a thinly veiled impatience at having to explain his ideas yet again. "Most instructional activities are more beneficial for the instructor than for the one being instructed," he says. "So we capitalized on this." If bad students were made into teachers, he speculated, it might help persuade them that they were not losers and permanent misfits. If they were valued by other people, especially smaller children, they might learn to value themselves. And they might not drop out of school. "To a certain extent," Cardenas concedes, "we are pulling the wool over their eyes. We depend on the tutor's concern for the tutee, but the hidden agenda, let's say, is changing the behavior, attitudes, performance of the tutor. We just say something that is true, that we're interested in their assistance in providing help for little kids, and we don't emphasize that in doing that, they are expected to do a lot of growing, also."

Cardenas needed a director to run the program, and his shrewd choice was Maria Robledo, an energetic young woman with a doctorate in education from the University of Wisconsin, a long list of academic publications on Hispanic education and a talent for presenting the program at academic conferences and workshops. Known universally as "Cuca," she combines charm and efficiency, with sparkling black eyes over round cheeks and lilting inflections testifying to her childhood in Laredo, right on the border.

Cuca Robledo had been working with Cardenas for seven years, and the two approached the dropout problem with a logical question: What makes kids leave school in the first place? Conventional academic wisdom holds that dropouts reflect all the economic and social woes of the disadvantaged minorities—poverty, low value placed on learning, family dysfunction and peer pressures. Not so, says Cardenas; in fact, disadvantaged kids will stay in school if they are doing well there. It's that simple: "The big factor in dropping out is performance in school." But performance in school is influenced by many related factors. So Cardenas and Robledo laid out six objectives for the kids in their program. Along with reducing the dropout rate, they would aim to raise the tutors' self-esteem, increase their academic achievement, give them a more positive attitude toward school, improve their attendance and get their parents and the business community involved in the process of education. That was a hugely ambitious set of goals, but Robledo and Cardenas reasoned that none of them could happen unless all the others came about, too.

With a $400,000 grant from Coke, IDRA set up its pilot program in 1984 in five San Antonio school districts. (Oddly, the city has no central board; there are thirteen independent districts.) Over the next four years, a total of 550 tutors were assigned, from both senior and junior high schools, to teach 1,600 elementary school pupils.

It was a hard sell. Schools tend to resist change anyway, and this idea was especially hard for traditional educators to stomach: teachers naturally favor good students, but Cardenas was proposing to reward bad ones by giving them the status of teachers. Even worse, he proposed to pay them, giving them the minimum wage for each hour they spent teaching their charges. That would be practical proof that they were truly valued, and valuable. But Cardenas must have it backward, educators said. "Many schools say, 'Yeah, we'd like to go along with you,' " Cardenas says. "But then they say, 'Let's make a slight change. Let's put the valedictorian in there, because he's the best qualified to do the tutoring.' "

This objection is not crazy: After all, rewards should have something to do with incentives for good behavior, and the idea of handing out prizes for low achievement remains a little disturbing. It may be significant that at least one good student who was rejected for tutoring in the program started skipping classes in order to build a record bad enough to qualify. Cardenas argues patiently that the program is aimed at preventing dropouts, and very few valedictorians drop out of school. But even after that, the resistance tends to persist. Every year, teachers protest that it's the good students who deserve to be singled out, and surely they would do the job better. Even that point, however, is debatable. There's some evidence that slow learners actually do better than honor students as tutors—perhaps, the program's defenders argue, because they understand better what hampers underachievers and thus have more patience.

The pilot program proved that the basic idea can work with tutors at both senior and junior high school level. But as a pragmatic matter, says Robledo, "By the time they get to high school, we've already lost 50 percent of the potential dropouts." So the senior high programs were phased out, and the Valued Youth Partnership focused its energies at the middle school level. At that stage, says Cardenas, "We're looking at kids who have been eight or nine years in school, and they don't know the basic skills that you're trying to get the tutors to apply. They were taught reading, and they didn't learn to read; they were taught arithmetic, and they didn't learn that either." Why then will they learn now? Cardenas argues that when the tutors are confronted with a small child who must be taught reading or arithmetic, "for the first time they feel, in very practical terms, the necessity for learning."

But when the student is ready to learn, the school may not be ready to accommodate him. "Let's say a junior high school student says, 'Tomorrow I have to tutor a kid in subtraction,' and goes to the school and says, 'I need to learn to subtract,' " says Cardenas. "The school says, 'Well, subtraction is something we teach in the third grade.' His own math teacher is working on percentages or algebra or whatever, and may not have the time, the inclination, in some cases the interest even, to teach the kid."

That dilemma showed just part of the need for a support system for the tutors. If a small group of kids with problems were to be chosen from a junior high school and assigned to work with children from a nearby elementary school, they would have to have a teacher working at least part-time to select tutors, teach them what they needed to know and help them on the job. But somebody also had to handle liaison with the tutors' homeroom teachers and the elementary teachers. Somebody had to make sure everybody was in agreement and see to all the logistical details of getting the tutors to the right place on time, making sure as little as possible went wrong. The elementary teachers working with the tutors also had to be trained in how to use their new aides. All that led Cardenas and Robledo to the notion of a coordinating teacher, selected from the staff of one of the paired schools, as the centerpiece for each group of tutors.

The tutors clearly needed a lot of help, especially since most of them were reading two years below their grade level. To make sure they wouldn't be hopelessly behind their own pupils, it was decided that tutors should be at least three years older than the children they taught and that they should get at least a day's notice of what they would be expected to do in class. If a tutor didn't feel up to multiplication drill, she could go to the coordinating teacher for emergency review. The tutors would spend at least two weeks observing in the elementary classroom before they started teaching, and would get some basic educational training—not in specific subjects, but in how to communicate, how children learn and why they want to. And it worked out best to use the tutors for actual teaching in one period four days each week, with the Friday session reserved for a class with the coordinating teacher to brush up academic skills, discuss problems that might come up with pupils or with the classroom teacher, and generally let the tutors share experiences and encourage each other.

The program doesn't stop there. Cardenas thinks it's essential that the tutors and their pupils should go on field trips to visit local businesses, government agencies and museums and generally see the world outside the school. Successful adults who can be role models are invited to speak to the tutors at some of their Friday sessions. The tutors' parents are encouraged to take part, giving written consent to the program and attending evening workshops on parenting issues. And the tutors are given conspicuous recognition and encouragement through school assemblies, an annual dinner ceremony, local press reports and the like.

The Valued Youth Partnership has been an enormous success, recognized nationally. The Department of Education has provided funds to continue it in San Antonio, and Coca-Cola has put up an added $1.3 million to extend it to five more districts in Texas, California, Florida and New York for the next five years. Its boldness and counter-intuitive leap make it irresistible to journalists: the program has been written up in national publications including *Fortune, The Washington Post* and *The New York Times,* and has been featured on national television on NBC and ABC. All indications are that the tutoring actually helps the smaller children, whose grades and achievement test scores improve significantly in every subject. But VYP is most spectacular in its effects on the tutors.

They do stay in school, raise their grades and improve their attendance; an outside study found the tutors' reading grades rising by 35 percent in the first year of the program and 34 percent the second year. They also generally feel better about themselves. Many of the tutors change their way of dressing and their choice of friends. They learn to see the teacher's viewpoint, urging their small charges to do their work, pay attention and get organized. If they are going to be absent, some tutors even call the teachers to give notice. They use their biweekly paychecks to help with the family budget, some by taking care of their own clothing and other purchases, others by turning over part or all of the money to their parents. Many extend their tutoring to their brothers and sisters. At least one helped tutor her mother in pursuit of a graduate equivalent degree.

Their own words may be the best testimony. Like the chorus of students from Parkway North's enrichment program, the Valued Youth tutors are predictably enthusiastic about the program itself, saying it helps them to raise their marks and even to enjoy school. But there is another similarity in the sea change caused by the Valued Youth program: The tutors feel truly valued; they have learned to value themselves. Among many comments gathered by researchers and journalists over the years:

"I have to come and teach the kids. I don't miss too many days because the students ask me where I've been, and tell me that they miss me. Every time I'm absent, like last week, they ask me, 'Where were you?' I really like those kids. If I hadn't been a tutor, I would have missed more school."

"I made something good happen with Rosa. Now she raises her hand in class and gets her work done."

"My mom and dad are proud of me."

"I've been teaching Jose Luis, a third-grader. His grades are going up. He was having trouble in social studies. Now he's going to pass. The same thing happened to two other kids last year. Because I helped them, they passed."

"I have learned that I am really smart."

"[I] try to improve and be the best tutor that I can be, because you can never know, maybe some day when I'm old, I may need to go to a doctor and find out that I used to tutor that doctor."

The Valued Youth Partnership has both new and long-established programs. It's useful to look closely at one of each: the older pairing of Abraham Kazen Middle School with Antonio Olivares Elementary in South San Antonio, and a new one, Southwest Elementary School with the Enrichment Center for troubled middle-schoolers. Both stick to the formula that VYP has settled into: some twenty-five middle-school tutors working with about seventy-five elementary children.

In practice, the process begins with choosing the tutors—and like everything else in life, this involves a series of compromises. Honor students are ineligible, and "We don't even want the average kids," says Cuca Robledo with her lilting touch of accent. "We want kids who are really at risk." But certain obvious risks must be ruled out. It was clear from the beginning that all the tutoring would have to be done in the controlled atmosphere of the elementary classroom. And tutors with any record of drug use, for instance, or tendencies to abuse smaller children, simply couldn't be used. Even with those guidelines, recalls principal Victor Ortiz of Olivares Elementary School, "The first year was rough. We had a pretty rough bunch of kids."

The tutors were never any trouble in class. In fact, there has never been a major disciplinary problem with a tutor in any elementary classroom in the history of the program. But they didn't turn overnight into model students. Ortiz says some tutors occasionally vanished on the short walk to the Olivares campus from Kazen Middle School next door. There were fights among the tutors, and they used rough language. Once a couple of elementary pupils reported that they saw some tutors in the bathroom, pushing at a ceiling panel as if they were hiding something there, or maybe getting something out.

After that incident, Kazen's principal, Manuel Bejarano, took a hand in choosing the twenty-five tutors. Bejarano and Louise Gaitanos, the elegant, grandmotherly coordinating teacher for the two schools, maintain that their new standards didn't significantly change the tutor mix. "We still get some of those that we used to see constantly in the office for discipline problems," says Bejarano. He is a short, vigorous and round-faced man, with graying hair and the wary look of a longtime principal. "The rest are not bad kids, but they had kind of given up—they were saying, Why try to do anything, I'm gonna fail anyway. You have to pick the kids who are not going to make it, but you also pick those you feel will benefit." Louise Gaitanos, smartly suited in her classroom decorated with her tutors' drawings and poems, puts it just a little differently: "Most of them have failed somewhere along the line. They can be barely C students and still be good tutors, but they have to have some spark of desire to do something."

It is a delicate balance, and to some extent the choosing skews the results of the experiment, in the same way the voluntary feature of Carol Kolar's Skills Tutorial distorts that program. Just as the least motivated of Parkway North's low achievers can choose not to take part, so the Valued Youth tutors aren't a true cross section of the kids at risk, but in some ways the most promising slice. To that extent, VYP isn't rigorous proof that hard cases make good tutors. But as far as the educators are concerned, the aim isn't experimental precision, but helping kids. It's hard to quarrel with them.

After that first year, rules for the tutors' conduct at Olivares were also tightened up. VYP now requires that the tutors have an escort while walking between the schools. Gaitanos refuses, as a matter of principle, to do that, but she makes sure each boy and girl is logged out of Kazen and logged into Olivares within five minutes. To prevent any more bathroom incidents, the tutors are to use the toilets at the middle school before they leave. There is a dress code at Kazen, and it is a bit stricter for the tutors than for ordinary students; a girl with a skirt deemed too short, or a boy whose T-shirt message is too provocative, may be kept in the counselor's office during the tutoring class and docked a day's pay. It rarely happens. Almost instinctively, the kids seem to know what's expected of them. Without even being prompted, one eighth-grader recently removed his gold earring on the way to tutor his class.

The rules are a bit stricter for the tutors in the Southwest independent district, in part because they come from the tough Enrichment Center. In the first year of the program at Southwest, the Enrichment

Center was also new: an experimental middle school, intended as a last-ditch effort to reach a limited enrollment of two hundred troubled kids who still have a chance to be redeemed before they are sent to the Alternative School as confirmed delinquents. The "enrichment" consists of a curriculum built around archeology, the aim being to get students interested in lessons providing cross-disciplinary teaching in science, math, English and social studies. The school was still too new to measure results, said principal Laura Yzaguirre, but "I'm seeing a significant change in a lot of the kids." She is slim, gracious and smartly dressed, an incongruous figure for a principal of what most folks would still call a reform school. But the kids say that when she has to face down some adolescent tough, the eyes behind her big glasses can become ball bearings.

Some of the biggest changes among her students have been in the tutoring group. They tend to come to the center like all the others, wary and sullen, kids who wear labels as losers and troublemakers. For many of them, the only redeeming factor is that the center is a "choice" school, meaning that students and their parents must choose it and also that the school can choose not to accept them. When the VYP program was explained to them, a few seventh-and eighth-graders volunteered. All the volunteers were accepted, and the group was filled out with draftees. "We're not looking for angels," says Gilbert Garcia, Southwest's assistant superintendent. "These kids tend to be the leaders, in problems as well as other things."

As at Kazen, the standards are flexible and pragmatic. "I don't think we need pregnant girls going over there to be role models," says Yzaguirre dryly. "It might be hard to explain to the elementary parents." But the tutors start with fairly deep handicaps, and perhaps predictably, those from the Enrichment Center have run into more trouble than tutors from Kazen. Four of the original twenty-five were expelled for using drugs; two others served stints in the Alternative School for discipline problems, but then returned to the center—and to their tutoring chores.

"I see tremendous growth in their self-esteem and self-confidence," says Sylvia Glass, the deceptively formidable principal of Southwest Elementary school. At first, she says, "They were loud coming in the door" after the two hundred-yard walk from the middle school. "But after a few weeks I didn't hear them anymore." The tutors punch in on a time clock, greet the principal quietly and go to their assigned classrooms. And once there, they become young adults, addressed with the honorific "Miss" or "Mister" and uniformly adored by their young charges. Children who aren't being tutored sometimes get jealous of those who are. "The others will sometimes come up and say, 'Don't teach them, teach me instead,' " says a tutor. But the tutors themselves took the lead in defusing such situations: A couple of them volunteered to read aloud to their entire classes.

At first, the elementary school teachers were understandably dubious about the help they were being offered, and coordinator Nelda Wiest had her hands full placing the tutors. One teacher opted out of the program, and three more, after brief trials, said they didn't find the tutors useful. But the others, like Kay Farmer, are enthusiastic. If more tutors from the Enrichment Center become available, there is a waiting list for their services.

And problems, at least in the classroom, do seem minimal. The tutors have grown into their job as teachers' aides, even volunteering after school to help get the elementary children loaded into buses. There are stories of bewildered parents being introduced to "my new teacher, Mr. Alvarez," in chance meetings at a shopping mall, and being won over by the grave courtesy and sudden dignity of the teenage tutor. "It's really neat to see those little kids running after the tutors, yelling "Miss Estrada! Miss Estrada!" says Nelda Wiest, a large and rumpled woman with a glowing smile and an obvious affection for her charges. "I swear the tutors grow at least two feet taller on their way over here."

But in large part, like all the other small-bite programs, the Valued Youth Partnership works because its principals and teachers work so hard at it.

The first necessity is for principals at each of the paired schools to be solidly behind the program. They must mesh their schools' schedules to accommodate the tutoring, keep an eye on the logistics and maintain a constant dialogue to deal with problems and misunderstandings. "You have to have both principals gung ho, so they'll give me a free hand to walk in and contact the teachers to sell them the idea that these students will be useful," says Louise Gaitanos at Kazen. "I worked in another school where I didn't get the backing. I got a little storage room to work out of and one of those limp handshakes from the principal. So I had to talk a lot harder to the teachers." The principals are essential in matching tutors with teachers, correcting mistakes, enforcing the rules and pushing past the inevitable problems. But they must also be flexible enough to live with imperfection and tolerate each other's foibles. In the Southwest system, Sylvia Glass has imposed a ban on Bart Simpson T-shirts, on the ground that Bart conveys altogether the wrong message to elementary kids. "Oh, loosen up, Sylvia," teases Laura Yzaguirre. "It's only a cartoon." But the rule stands.

The second essential is to find coordinating teachers like Nelda Wiest and Louise Gaitanos: dedicated, motherly and willing to spend long hours at a frustrating job. "They have to be moms, mentors and white knights on chargers. They've got to see these kids as savable and lovable," says Merci Ramos, the VYP official who oversees the South San Antonio program. She is short and merry, with hair like an electric storm and energy to match; she shares with Cuca Robledo the chore of presenting the program at academic gatherings. "Many teachers, you couldn't pay them enough to do this job."

Gaitanos, for instance, teaches nearly a full load, with her coordinating activities counting for just one period a day. (Ramos would like to see that doubled to two periods, to make up for some of the extra time Gaitanos spends on VYP, but that remains a dream.) She works with the elementary school teachers, making sure they understand how to use their tutors, how to plan lessons for them, and how to intervene if a lesson isn't working or a tutor loses control. "When Plan A goes wrong, there always has to be a Plan B ready," says Ramos. "The teacher has to understand that this is not going to make her life easier right away, it's going to make it more complicated." Gaitanos also serves as a link between the elementary and middle school teachers, and she stays in constant touch with the tutoring classes, intervening when she sees problems and helping her tutors over the hurdles of dealing with smaller kids and adult teachers. "Maybe a kid is talking too much in class and getting into a conflict with the teacher," she says. "Maybe a tutor saw something that she thought was wrong going on in her classroom."

Gaitanos will intervene if necessary, counting on her warm presence and obvious sympathy to enlist support for her kids. In extreme cases, she will call in the principals—as she did when a strong-willed tutor (call her Maria) clashed disastrously with her teacher. Maria was switched to another classroom, where the teacher proved more flexible. Not all stories end happily, however: Maria herself dropped out of school, one of VYP's rare lost sheep.

The tutors themselves must be constantly mentored. The regular Friday classes are used to reinforce their training, discuss classroom problems and teach new techniques such as making flash cards for math review. Guest speakers furnish role models; one of Louise Gaitanos's most successful speakers was a glamorous local television reporter whose first job had been as a field hand. Gaitanos stresses the crucial dividing line between tutoring and counseling. Like the mentors of Fannie Mae, the tutors have to learn that they are to be friends and helpers, but they can't be responsible for their pupils' lives and they must respect the children's privacy. "Don't tell tales," Gaitanos says. "If a child tells you bad stories about his home life, it's not your responsibility to try to do anything about it. You can sympathize, but you tell only me, and if necessary I'll talk to the principal."

Such a case has come up only once, and Gaitanos won't discuss it—except to say wryly that she learned that such problems must be dealt with immediately, so that a tutor doesn't take them home and get her parents involved. But her Friday sessions usually emphasize positive things: what the little kids have learned, or how good it makes the tutors feel to be loved. She tells them about Monica, only two years out of Mexico, who went to an educational convention in Austin and gave a speech without a script to a roomful of school administrators. "I was so proud of her," says Gaitanos. She and her Kazen School tutors wrote, illustrated and published a seventy-nine-page pamphlet on how to be a tutor, and they write journals about their experiences. Among the poems on her wall is one by Anthony Medina, which concludes:

When we start leaving they all yell Bye
And some start to cry.

The tutors sometimes have to be taught odd facts of life. One boy from the Enrichment Center complained to Nelda Wiest that the little kids bugged him, always fighting over who got to sit next to him. "That's because they love you," she explained, and it came as a new thought to him. Another boy got in trouble with Sylvia Glass over showing his pupils a fan magazine she had banned. Okay, he said defiantly, "I'll drop out of the program." No, she told him, you just need to learn to think. But a little later she found his tutor's notebook and lapel ribbon in a trash can. She fished them out and gave them to Wiest with a message: she wanted him back. He came back—and after that, he made a special point of greeting her in the halls.

By and large, however, the kids aren't the real problem. If you put them in the right position and back them up, says Cardenas, the program will work just fine. The problems come from the grown-ups.

The tutors' parents, for instance, have never taken as big a part in the program as Cardenas and Cuca Robledo would like. "A lot of parents are losing their grip on their kids," she says. "And they don't see themselves as part of the solution." But it's hard to reach them through community meetings, talks with teachers and parent networks.

"This is my weak spot," says Gaitanos. She has a slight tremor in her voice, and it deepens when she talks about problems. "Parents are eager for their kids to be involved, and they plead with us to choose them. Those paychecks are important to the family finances. But they have to work all day so they can't come to school, and it's hard for me to make time for meetings in the evening." There are also a lot of single parents these days, frantically trying to balance work and family duties, and there is the chronic problem of absentee husbands leaving wives to cope alone. At Olivares Elementary, says principal Ortiz, the children are young enough that their parents still feel involved with them. But the parents who come to conferences are usually the ones whose kids don't get into trouble. Nobody knows how to reach the others. And to that extent, the success of VYP seems to prove that Cardenas and Robledo were wrong in at least one of their original assumptions: It turns out that at least some children can improve their school performance even if their parents don't become involved.

Teachers can also pose problems. As in the 1960s when teachers' aides first came into widespread use, some teachers resent or misunderstand the tutor system and try to use their new helpers as gofers: "Take this book and run it to the library, and get me a Coke on the way back." So VYP has decreed that tutors aren't to be used to correct papers or do chores around the classroom. "It's probably going to happen anyway," says Merci Ramos; the only answer is for the coordinating teacher to keep an eye on the problem, along with everything else going on. But this too has led to misunderstandings. In one case at Olivares, Gaitanos protested when a teacher had her tutor grade some papers. When Ortiz looked into it, he found that the teacher was only trying to help the kid understand teaching and the need for high standards and firm rules. Gaitanos knows Ortiz as a good principal, one of the rare ones who remembers kids from years back and recognizes their brothers and sisters when they come to school, and she had no problem with that explanation.

The middle-school teachers can be hardest to deal with. Laura Yzaguirre says some of her Enrichment Center teachers still don't understand that tutoring isn't a special favor. They complain that better students ought to be allowed to do it, and that a tutor who misbehaves in class or doesn't do homework should be punished by not being allowed to tutor. "I have to tell them this isn't a privilege, it's part of the tutor's curriculum," the principal says. Even worse, the middle-school teachers don't get to see the transformation of their problem students into genuine role models. Thus they tend to treat them with all the wary suspicion that their previous records have earned. That's natural enough, but it undermines the tutor's new self-esteem and reinforces the old impulse to act up. In effect, the tutor is living two lives, one as a reborn figure of dignity and worth, the other as the proverbial dog with a bad name.

Nobody's sure how to solve that problem, but Nelda Wiest has an idea. She wants to volunteer to take over classes for the Enrichment Center teachers, one at a time, during the tutoring hour so that they can go over to the elementary school and watch what goes on. If Juan Gonzales's teachers can see him with the little kids, she thinks, they will be a lot less likely to see him as the same tattooed skinhead in their own classes, and maybe Juan will get the chance he needs to succeed. It's a promising idea, but she hasn't been able to try it; there have been too many bureaucratic stumbling blocks in the way.

What does the Valued Youth Partnership cost? By Jose Cardenas's reckoning, the most expensive feature is the pay for the tutors, which comes to less than $20 a week for each of them. As it works in San Antonio, where the paired elementary and middle schools are within easy walking distance, there's no need for special transportation to get the tutors to work. But even if busing were needed, the trip would come at a time of day when buses are usually idle. The program must pay part of the coordinating teacher's salary; if that came to one period of a six-period day, it would be $5,000 to $6,000 a year, spread among twenty-five tutors and seventy-five younger children. All told, Cardenas estimates that VYP costs about $200 a year per child, including both tutors and their pupils, but not counting pay for Cuca Robledes and her staff, who are funded by Coca-Cola or the Department of Education. The portion of their salaries devoted to VYP would bring the cost per child to $300. It seems a remarkable bargain.

Can the program be adapted for use in other schools? Almost surely, the answer is yes. Robledo has even compiled a list of which of its features are critical, which important and which merely desirable. The first essential is another small-bite principle: a school must be realistic in assessing its problems; it is useless, for instance, to define a problem as "poor grades" without conceding that the school isn't teaching basic skills well enough. After that, says Robledo, "the principal is the key to the success of the project." If a principal doesn't see the program as useful or important, it will fail. Given clear thinking and commitment, these are among the other critical elements of Valued Youth:

• **Training.** Tutors must be given a chance to observe elementary classrooms before they start work, and must get at least thirty weekly training sessions each year. A coordinating teacher must design the program and ride herd on all of its complications.

• **Small classes.** Tutors should have no more than three pupils, with as few changes as possible during the term, for at least four hours but no more than eight hours a week. They must work under the supervision of an elementary teacher who wants their help, plans their work and provides feedback.

• **Wages.**   Tutors must be paid for their work, as concrete proof that they are truly "valued."

• **Field trips.**   Two to four educational excursions should be provided each year for tutors and their pupils.

• **Speakers.**   Tutors should have three to four guest speakers each year to provide positive role models for success.

• **Honors.**   Tutors must get individual as well as group recognition for their services in a year-ending event attended by the tutors, their teachers and school administrators.

By definition, the Valued Youth Partnership was designed to fight the dropout problem among Hispanic youth. Jose Cardenas makes no claim that it will work in other ethnic or demographic groups, and he warns dryly that it can't be stretched to its logical conclusion as a universal cure. "The solution for the educational problems of this country," says Cardenas, at his most professorial, "is not going to be to have half the students tutoring the other half." Granted, and obvious. But there is no reason why some failing students can't help some others, no matter what part of society they come from. At its core, the program proves that underachievers can improve their performance in school by tutoring younger kids, and that is a useful idea, whether the goal is to reduce dropouts, raise attendance, improve self-esteem or simply help kids get better marks. They all go together anyway. And that's one definition of improving a school.

5.

When Archie and Veronica Need a Friend

If the Valued Youth program of San Antonio is an unexpected and counter-intuitive use of students in educational programs, the most predictable way to use kids would seem to be in programs dealing with drug and alcohol abuse and the rest of the social ills plaguing American schools. It's so obvious that it almost doesn't bear repeating: Kids confide in each other far more freely than they do in their parents, or most other adults. Kids also see each other in the situations where such problems occur, and for adolescents, peer pressure is far more effective than parental lectures in changing behavior. So naturally, most student assistance programs must be built around peer helpers, who can spot problems and talk their friends into treatment, right?

Wrong. There are student assistance programs in an estimated 1,800 school districts, about 10 percent of the districts in the country, but a survey by the National Organization of Student Assistance Programs and Professionals found that only 12 percent of a random sampling of them claimed to have peer helpers as part of the program. Reasons vary for keeping students out. Some administrators say information on troubled kids is too sensitive and confidential for their peers to know; others say parents don't want their children getting involved with kids in trouble, not even to help them out of it. But people in peer helper programs scoff at both excuses, arguing that the kids know most of the facts anyway and that parents seldom really object. It's likely that another factor is at work: Just as the teachers of Valued Youth tutors doubted that the troublemakers they knew could teach anything, a good many educators cling to their traditional authority and instinctively reject the idea that students can be part of the power structure.

Whatever the reasons, Jim Thom thinks they're wrongheaded— and the program he has set up in Moorhead, Minnesota, tends to bear him out. Thom's peer helpers have been instrumental in reaching hundreds of students with problems ranging from drug and alcohol abuse to grief, sexual problems, teen pregnancy and thoughts of suicide. In addition to making creative use of the students, the program illustrates several other small-bite principles. It borrows ideas liberally from others, addresses real problems, reaches out for community support and gets nearly half its funding from outside the district's budget. The program has also won national recognition and is expanding from the high school through the Moorhead school system.

When people worry about drugs and kindred problems in the schools, Moorhead doesn't exactly leap to mind. The town is tucked away on the western border of Minnesota—it's actually a suburb of Fargo, North Dakota—where Canadian air masses regularly blast the winter temperature to a purging 20 degrees below zero. The high school is modern, tidy and graffiti-free. Ninety percent of the students are white, 75 percent of them go on to higher education and only 2 percent drop out. The place seems scrubbed and downright wholesome, a throwback to the '50s. Walking the wide, well-waxed corridors with their showcased trophies, well-tended bulletin boards and brightly painted lockers, it wouldn't surprise you a bit to run into Archie, Veronica, Jughead and Betty.

But if you did, at least one of them might well have a problem. The fact is that drugs are in all the nation's schools, reflecting the larger ills of a complex society. To be sure, Moorhead is a long way from the Chicago projects. Crack cocaine has made only minuscule inroads in Minnesota, and alcohol is the drug of choice. But there is a whole lot of choosing going on. When the state surveyed its students in 1989, the results in Moorhead reflected the state as a whole, which wasn't much different from many other states. Three out of four twelfth-graders and nearly half the high school freshmen in Minnesota said they had used alcohol. Excluding alcohol, 22 percent of the seniors and 15 percent of ninth-graders admitted using illicit drugs, mainly marijuana. More than half of the users of drugs and alcohol alike indulged regularly, once a month or more. And those figures reflected troubled lives. A quarter of all Minnesota students had to deal with substance abuse in their families. Twelve percent said they had been beaten, and nearly as many reported sexual abuse by family members or outsiders. Fully 38 percent had thought about killing themselves, and 13 percent said they had tried.

That survey merely confirmed what Jim Thom had been finding out ever since 1977, when he first tried to start a drug and alcohol prevention program in one of Moorhead's junior high schools. Like many another drug and alcohol counselor, Thom came to it the hard way: While he was never a caricature rolling-in-the-gutter alcoholic, he had had drinking problems bad enough that he flunked out after two years at Bemidji State University. He held his life together well enough to serve in the Army reserves, marry, graduate from Moorhead State University and go into teaching, but he didn't stop drinking until 1976. At that point, the troubles he had gone through persuaded him to switch from teaching English and language arts to counseling, and eventually to dependency counseling.

His first program was built around peer helpers largely because there wasn't much money for hiring staff, and experiments in other schools were hinting that students could be useful in solving each other's problems. But that first effort was fumbling and unsuccessful, a flawed concept that had poor structure, no backing from the faculty and no real niche in the school. It took him a decade of hard thinking, slow evolution and skillful building of support to make the program what it is.

The peer helpers are still the core of the student assistance program at Moorhead. They don't do counseling; Thom knows better now than to think kids can function as social workers, psychologists or experts at substance abuse. Even if they knew all the facts and techniques, they are far too vulnerable and just plain young to be put in that kind of position. But they can see problems, offer an ear to their friends and steer them to adults who can help; and with the right training and backing, they can do all that without any taint of being narcs, stoolies or even teachers' pets. As the school's dependency counselor and head of the assistance network, Thom takes seventy-five to eighty troubled kids under his wing every year. Most of them are still referred by teachers, parents or the local cops who have caught somebody drunk or carrying drugs. But more than a quarter of the students in each year's new crop come in after talking to one of Thom's forty-odd peer helpers. And other kids, perhaps fifty a year, go to the peer team with other problems: worry over their parents' marital fights, for example, or fear that they may be pregnant. The program now wrestles with most of the social problems afflicting modern students. All told, at any given time Thom is dealing with about 120 kids—a tenth of the high school's enrollment.

Call her Clarissa. She has a reputation around the school as a drinker, and she's been missing a lot of classes. One day she turns up in biology lab with several scratches on her wrist.

Leah spots that immediately; she's a peer helper, and it's one of the warning signs she learned about in her suicide assessment workshop during sophomore year. Leah has been worried about Clarissa for some time, and now, leaving the class, she falls into step with her and starts probing.

"Hey, what happened to your arm?"

"I just scratched myself," says Clarissa.

"Three times?" says Leah. "Why?"

"Ah, nobody cares," says Clarissa. "Nobody cares what I do anyway."

"Hey, listen, I care," says Leah. "You want to talk about it? Let's go to Pizza Hut for lunch today, okay?"

"Okay."

"And listen," says Leah. "Will you promise you won't do anything else to yourself before we talk?"

"Okay," says Clarissa. "Don't worry."

Leah knows from her training that Clarissa will almost surely keep her promise until lunch; such contracts have real force. But any hint of suicide is serious business. She has to find out whether Clarissa really means it, and especially whether she has a specific plan, along with the means and an opportunity to try to kill herself. Ordinarily, whatever Clarissa tells her is privileged and confidential until Clarissa is ready to go for help. But if there's a suicide plan, Leah will have to tell Jim Thom, and he will make sure Clarissa doesn't hurt herself.

It turns out over lunch that there isn't a real plan. But Clarissa is confused and depressed, and the more she talks the clearer it is that she has big problems. "I just don't want to go on living," she says. Leah keeps saying, Why not talk to Jim? Clarissa doesn't want to, but Leah says it's no shame to need help, everybody needs help sometimes. Jim won't yell at you or throw you in jail or anything like that, he just helps you figure out what's wrong and what to do about it. Clarissa just won't do it; all she does is lament to Leah, and she keeps doing that between classes and before and after school for two days, until Leah is drained and helpless.

So she goes to her core team, three other peer helpers who can back her up and give advice in an emergency. It sounds like a classic case, they agree: Clarissa has fastened onto Leah, and if she can't disengage, Clarissa will just keep draining her. The thing to do is tell Clarissa that Leah can't help her, that the only one who can help is Jim Thom, and then gently walk away. It's about the hardest thing Leah has ever done, but she manages to tell Clarissa that. And after a day of indecision and a night when she gets drunk, Clarissa finally goes to the small windowless office at the top of the stairs.

She has seen Mr. Thom around the school. His name sounds like a lisp, with the soft *Th*, but he has always seemed a little forbidding: medium height, fortyish and somehow military looking, trim and intense. He isn't one of those teachers who kids around a lot, and he uses a lot of big words. But close up, she decides, he's more likable. He has a nice, gap-toothed grin, his dark hair is getting thin on top, and his voice matches his eyes, steady and quiet. He listens to her as if he is really hearing what she says, and he doesn't lecture her or anything. He doesn't even seem surprised by anything she tells him.

He tells her he's going to do a "preassessment" for her, to see if she needs a "prescreening." It's sort of reassuring that everything sounds so preliminary and tentative, as if she could back out anytime. He has her fill out a questionnaire about her drinking, and another one about her parents' use of alcohol. She's calling him Jim by now, and she finds herself telling him the truth, pretty much, even about her dad getting loaded all the time and how much she worries about that. But when Jim asks her about pot she says no, she doesn't do drugs.

When the ninth grade was switched over to the high school in 1981, Thom brought the student assistance program and the peer helpers with it. The helpers hadn't been totally ineffectual; they were finding kids with troubles. The problem was what to do after that. The high school's psychologist was in favor of the program, but the guidance counselors were '50s-vintage people with no training in group work or chemical abuse, and they didn't want any part of it. The faculty didn't understand the program and resented the way kids got pulled out of class for training workshops in something that wasn't even officially recognized as an extracurricular activity. The chairman of one department told Thom, "I wouldn't let my kid be part of that program."

So Thom was rethinking the program from the ground up, beginning with his own role, and doing a lot of reading in psychology, sociology, substance abuse, dependency and group therapy. All that has left him with what might be called a replacement habit for his drinking, a kind of jargon addiction. His native tongue is basic Midwest, but there are times when he sounds like a cross between a flight attendant and a psychology text, all multisyllabic verbs and pompous abstraction. Right after describing an idea as "real neat," Thom will say something like: "We have the capability of implementing some facilities that perhaps others haven't got the capabilities." Like many people who spend much of their time dealing with substance abuse, he also tends to see the world through that window. When a student is referred to his attention for drinking or taking drugs, Thom's question isn't whether it's true, but how bad it is; by definition, the kid wouldn't be there if there weren't a problem. And no amount of lying, rationalizing, evading, backsliding or relapsing can surprise him. He has seen it all. Still, Thom has none of the cynicism and contempt that seasoned narcotics cops often develop. At bottom, he really likes kids, and understands them.

He figured out early that his peer helpers couldn't be asked to do counseling for their troubled friends. Like most of Thom's conclusions, this was hardly original. He takes ideas where he finds them, and tests them against his own experience. Both study and experience told him that kids are terribly vulnerable, particularly when manipulative personalities are at work. Thom recalls one boy who tried to keep a friend out of trouble by going to a party with him. The helper wound up matching his friend drink for drink and passing out—waking later to torments of guilt and shame. So the program had to be a referral network, with the helpers being used to spot troubles and lead their friends to treatment. They could also be missionaries and role models for younger children, taking the message about saying no to elementary and junior high schools. They would have to be trained to recognize the signs of addiction, depression and other adolescent woes, but they mustn't try to provide treatment themselves. Therapy couldn't be done in schools, Thom concluded; education is what's appropriate there.

If the helpers were to avoid the taint of narcs and informers, confidentiality was essential. And that meant that kids with problems must be referred to an adult inside the building, who could then develop his own information without betraying confidences and decide whether outside doctors, social workers or treatment centers were needed. As Thom sums it up, the helpers had to know that "they aren't sending their friends to a stranger but to someone in the school, and they had to know and trust that person."

But that forced him to rethink his own role. The traditional dependency counselor is an ominous figure. Students don't see him as somebody there to help, but as a cross between a snoopy, officious cop and a hanging judge. The counselor usually gets called in when a kid is in trouble, often because the local cops have caught him drinking or carrying drugs and agreed not to press charges if the school will take action. What follows is an interview with the counselor that doubles as a trial, followed by a sentence, usually to treatment with no option for appeal. Predictably, most students resent the whole process and resist the treatment.

"We needed a more nonthreatening process, one that would bring the kid along with us," says Thom. To begin with, he wanted to be less judgmental and more diagnostic in his counselor's role. The student should be made to see that there was an objective basis for Thom's decision—that she hadn't just been unlucky and got caught, but actually had a problem. Thom learned that a program in nearby Fargo used questionnaires to gauge the severity of drug and alcohol problems, and he seized on that as a helpful tool in the first round of dealing with kids in trouble. He called that first round the "preassessment," to emphasize that it was nowhere near final judgment, and he broadened it out to include formal participation by parents and teachers as well as the student. All of them would get questionnaires and be invited for interviews. Thom developed a whole battery of forms, adapted from other programs and from books and journals on student assistance.

He has a liking for the seeming precision of multistep outlines, flow charts and elaborate lists of procedures, and he has formalized preassessment almost to a mechanical fault. He charts substance-abuse problems in four stages (experimentation, regular use, abuse and dependency), according to how many boxes are checked on the questionnaires and how many real-world "consequences" a student has triggered. (Among them: lost friends, athletic suspensions, failed tests, arrests.) A student who drinks or smokes pot more than once a month has progressed from experimentation to regular use, but he might indulge as many as 104 times a year without crossing the next line into abuse—as long as there is no use on weekdays. In theory, twenty-eight positive answers on the "Youth: 40 Questions" form would indicate late-stage dependency. But in practice, no kid with a habit that big could meet Moorhead's academic standards, and would have flunked out or left school before getting that far. Thom knows that the precision of the boundaries is phony, and mainly for show. The real value of the forms is to force a student to agree with the diagnosis and go willingly to treatment. It's hard for a kid to argue that there's nothing wrong if her parents have recorded three episodes in two months, two teachers have checked off behavior changes and slipping grades, and the student herself has said she drinks twice a week and flunked a test because of a hangover.

But even under that kind of pressure, kids tend to part with their secrets slowly and reluctantly. The preassessment process needed something that would get them talking more openly, and Thom found it in a county program that used discussion groups. For students, the peer pressure of a group works far better than one-on-one counseling to break down resistance, winkle out honest answers and change behavior. There was another advantage. Groups are efficient. A counselor conducting a group is working with six or eight kids in an hour, as many as he could see all day in individual sessions. But there was a familiar line that shouldn't be crossed; these would be support groups. They could encourage insight, probe feelings and explore new coping skills, but they should stop short of trying to resolve basic issues, which would be therapy.

So preassessment became a six-week procedure, with each student's interviews and questionnaires backed up by at least five weekly meetings in a support group. From there, Thom could refer a student to what he calls "prescreening," a formal evaluation by qualified diagnosticians at a local treatment center, which would probably lead to some kind of outpatient treatment. Or if he thought the problem wasn't severe enough to call in the professionals, he could recommend that the student sign a formal contract, promising not to use alcohol or drugs and to continue weekly meetings with the chemical abuse support group.

Thom was also rethinking his basic idea of dependency. The problem wasn't simply drug and alcohol abuse, he decided; you couldn't deal adequately with those unless you worked on whatever had caused them. He was also learning about codependency—the way a whole family's behavior can be affected by the problems of a single family member. Then too, "We were running into students for whom chemicals weren't the issue at all, but their problems were just as serious." So the support groups at Moorhead multiplied, stretching beyond chemical abuse to grief, divorce, sex abuse, codependency and a vague "concerned persons" group where a student could sort out what his real problem might be.

Clarissa has started in what Jim calls a transition group, meeting once a week with seven other kids who have problems of one sort of another. She knows a couple of them. Sam had been to a lot of parties she went to, before he was sent off to dry out, and now he has come back to school and goes to Alcoholics Anonymous (AA) meetings as well as the group. Rachel's stepmother has been giving her a hard time, but it sounds to Clarissa as if what bugs Rachel isn't so much what the woman says as the fact that she exists. Rachel hasn't got over her parents' divorce. Jim talks a lot about grief and codependency. One day Clarissa tells the group about her dad's drinking, and then she finds herself confessing about the pot—that she's been smoking for five months, and lately it's every day.

That changes things. She has crossed two lines, from regular use right through abuse to early-stage dependency. Jim makes her fill out another questionnaire, and he wants to know what she is going to do about it. Does she want to be hooked on drugs? She guesses not. What does she want? She doesn't know. He says he has to have a conference with her and her mom and dad. The rules are that what she has told him is confidential, and he won't tell her parents what she wants to keep private, but she'll have to decide how much to tell them. And he will have to make a recommendation. He can suggest a prescreening or the contract route. Which does she want?

Clarissa agrees to a modified limited hangout: she will tell her mom and dad about the marijuana, but not the daily use. The meeting with her parents turns out to be easier than she was afraid it would be. Her dad, who can be pretty stormy, is unusually quiet; he just seems glad to do whatever Jim suggests. And they settle on the contract option. Clarissa promises to stay clean, and she will switch to the chemical abuse group for weekly meetings. How long that will last, Jim says, depends on her.

What Thom was evolving at Moorhead was a whole new structure for addressing nearly all the social problems that put modern students at risk. It needed a name, and he wanted one that wouldn't be limited to the usual drug and alcohol issues. But he also wanted to avoid words like "crisis," "abuse" and "prevention." He came up with a label so bland as to be totally forgettable: it was to be a "Student Assistance Program." That turned out to be prescient. Other counselors had been moving in the same directions, and within three years, the diverse field was converging as the student assistance movement, complete with annual conventions, a bimonthly *Student Assistance Journal* and two professional groups, the National Organization of Student Assistance Programs and Professionals and the National Association of Leadership for Student Assistance Programs.

Thom also needed political support for his program, both inside the high school and in the community at large. He has a somewhat prickly relationship with his principal, Donovan Dulski, a tall, craggy man who cherishes firm, uncomplicated convictions. Dulski argues that TV sex and violence have warped values, for instance, and thinks kids shouldn't have part-time jobs that get in the way of their schooling. Dulski believes in being honest with parents; there's no point in telling them that Johnny can do better by hard work "if the kid is next door to a rock and can't compete." But he and Thom don't always see eye to eye. It isn't that Dulski is an enemy. He recognizes that Thom's program helps students and reflects well on his school. It's just that he doesn't see all the problems from Thom's point of view, and can't be counted on to support, say, Thom's efforts to set up an assistance plan for teachers, even though it's plain that the usual percentage of them have problems, too.

Thom has made firm allies among Moorhead's staff of counselors, who gladly sit in on some of his student groups and count the time well spent. The school's teachers are mostly resigned to the time his peer helpers spend in training, thanks to a system that lets each helper choose among three weekly workshops to find the time slot least disruptive to academic schedules. And Thom has set up an administrative core team of teachers and administrators to supervise the program inside the school and give him some political cover.

Thom hasn't yet learned to be as effective as the professionals at Fannie Mae in getting local publicity for his program, but he knows that it needs to be politically connected and seen as necessary—as he puts it, he has to make sure "the community has a sense of ownership in this." So he has recruited a steering committee to build support for programs beyond the high school, with representatives from the board of education, other district schools, the police department and county and city social workers. The steering committee is extending the student assistance network to the lower schools and working on ways to manage crises that have an impact on students. These could range from the crib death of a single baby to events that could affect children throughout the district—a major fire or industrial accident, for instance, or a national crisis with local reverberations such as a war, another space shuttle disaster or a presidential assassination.

But the peer helper system is still the core of the program, and Thom has learned from his mistakes along the way. Perhaps the first lesson was that he couldn't assume that kids who volunteered would be ideal for the job. Just as Thom himself was drawn to deal with his own problem, some teens inevitably gravitate to fight the tendencies they feel in themselves. "Our very first referral," he recalls, "was made through a peer helper who was in treatment herself a year later." These days, the chosen volunteers are routinely put through the preassessment process to turn up any hidden drug or alcohol problems. A tendency doesn't bar them from the team, but about 10 percent of the recruits wind up in some sort of support group or treatment.

In the early days of the program, Thom picked his helpers from a list of candidates nominated by teachers, administrators and student leaders. But he soon realized that this amounted to an elite group, already stigmatized to some extent as nerds and teachers' pets and easy for other students to dismiss as narcs, stoolies or worse. Kids might be willing to talk to their peers, Thom concluded, but they would have to be genuine peers. What he needed was a cross section of all the cliques in the school—not only the leaders and top students but the politicians, the band, the jocks, the cheerleaders (known at Moorhead as "bips"), even potential druggies and "loadies" (kids who get loaded every Friday night). So he set out to recruit them.

Recruiting starts with a formal presentation of the program to the incoming ninth grade. The peer helpers talk about what they do and show a video illustrating it. They play out some of the refusal-tactics skits that they take around to the junior high and the four elementary schools, showing kids how to say no without losing friends or face. They explain what the program means to them and what they get out of it, which for most of them is just the satisfaction of helping people. Then they ask for volunteers. They usually get about seventy-five applications, and in most years, these have the makings of a real cross section of the school's 1,400 students. If there's a shortage of jocks, nerds or bips, some discreet solicitation may be needed. The peer helpers interview the candidates and make their recommendations; then Thom reviews the record and makes the final cut. He usually picks ten freshmen, to bring the group to a total of forty. If upper classmen leave the school or drop out of the program, they are usually replaced from their own class. But a senior who drops out will be replaced by a lower classman, to avoid wasting the training.

From early on, the helpers were steered away from any counseling efforts and told to refer problems, not try to deal with them. But handling a troubled friend is always hard, and kids tend to get involved. It was to help deal with those situations that Thom set up the helpers' core teams, to talk over tactics or help a team member disengage from a clinging friend. Sometimes a helper has to be given permission to let go—to be told, "Drop it. You did what you could. Maybe she'll come back to you later." And sometimes, as with Leah and Clarissa, it's only after a helper disengages that a troubled teen can work up enough initiative to take the next step.

Clarissa's mother is on the phone with Thom. She has just found out that Clarissa has deliberately skipped two of her group meetings. The woman is obviously upset and worried; in response, Thom is quietly concerned. He says the breaking of the contract is serious, and it may be time to put Clarissa into prescreening. That may mean some sort of outpatient treatment, he says. The mother doesn't want to hear that. "Well, talk it over with your husband," says Thom. "Let's see what happens. No matter what, we'll have to have another talk with her together."

He hangs up. You can alienate parents easily, he says, and then they stop cooperating and sharing information, so, "I won't push. I won't come down on them—'I expect you to follow my recommendations,' like that—I'll go slow and let her wear her parents down a little bit. And I know she will." A broken contract is a cry for help, he says; if the parents don't respond, something more dramatic is sure to follow.

The peer helpers concentrate mainly on drug and alcohol abuse, with a strong sideline in suicide prevention. But as Clarissa's case shows, problems rarely fit neatly into a single category, and the helpers are available to listen sympathetically to their friends' troubles ranging from a parent's job crisis to a death in the family. At their own weekly training workshops, the helpers are taught listening skills: how to win trust, how to maintain eye contact, how to detect evasions and omissions, how to avoid being judgmental, how to frame hard questions sympathetically. They learn a little about confrontation, family dynamics and adolescent development. They are taught the basics of the problems Thom sees as major issues for kids today: grief, codependency, family crisis, suicide assessment, sexual abuse and violence. And they are briefed on the kinds of treatment the community can offer, on a scale ranging from group therapy to hospitalization and permanent membership in an antiabuse program such as Alcoholics Anonymous.

The helpers are always on duty, in the sense that they are alert to what's going on around them and ready to listen. Taking initiatives is left to their own discretion: It's seldom productive to challenge a drunk in the heat of a party, and the assumption is that the helpers themselves know best when they can be effective in their main role. But they also play a part as missionaries to their classmates and the community, delivering an antiabuse message while trying to steer clear of sanctimony. Their skits are clear and often funny, designed to underline simple techniques for staying out of trouble, having fun and keeping friends. In one such playlet, Amy Cermak, vivacious and assertive, plays the part of the temptress; Sara Forsythe, slender and quiet, is deflecting the invitation.

"Hey, Sara, my mom and dad have gone to Chicago. Are you up to go over to my house for a little real fun?" says Amy.

"Like, what would we do?" asks Sara. The rule: *Always ask specific questions. Never get into a situation you don't understand.*

"There's a lot of vodka in the liquor cabinet," says Amy. "And my mom has some pills that really blow your mind."

"That sounds like trouble," says Sara. "Pills can make you really sick, especially if they don't mix with alcohol." *Name the trouble.*

"Oh, come on," says Amy, getting into her role. "The world could blow up tomorrow, too. Don't be such a dweeb."

"No, really," says Sara. "If I got caught doing something like that, I'd get thrown off the swimming team and my folks would ground me for three months." *Name the consequences.* "Listen, I'm going down to shoot some baskets. Want to come along?" *Suggest an alternative; start to leave.*

"I don't want to shoot any dumb baskets," says Amy sulkily.

"Well, if you change your mind, I'll be in the gym," says Sara, walking out. *Leave the door open.*

Sara hasn't been judgmental, merely practical. She avoids alienating Amy with any righteous pieties or priggish denunciations, and she keeps control of the situation. But in a second skit, the situation is already out of control, and Amy, this time playing the pressured role, has a more serious problem. She is Hans Nielsen's date; they are in his car on a lonely road, and he is trying to bully her into having sex. Her solution is the technique called the "broken record." No matter what he says, she merely repeats one plaintive line: "I'm just not ready for this." Again, she makes no moral protest, no accusation, nothing that puts him in the wrong. She just keeps pleading incompetence, a passive resistance designed to deflate the randiest libido. He reacts first with a leer: "Baby, you just leave that to me, I'll make sure you're ready." She sounds her one note again, and he tries argument: "But how do you know you're not ready?" He goes through more debate, then ridicule, then the threat to strand her miles from home. She all but wrings her hands: "I'm just not ready . . ." Finally he erupts furiously: "Goddammit, can't you say anything else?" But in the end, if he's not prepared for an outright rape, he has to give up. Without getting into a power struggle, she has sapped his power; but she has avoided any confrontation that might give him an excuse for real aggression. It's an impressive display.

Now it's Clarissa on Thom's phone: "Did my mom call you?" He is straight, calm, matter-of-fact. Yes, he says, she told me you've skipped two groups. What was that about? He listens, mutters a couple of uh-huhs; then:

"Clarissa, we ought to have a talk, but let me be straight with you. I think you should go to prescreening, no more messing around. What do you say?"

She stalls for a minute, then consents. In fifteen minutes he has set up an appointment at a treatment center in Fargo for two o'clock this afternoon, and called Clarissa's mother to invite the parents. "I've talked to Clarissa, and she agrees it's the right thing to do. . . . He may not be able to? Does he have something more important to do today? . . . I'll see you there, then."

Jim hangs up. He took a chance, he says, pressuring Clarissa like that, but the call seemed to tip the balance: She was asking for help.

Prescreening is real neat, and free to the family. A counselor will spend twenty minutes with Clarissa, take her drug and alcohol history and compare it with what she said in the preassessment. Then he'll discuss it with the whole family and Jim, and recommend treatment. It's fast, professional and objective. The trick may be to get the parents to follow through.

As a realist, Thom knows there are some battles he just won't win. He remembers a peer helper, Jody Olson, who intervened at a party where a drunken boy—call him Bill—locked himself in the bathroom and threatened suicide. Jody called Bill's parents, and they came, but Bill came out of the bathroom and said it had all been a joke. She talked to Thom about it next day, and he advised her to find another friend of Bill's and talk to him again. This time, sober, Bill said he had meant it, and still intended to kill himself. And he had a plan. His dad kept a gun, and his parents were leaving for the weekend. Jody relayed that to Thom, who called the parents, and they followed his process to the point where treatment was recommended. But instead of following through, they bought Bill a racing motorcycle. At Thom's last report, the boy had ridden it between two cars on a two-lane road at eighty-five miles an hour, but he wasn't dead yet.

"But Jody did fine," he says. If it seems harsh to put a teenager like Jody into such a situation, well, she was already there; so were all the kids at the party, and they would all have felt the guilt if anything had happened to Bill. Jody knew how to take the initiative, and when it foundered, she had a program to reassure her that she had done all she could. "If there was a similar situation again," says Thom, "I'd advise her to call the cops at the first threat, not the parents. But that's a tough call. What she did was totally okay, especially the next day, and I was proud of her."

For all the losses, mistakes and false starts, Thom is justifiably proud of his whole program. In their areas of training, he says, "I'd stack up my peer helpers against any faculty member in the building when it comes to understanding kids. These kids know their limitations, and they do pretty good work." The program has a widening reputation in the Midwest, where Thom is increasingly being invited to discuss it at conferences and consult on clones for other school systems. It has also won national recognition: In 1990, Jim Thom was named one of the Reader's Digest Heroes of the Year in education, with a $5,000 prize for himself and $10,000 to be spent on his program.

The program can always use money, and Thom has long chafed at his school's sense of priorities—he recalls scraping in vain for $150 for his helpers while the school was spending $5,000 to send the band to a one-day state competition. So it's a relief to have a discretionary fund of his own. He earmarked part of the prize for some of his peer helpers to attend the National Student Assistance Conference in New Orleans, and another chunk to send them for intensive training in a weeklong summer camp run by a professional training group, the Partners Institute.

But in fact, the Student Assistance Program isn't expensive. True to the small-bite principle of scooping up all available funds from outside the school system, Thom gets $22,000 a year from the federal Drug-Free Schools program and another $4,000 in state funding, and the program earns $10,000 a year for services he provides to a regional school coalition. The outside money pays for an outreach worker, Kathy Bossart, and part-time work by Lynn Sipes, a social worker on the school district's payroll. Thom's own salary is the school's only direct expense. All told, the program costs just $475 for each of the 160 students involved in it; excluding the outside income, the cost to the board of education is only $250 per child.

Whatever his differences with Donovan Dulski, Thom and the principal agree on one point: It would be better to reach troubled kids earlier in their school career, before their problems become overwhelming. "Every dollar saved in elementary school costs two dollars here," says Dulski, "and it's not as effective. By the time the kids get to us, the damage has been done." Thom and his steering committee are working to set up support groups and a student assistance program in the junior high school and the district's four elementary schools, and the pilot projects are in varying stages of development. A separate offshoot of the high school program, Student Match, is modeled on a Canadian program and aims to use peer helpers from the high school as big brothers or sisters for elementary students who are considered at risk. After a pilot phase with just fifteen pairings, to work the bugs out, Thom hopes to expand the program and perhaps recruit high school students who aren't already peer helpers.

What does it take to start a student assistance program? Some of Thom's fans think the answer is to clone him. "He's one of a kind," says Russ Henegar, the head of Moorhead's counseling staff. Kathy Bossart, the outreach worker who runs some of Thom's support groups and monitors the elementary-school pilot programs, thinks he should go into business training people to run programs like the one he developed. But Thom scoffs at the idea that he is unique, and believes there is room for any number of variations on his formula. A program has to be tailored to its school system and to the talents and strengths of the person running it, he says. But that person should seek out advice, read the literature of the professional student assistance groups, learn from experience and be open to new ideas.

Within those broad guidelines, he and his colleagues agree, there are several essential features:

• **Structure.** A student assistance plan must have strong central leadership, from a thoroughly qualified counselor, and that counselor must have backing from the school's faculty and support in the community.

• **Limits.** Peer helpers must not try to function as counselors or therapists; they must refer troubled students to the program's director, who can get professional help from outside the school.

• **Training.** Peer helpers must be given training and backed up by core teams.

• **Backups.** There must be support groups within the school to help diagnose student problems and supplement outside treatment.

It's probably a good idea, the Moorhead team agrees, to start a new program at the elementary school level, mainly because the problems of small children tend to be more manageable than those of teens. Such a program could naturally follow children into middle school and then to high school. But at whatever level, the rest of the advice is familiar: start small. Find a counselor who can put together a peer helpers' group in one school. Expand cautiously, making sure the problems are worked out and that everyone is on board. In a program like this, it's possible to do lasting damage, and that danger must be constantly remembered. But the potential rewards are big, too.

It's only 3:30 in the afternoon, but Thom is already back from Clarissa's prescreening session. He wears a beatific grin. "You should have been there," he tells a visitor. "This is the best prescreen I can remember."

The counselor at the treatment center was a new guy, one Thom hadn't seen before, and he was fine. "He backed me right off," Thom says. "I was talking too much, and he said, 'The young lady can speak for herself.' It was really neat." Then Clarissa's dad came in, smelling of liquor and emotionally shaky, conditioned by the crisis to be ready to face his own problem. The counselor picked right up on that, and by the end of the brief session, father and daughter had both agreed to go into treatment. The mother was shedding tears of joy, and Thom's own eyes were moist.

"That's the best prescreen ever," he keeps saying. "I don't see how it could have worked out better. These are the days that make it worthwhile."

6.

Ringing the Preschool Bell

Driving along Interstate 69 through the gently rolling farmlands of northeastern Indiana, you see a bright yellow water tower, one of those mushroom-shaped tanks maybe eighty feet high, supported only by its improbably slender stem. This one has a happy face painted on it, with the Orphan Annie eyes and button nose and the inane grin, beaming at the interstate traffic. It is a Hoosier totem of friendliness and somewhat vapid cheer, and that marks the turnoff for Hamilton.

Becky Norris took that turn back in 1985, heading with her husband, Don, into a new life. They were moving down to Hamilton from Union Lake, Michigan, where he had been an engineer in the auto industry and she was what she calls a "domestic engineer," running the household for thirty years and raising four sons. Union Lake is well out in Detroit's exurbia, west of Pontiac, and Becky never got involved in the country-club-to-shopping-mall routine of the stereotypical auto executive's wife. Her life was bound up with her boys, from camping trips and Pony League baseball to school activities and above all the PTA. She always figured that the more she hung around the schools, the better chance her kids would have. One year she was president of two separate school PTAs and a regional PTA association, all at once. But now Don had taken a job as vice president in the suburban Fort Wayne plant of Eagle-Picher, an auto parts maker, and Becky knew she was going to have to start over, making the effort to get involved in church groups and community affairs in order to build up a circle of acquaintances. She still had one son in school, in the sixth grade, and he would be her ticket to school affairs. She had kept up with newspapers and magazines in education, and she had some ideas, particularly about getting parents involved in the schools. It's a major principle of small-bite programs that it takes only one person to start making a difference, and in Hamilton that turned out to be Becky Norris.

She felt comfortable in Hamilton. It was a smaller community than she was used to, a bit less sophisticated and more conservative, but she got along well and her campaign to fit in was a success. She is a cheerful, likable and confident woman, comfortably upholstered, with her graying hair nicely coiffed and her wardrobe running to smart print dresses topped off by a jacket and a Helen Hokinson sort of furbelow at the bosom. In Hamilton she's upper-crust, but she doesn't flaunt her position. She has no pretensions to expertise, and only a two-year secretarial degree as her own higher education.

Hamilton has no pretensions either. It is little more than a hamlet, a community of 850 people living mainly off the summer colony at nearby Lake Hamilton. There are quite a few farmers, but farming is increasingly a part-time occupation in northern Indiana. There are a few small local factories; many people commute to jobs in Fort Wayne, thirty miles south. And there are growing numbers of retirees, attracted by Hamilton's tranquillity, slow pace and low living costs. The community schools have just 675 students, drawn from a population of five thousand spread over three townships. All the kids, from kindergarten through the twelfth grade, go to a pair of connected buildings on the south side of town. The 1964 construction is boxy and plain vanilla, with concrete block walls and well-waxed asphalt tile corridors, bright artwork on display and tiny boots lined up in pairs outside the kindergarten room. A fourth of the elementary students are poor enough to qualify for federal lunch money, and only 40 percent of the high school graduates go on to higher education, most of them in state universities or community colleges.

Hamilton is not a simple place. Hoosier friendliness can mask narrow-mindedness and even bigotry; back in the '30s, this part of the world was Klan country. To this day you may hear a man at the next table in the tiny cafe talking with undisguised indignation about "what the niggers want." Most Hamiltonians are thoroughly decent folk, of course, churchgoers and family people with respect for hard work and solid values. Even the remark in the cafe reflects mainly old fears and ignorance, with no real knowledge or even acquaintance of black people. After all, there are no black families in town. But the school mirrors the town; the school board members live within the same narrow horizon and resonate to shared values. The board has traditionally run to farmers, small shopkeepers and blue-collar people, with only an occasional executive or professional man. Its members tend to be deeply conservative, tight with a buck and suspicious of any educational frills that won't improve the basketball team. They want their children to do well, but they think of schooling as a means to an end, a meal ticket. They distrust intellectual pretensions. Serving on the board has been a job that confers some prestige, but at the same time isn't much sought after.

Becky Norris saw that as her opportunity, and she made her move in 1988. She avoided any campaign charges that the board wasn't good enough, and she didn't present herself as any woman on horseback. What she could give to the board, she said, was "not a background in education, but an informed interest." She was seen as a benign touch of new blood for the board, no threat to the old standards, and she didn't have much trouble: she made about seventy-five phone calls and got elected. A year later she was the board's president, and all but one of the five old members had been unseated. But by then she had already made the suggestion that led to the program called "BELL." Nobody in Hamilton realized it at the time, but they were following another small-bite precept by borrowing an idea—an insight that has changed preschool education in towns and whole states across the country. They went on to create from the ground up a program that already exists in several national models. The progress of their modest idea provides an intriguing comparison with the larger-scale model that the Hamilton group eventually joined.

*   *   *

The first trick is to identify a real problem, and it was Beth Muntzinger, the kindergarten teacher, who did that. It was a perception that crystallized over several years: the children coming to her class just didn't seem as well prepared as the kids of twenty years past, when she had started teaching. Their vocabularies were smaller, and a lot of them couldn't count; some of them got their colors mixed up and got confused by simple tasks, like putting the little block on top of the big one. Parents didn't seem to be reading to their kids anymore, or even talking to them. Talking it over, the teachers thought vaguely that the decline might have something to do with television, or maybe divorce and the breakdown of family values. Even in Hamilton, the last three decades have left their mark. The elementary principal, Steve Keeslar, estimates that 60 to 70 percent of the district's children now come from families that don't fit the old nuclear norm. Whatever the cause, the results weren't good. The kindergarten kids weren't scoring well on the Early Prevention of School Failure test, which they take at the beginning and end of each school year. The school had to set up a special "readiness" class for seven to ten kids every year who weren't prepared for first grade even after a year of kindergarten.

Keeslar mentioned that problem at Becky Norris's second board meeting, and Norris was ready. In her reading about education, she says, "I was seeing a lot of programs being put in the secondary schools to correct problems that could have been avoided in the first place. I felt that, with a little help and cooperation between families and the school community, some of these problems could be solved early." Her idea was both simple and matter-of-fact, a classic small-bite insight: If the children weren't ready to come to school, why couldn't the school reach out to help parents prepare them? It wouldn't have to be very elaborate. Perhaps a teacher could visit with mothers, give them information on child development and generally help them with the job of teaching their own preschool children. She made the suggestion a bit diffidently, conscious of the risk of coming on too strong too fast. "I was sitting there quaking and thinking, 'Should I be doing this already?' I didn't want to bluster my way in, but it was just something I felt needed to get done. Why wait around on it?"

"I wasn't real used to that," says Keeslar. He is a stocky, earnest man, a nonsmoking, nondrinking churchgoer who is a member of the Gideons and shuns even coffee; he takes his job seriously and is proud of his school, but he had long ago given up any thought of serious initiatives coming from the board. "I've been here twelve years, and no board member had ever asked me to look into anything if it wasn't some personal problem," he says. "So to have this question asked was a real flag to me." True again to small-bite principles, Norris had started the ball rolling with her suggestion, but she realized that the pros had to pick it up, and she left them to it. Keeslar called in Beth Muntzinger, and the two of them quickly sketched out a preschool education program to be built around home visits. And in the modern educational fashion, they baptized it with an acronym. "I've always liked the idea of the school bell, so I thought up the name just like that," Keeslar says. At first it stood for Beginning Early with Little Learners; later the title grew slightly smoother, Begin Educating Little Learners.

"So in fifteen minutes we set up the BELL program as you see it right now," says Keeslar. "It's all blossomed from that one meeting." In fact, Muntzinger recalls, "It clicked together in the next three or four weeks." Because it's a small school and the only one in the district, there was no need for elaborate politics to get other principals and teachers on board. And Keeslar and Muntzinger knew they could count on support from the district superintendent, A. Gary Nordmann. A tall, tweedy and easygoing man, Nordmann is Hamilton's main force for innovation; he has installed programs ranging from a new vocational course for future marina workers to a high-tech cooperative venture with Ball State University, beaming in college lessons in physics and Chinese for bright students in Hamilton. With Nordmann's blessing, the school board approved the preschool idea at its next meeting, and Muntzinger started assembling educational materials to be handed out to participating parents.

Keeslar and Muntzinger decided early that their program should start as soon as possible after a prospective pupil's birth, to take advantage of the high-speed early learning years and to get parents involved while they were still excited about having children. Since there were about fifty kids in kindergarten every year, the potential population of preschoolers in the district must be five times that many, about 250; allowing for the fact that some of them were siblings, there were perhaps 170 families to reach. The key to the program would be visits by teachers, who could tell mothers things that can't be taken for granted these days—the importance of reading aloud to children, how to recognize hearing and vision problems, what's normal at what ages, and how to teach concepts, play number games and make educational toys out of simple things like Clorox bottles. The teachers could also pass out pamphlets on health and child development, and inexpensive kits of educational materials. Parents could be invited to regular meetings at the school, to exchange information and get to know each other; that might break the ice for getting parents involved in the schools later on, when their kids came of age to attend. They could be encouraged to use the library, with books on parenting and a new section to serve preschoolers. The idea was growing.

Keeslar and Muntzinger started planning in February, and that summer she made her first home visit. She went to see four-year-old Michael Hurraw and his mother, who had older children already in school. Muntzinger hadn't got home before the word of mouth was operating: Her husband John fielded a telephone call from the parents of Michael's cousin, Kileigh Buell, asking how to get him in on the program.

They had been working on it for six months when Keeslar and Muntzinger discovered that their idea wasn't original. "I saw an ad in one of the educational magazines for something called Parents as Teachers," he recalls. "I had no idea what it was, and when I looked into it, it sounded exactly like our program. I was dumbfounded."

It was as if Abner Doubleday, fooling around with a bat and ball on a sandlot, had suddenly found himself in Yankee Stadium. In fact, Parents as Teachers (PAT) is the big league of preschool education, a sophisticated organization based in St. Louis with its roots in a statewide Missouri project and more than two hundred offspring programs in thirty-five other states and Australia. BELL was to become one of them, with Muntzinger and three colleagues making the trip to St.

Louis for training and accreditation in PAT's methods. BELL retains its own identity, less ambitious, less coherent and probably less effective than the parent program, but decidedly worthwhile; as an example of hometown initiative, hard work and willingness to experiment, BELL shows how PAT's ideas can be applied in one kind of community. But PAT has the research, the experience and the statistics to prove its case, and it shows what BELL might one day become.

Preschool education is far from a new idea, or a new reality either. In educational theory, the three years starting at birth are all-important, the crucial beginnings and foundation of a lifetime of learning. Wealthy parents have long sent their children to nursery school to get the right start in this process, and in recent years the federal Head Start program has reached at least some poor kids, but they remain a minority. In practice, most new parents take their baby home from the hospital and have no contact with any educational establishment until the child reaches five years old and toddles off hopefully to kindergarten, to soak up the elixir of professional education.

In the past twenty years, there have been several attempts to fill the gap. A program that started in Israel forty years ago, the Home Instruction Program for Preschool Youngsters, has spread its acronym, HIPPY, into thirteen states. The Family Oriented Structured Preschool Activity, FOSPA, claims 146 clones in seventeen states. But most such plans are aimed at three-to-five-year-old children, specifically to prepare them for school. PAT starts with the idea that the Hamilton crew intuitively understood: parents are a child's first and most influential teachers, all-important during the early months and years when infants learn most and fastest. PAT tries to contact women during pregnancy and follow the children through the preschool period, with emphasis on the first three years.

PAT goes back to 1970, when a suburban St. Louis teacher, Mildred Winter, began offering a range of activities for preschool parents in the Ferguson-Florissant school district. Two years later she was named to head a state office on early childhood education and joined forces with Burton White, a Harvard educator who had been working in early childhood development. White's theory began with his perception that parents get no real training for their most important job. "You get more information with your new car than you do with your new baby," he said. In the tradition of much academic research, he set out to document the obvious: that children soak up learning ferociously from the time their senses start operating. Sure enough, he found, they do. But his research also showed that a child's abilities at the age of six could be predicted three years earlier. That meant that by the age of three, the most important stage was already over.

"Our education system essentially ignores the formative years," Winter preached. Furthermore, White was finding that what a child learns easily in the early years is much harder to teach later if the first opportunity is neglected. The lesson was an old story, easy to grasp: a dollar spent early could save a lot more later on.

But that wasn't an easy sell. Missouri, the "show me" state, ranked among the five lowest states in per capita spending for education, and new ideas were suspect. It wasn't until 1986 that kindergarten was made mandatory in Missouri; the idea of starting public education at birth was so radical that it seemed hopeless. But Winter and White started a pilot project with funding from the Danforth Foundation, and got sensational results with children from 390 families. Measured against a control group, children who had been in the program scored consistently higher in language development, problem solving and intellectual development. They also had better relationships with adults. Families at all social and economic levels benefited from the help. "This is the strongest stuff I've seen in twenty-eight years of working in child development," White told *The New York Times*.

What he and Winter wanted next was a statewide program, aimed not just at the poorest families but available to everyone. For one thing, Winter argued, programs targeted at the poor create a stigma for the people in them. But just as important, White's research showed that rich people need help, too. "Parents with two Ph.D.'s can be basket cases when it comes to parenting," Winter said. She made a key early convert in Christopher "Kit" Bond, who became a father in 1981 during his second term as Missouri's governor. Bond backed a bill to establish PAT as a statewide program, but met heavy opposition. Right-wingers led by Phyllis Schlafly denounced it as a communistically inspired scheme, designed to undermine family values and indoctrinate children. But the PAT forces had their own hardball tactics: By some accounts, Bond passed word that if the bill didn't go through, he would veto a legislative pay raise. The bill passed in 1984.

At recent count, PAT had more than fifteen hundred trained educators making regular visits to sixty thousand families in the Missouri program, beginning if possible in the third trimester of pregnancy. The program also includes group meetings for parents and developmental screening of the children, to keep track of their growth and language development and identify any hearing or vision problems. Most of the "parent educators" have a background in education, psychology or social work; they go through thirty-four hours of training, with added instruction in following years. They visit each family every four to six weeks, coaching the parents on how children learn and listening to their problems. Parents are taught how important it is simply to talk to infants, to make sure they have books with pictures to look at, to read aloud to their children and take them to story hour at PAT centers and at the local library. As a child comes to a new stage, the parents can be shown how to deal with it. The parent educators answer questions as concerns come up and encourage parents to go to group meetings, where they can share problems and successes. And if the visitors find needs for medical or financial help, they have a network of community facilities where they can send the parents.

The program is both effective and economical. Outside studies have found that children in PAT reach the age of three with a significant advantage over nonparticipants in language development, intellectual abilities and social skills. Children with development problems can be helped to overcome them, and parents in the program learn about child development and become more active than non-PAT parents in their children's education. But the expense is just over $200 a year for each family. The modest cost and the haste to expand the program actually alienated one of its founders: Burton White pulled out, complaining that caseloads of as many as eighty families were too high for the parent educators and that much more extensive contacts and training were needed if PAT were to succeed. The pilot program worked, White said, because it spent $800 to $850 per family, and the full-scale project should match that. But Mildred Winter argues that fast growth was "a blessing in disguise" and that White, like many researchers, has allowed the best to become the enemy of the good. "We would like to have the ideal funding," she says, "but if you don't have the maximum dollars, you learn to work with what you have."

PAT's results are impressive enough that similar programs have been funded in Connecticut, Illinois and Ohio. Kansas has passed enabling legislation, and pilot programs in Texas, Rhode Island and Delaware are being expanded. Kit Bond, now a U.S. senator, has introduced a bill to fund pilot programs introducing PAT in one thousand school districts across the nation. Mildred Winter is now director of the Center for Parents as Teachers at the University of St. Louis, overseeing the state's program, training its parent educators and offering training and materials for offspring programs in other communities. And Beth Muntzinger came from Hamilton to take the course in 1989.

Most people have had at least one teacher like Beth Muntzinger. She's cut from the classic pattern, kindly and strict, with perky intensity and eyes in the back of her head for children who fool around when she's writing on the chalkboard. She is short and slight, a bundle of energy and electric blond hair, with spectacles and insistently rising inflections and the teacherly habit of referring to herself in the third person: "Will you do that for Mrs. Muntzinger? Will you? Well, all right then." Meeting a new child, she has a tendency to gush: "Well, isn't this *nice*! Now, let's play *another game*!" But her affection for children is warm and genuine. She sees them as real people, capable of learning and feeling. She corrects them matter-of-factly—"Backward letter, Alison"—and praises them generously: "Good *job*!" She is both pleasant and shrewd, a good friend and a good teacher.

Her colleagues think so, too: in that summer of 1989, she had just been voted Hamilton's Teacher of the Year. The honor was ratified by the parents' organization and the Board of Education, and it brought a $500 grant, to be used for her professional advancement. Muntzinger had just heard about Parents as Teachers, and she chose to spend the money on the PAT training course. The school board picked up the rest of the $900 tab for the five-day trip, and Muntzinger flew off to St. Louis, leaving her husband John, a tool and die maker, to take care of their lakeside house and two teenagers.

PAT offers the course several times a year, training about one hundred new parent educators at a time, and Muntzinger remembers it as pleasant but intensive. The University of St. Louis was in its summer mode, relaxed and empty of students. There was an easy camaraderie among the trainees, a mixed lot, some of them teachers or former teachers, others from nursing, psychology or social work. And as a kindergarten teacher, she found most of the actual instruction familiar: the stages of childhood development, language skills, visual and auditory skills, gross motor development and fine motor movements, the telltale signs of impairment in sight, hearing or speech. The class spent one full day on each of the first three years of life, learning how children develop and how to communicate what was going on in terms that a parent could take in. They learned about group dynamics and the psychology of the home visit, and heard from experts on screening for learning and medical problems. They took turns playing roles in a simulated family visit and then got to watch a real one. Muntzinger found it reassuring that PAT so evidently meant business in its own teaching. For all the relaxed summer atmosphere, there was homework to be done every night, with lists of suggested additional outside reading, and there were daily tests to make sure everybody was getting the material. Nobody actually flunks out of the course, but some have to take the tests repeatedly until they manage to pass.

Back in Hamilton, Muntzinger started applying what she had learned. There would be home visits throughout the year, concentrated mainly in the summer months, and she lined up two more teachers, Lynn Bercaw and Randy Shoemaker, to help out. They paid sixty calls that first summer, and they were paid for the extra work at hourly rates based on their annual salaries. Steve Keeslar found some federal grant money to cover that cost and about $8,900 in start-up expenses, for books and materials. There wasn't any public library in town, so the school library had to put together the books, pamphlets, games and puzzles for the parents to borrow. This turned out to be the biggest single expense of the program, but it also turned out that a lot of the materials needed were free or came at minimum cost of perhaps $2.50 for a pamphlet, and that many educational organizations allow reproduction of their materials with no fussing over copyrights. There was also help available when Muntzinger, Bercaw and Shoemaker ran into children with special problems. Organizations for the illiterate and the hearing-impaired respond eagerly when somebody locates new clients for them. Hamilton's Lions Club already had a program offering glasses and hearing aids for the needy.

The biggest problem turned out to be finding families with preschool kids. You might think that would be easy in such a small community, Keeslar says, but it's surprising how people move in and out. He sent bulletins home with all his current students, letting their parents know about BELL and asking them to spread the word to their neighbors. He asked local real estate agents to tell home buyers that help for their children was available. He put ads in the local paper, which also wrote up the program. "In the summer, I spend a lot of time at the baseball diamond in the park," says Muntzinger. "Sooner or later, everybody in town turns up there. When I see some little kid I don't know, I ask, 'Who does that one belong to?' " Keeslar is also active in the Boy Scouts, helping candidates for Eagle Scout with their community service projects. When one of the boys needed a project, Keeslar set him to do a census of the school district. The scout enlisted his friends to canvass all the houses in 108 square miles and fed the results into a computer, producing the first detailed census in the district's history.

But there were differences from PAT's approach. Muntzinger agreed on the importance of the first three years in children's lives, but she didn't want to ignore the older preschoolers who would soon be coming to her class. So BELL would pay more attention than PAT to the three-and four-year-olds. The teachers were also uncomfortable with testing children's vision and hearing; after all, they said, they weren't qualified to get into medical issues, and what if somebody neglected to go to a doctor on the grounds that a child had already been tested? In practice, they gave up the formal screening, but if they saw something that looked wrong, they would just advise a parent to see the school nurse. Muntzinger and Keeslar also agreed that PAT's schedule of visiting every four to six weeks was unnecessary, perhaps even a bad idea. For one thing, there was a limited amount of information to convey to parents, and one visit per year ought to suffice for it. Then too, Keeslar worried that more frequent visits might infringe on the delicate Midwest sense of family privacy and authority—the same bugaboo Phyllis Schlafly had roused in Missouri. "I don't know that more visits would be useful," he says. "We're not here to run people's lives, and we don't want to give the impression that we're butting in. We have to watch out that parents know we're not trying to raise their kids for them."

As it is, parents tend to feel threatened when teachers come to their homes. Some sense implied criticism in every comment; some are embarrassed that they can't control their children perfectly, or that their housekeeping isn't immaculate. Randy Shoemaker, a pleasantly boyish young man with sandy hair and gray-blue eyes, recalls that one parent kept finding excuses to call off visits from Muntzinger. So Shoemaker dropped in without warning one day and brought off the visit, which turned out fine. Even so, he never got inside the house; the chatting was done over the picnic table.

In most cases, the atmosphere of a visit is casual and friendly. In one typical encounter, Muntzinger carries a tote bag of books, puzzles, games and homemade toys to the isolated onetime farmhouse where salesman Mike Moor and his wife Ellen live with four-year-old Libby and two-year-old Jacob. The living room is plain and comfortable, with furniture far from new and a big refrigerator carton being used as a playhouse in one corner. Muntzinger explores it with the two children—"Oh my goodness, your private little place! This is *nice*!"—before settling down to real business on the worn rug.

Jacob, dark-haired and shy, tries to cram eight fingers into his mouth. Muntzinger sets him to a puzzle, fitting a set of farm animals into their cut-out shapes in a plywood box. Libby, a skinny blonde coquette, gets a similar puzzle, this one featuring cut-out numbers. They both look good at it. But as Jacob continues to play with the animals, Muntzinger leads Libby through a quick interrogation. First Libby has to name the numbers as she fits them into their slots. Then, "Show me four fingers. Count them for me. Good *job*!" Muntzinger pulls a glove and two mittens from her bag: "Which is different from the others?" Different is an abstract concept, and Libby knows it. She also understands spatial relationships: Libby puts the glove on top of a chair, under it, beside it, behind it.

Ellen Moor is watching her daughter, smiling proudly, and Muntzinger tosses asides at her: "A clothespin is wonderful for fine motor coordination. Just sitting here opening it with one finger after another." Jacob's farm puzzle, she says, offers a chance to practice the sounds the animals make. Taking the cue, Jacob moos. His mother and Muntzinger laugh: The animal he is holding is a pig. Libby identifies some colors, and her mother volunteers that she tends to confuse green and orange. Muntzinger starts reading a story about a farmer and his hat, but it is remarkably dull and the children, quickly bored, lose interest. She abandons the story and has Libby draw pictures—the sun, with yellow rays, and a face, with hair on top. Libby writes her name: "Y P L P." Muntzinger tests Jacob's vocabulary: As she names them, he points in turn to a chair, shoes, an apple.

And so it goes. The visits are deceptively simple; there's a lot going on here, and the mothers (very few fathers sit in on these sessions) get a great deal of information. On another visit, Pam Harger, young, sparkly and a recent recruit to the program, has trouble getting a three-year-old to pay attention. She reassures the mother that her own daughter Katie tends to be overactive and hard to handle, too. "I was able to let her know it's okay and help her find creative ways to get her child interested," Harger says later. Lynn Bercaw warns the mother of a thirteen-month-old girl that she can expect some rejection in the next few months: "Negativism is perfectly normal. It's a sign that she's growing independent. She'll play alone, but she'll want you to be close by." The little girl is walking strongly, learning her own body, stacking blocks. Soon she'll learn to use a spoon and drink from a cup, Bercaw says—adding a casual thought that might or might not occur to a young mother: "and when you start giving her a cup, you wouldn't have it full, anyway." Mothers ask questions reflecting their own anxieties: How do you handle toilet training? Temper tantrums? Sibling rivalry? Why do kids get picky about their food?

In general, BELL's sponsors say they're pleased as punch about it. Keeslar is obviously proud of the program; he has presented it at educational gatherings and helped set up similar programs in four nearby districts, and he says the Fort Wayne schools are exploring the idea. By any measure, BELL isn't extravagant: it cost just $3,600 for the 1989–90 school year, or $26 for each home visit. That money was provided by the local Dekko Foundation and by a state summer school program, but even if it had to be paid from the district budget, says superintendent Nordmann, the funds would be found. "We're not going to let it die," Nordmann says. "The board is too committed to it."

But does BELL really work? Keeslar is trying to work out some objective measurements of success, but even if he had them, it's still too early to tell. Beth Muntzinger thinks it has helped her recent kindergarten classes, and Jill Mason, the first-grade teacher, says her first class containing kids from the program turned out to be exceptionally bright. There is anecdotal evidence that slow children have grasped ideas, shy children have learned social skills and parents have coped better. Sue Hile, herself a part-time teacher, credits Muntzinger with spotting the fact that her four-year-old daughter had a speech defect, not just a childish mannerism. Thanks to a speech therapy program, the child didn't have to lose a year of school. Parents are making use of the library, in modest numbers: In the 1990–91 school year, thirty-five books on parenting were checked out, and there were sixty-seven borrowers of children's books, games, puzzles and videos. And in general, parents are pleased with the home visits and grateful for the help. "She's full of ideas," said Ellen Moor after Muntzinger's visit. "All the things you can make for kids with just stuff around the house. I would never think of a clothespin for an educational toy."

The weakest part of the program is clearly the frequency of its home visits. It's hard to avoid the conclusion that BELL hasn't set its own standards high enough. For all Steve Keeslar's rationalizations about invading privacy, it's fairly obvious that unsophisticated parents can't take in all they need to know about child development in one visit each year. A mother is primed to hear about number games when her child is ready for them; she won't remember them if she hears them as part of an annual laundry list, and it's doubtful how much she retains from pamphlets and magazine pieces. It's also obvious that problems don't come up at neat yearly intervals. When the BELL program was described to her, Sue Trefeisen, PAT's training director, said she "would have a real question about that. How effective can it be, just one visit?"

Keeslar and Muntzinger aren't saying they were wrong, but the program is moving toward more frequent contacts with preschool parents. Pam Harger is pushing to concentrate her efforts on families identified as "at risk," with problems that indicate trouble ahead. In the 1991–92 school year, such families were to get a visit every other month. And Becky Norris, who started the whole thing, was moving cautiously back into an active role to encourage an expanded effort to communicate with parents. Specifically, she was pushing Harger's suggestion that the district might put out a newsletter for parents, like the one in the neighboring Prairie Heights district, using available materials on childhood development and tidbits of educational news. There's a publisher called Growing Child in Lafayette, Indianapolis, that offers a newsletter kit: regular infusions of information that can be pasted up and reproduced under a school's own letterhead or logo. An ambitious editor could combine the packaged stories with original news about her own program. The service costs just $24 a year.

Norris also likes the idea of making more use of the telephone: "We could have a contact person—not necessarily a teacher, maybe an aide or a parent—to call each family two or three times a year. 'Is this working? What do you need?' And we would have a file on the child's progress, whatever type of problems they have, and say, 'We'll send you something.' " It might be useful to start with parent volunteers on the telephone and gradually expand their role, perhaps even sending them for PAT training and using them for more frequent home visits. Keeslar sees possibilities here, but perhaps surprisingly, Beth Muntzinger disagrees. For all her efforts to make parents their children's first teachers, she has a firm sense of professional turf and the need for fencing it in. She uses volunteer mothers in her own classroom, but mainly to conduct drills and monitor small groups while she gives the real lessons to others. Parents could play a bigger role in BELL, Muntzinger thinks, but it would probably be for chores such as keeping records and assembling kits of library materials. "Let teachers do the teaching," she says.

One feature of BELL has been unequivocally disappointing: the monthly meetings for preschool parents. Keeslar had hoped that they would help to ease the intimidating effect schools have on parents and children alike, and would encourage parents to take a continuing role in schooling and school affairs. The meetings are intended to review progress and compare notes, share new learning materials and provide a bonding experience. "We try to do things that they'll identify with and have fun with," he says. And in time, "I think we'll see a lot of help coming from those parents. And that the families will stay active, help us raise funds for special events, things like that. A good parents' organization can do a lot for the school." But in practice, he concedes, "We haven't built that up real well." In the first two years, no more than twelve parents ever turned out for a meeting, and once there was only one. The next year, Keeslar changed the focus of the meetings to "parenting studies," and attendance rose to fifteen or so each month. But the same faces tend to keep showing up, and Nordmann suspects the meetings aren't reaching the parents who need help most, those so harassed by poverty and the hardships of single parenthood that they have no time for the program. Muntzinger says she'll keep trying— "I'll have a meeting if I have to talk to myself"—and she wants to experiment with varying the night of the week, trying daytime meetings and meeting at members' homes instead of the school.

But whatever BELL's shortcomings, the concept of parents as teachers is obviously valid, and the PAT system has proved its worth. Any school district could do a lot worse than try it. The essential moves:

• **Hook up early with PAT or a similar national organization.** The training is inexpensive and worth the cost, and the program can be a continuing source of information and support.

• **Start small, probably in just one elementary school, but line up all the community backing available.** Make sure the school board, the district superintendent and the principal are all on board and teachers are enthusiastic. Reach out to libraries, hospitals, day care and community centers. Contact local foundations and corporations to explore financial support. Line up local agencies that can serve handicapped children or families with special needs.

• **Inventory the available resources of books, toys and learning materials.** If they can't be assembled in a central location, they can be indexed and made available for circulation. Explore inexpensive sources of new materials and pamphlets: federal, state and local government agencies, back issues of magazines and newspapers, and corporate community-relations departments.

• **Try to reach as many young parents as possible.** Publicity is a permanent priority, and concise pamphlets and flyers describing the program should be widely distributed. As in Hamilton, real estate offices can help. Supermarket bulletin boards get surprising readership. Obstetricians and their office help should know about the program. Local social workers can help, too.

• **Accept help from all available sources.** Despite Beth Muntzinger's sense of turf, PAT has shown that it isn't only teachers who can teach; parent volunteers have their role, too. Be flexible, and work with what you have.

• **Use the program to strengthen contacts among parents, and between parents and the school.** It's a tough sell everywhere, but Keeslar's instinct is right: Having a strong parents' group improves a school, and preschool parents are a natural constituency. The program can lead to a permanent network.

In Hamilton, however, it has to be concluded that thinking about BELL isn't as clear as it could be. "We really want this to grow," says Steve Keeslar. But he has no schedule or detailed plans; even among themselves, the program's leaders haven't sat down for the kind of talk that clarifies long-term goals and the path to reach them. Nor have the people at PAT given more than token help. PAT officials say they keep track of their offspring programs and require that parent educators take systematic training every year in order to keep their accreditation. In practice, that rule has been scanted; Muntzinger says she still gets the organization's newsletter and orders materials through PAT, but none of her people have had additional training, and PAT has not monitored BELL's activities. PAT has been in a fever of expansion, more than doubling its list of affiliates in a single year, and it may be understandable that the modest clone in Hamilton escapes real scrutiny. But if PAT's program is to have credibility, attention must be paid.

None of this indicates that BELL is in trouble. So far, its problems reflect mostly the normal groping and exploring of ideas that go with any developing program. If it is at a crossroads, with a chance for both growth and failure, BELL also has dedicated and well-meaning leaders who have proved that they can think straight and act on their conclusions. The bet here is that BELL will thrive and grow, and has a chance to become the centerpiece of a lively parents' organization in a revitalized school system.

7.
The World According to Haskvitz

Nearly everything that happens in schools is done in groups. But it takes only one person to make a difference, and out in Walnut, California, in the dreary suburban sprawl of Los Angeles, Al Haskvitz has proved that small-bite principle again and again. Without special funding, without encouragement from his school board, without the support of a parents' group and with minimal backing from his principal, Haskvitz has used his eighth-grade social studies classes at Suzanne Middle School to make a real impact on the state and local scene. In the process, he has done even more for the kids. As one of his admirers puts it, "The most important thing they learn in his class is that they can change the world. Just by writing a letter or making a phone call, they can have an effect. Most of us grow up still not knowing that. We sit here and think, well, what can I do about the war in the Persian Gulf? Al's kids know they can do something."

Alan Paul Haskvitz is a likable, somehow cherubic man; he has a fringe of beard below plump cheeks and droopy eyes, and he is a fast-talking enthusiast who spews facts and ideas in great disorganized lumps. He can seem almost bashful, with an aw-shucks air; anybody, he tells you, could do what he does. But he is also a self-promoter and a zealot, a just man beleaguered in a world of complacency, bureaucracy, indifference and timidity. His destiny is to be a burr under the saddle of public officials, school bureaucrats, corporate male-factors—the whole apparatus of power, greed, stupidity and hypocrisy that refuses to see reason and do right. And his cause will live on in his students. "I just love the thought of creating all these little subversives," he says. "I can't wait for them to grow up and take over the system." But while they're growing up, he provides them with a steady stream of lessons in community activism. Among his works:

• On a routine visit to the polls on election day, the class found it hard to understand the official instructions for using the voting machines. Using a word-and-syllable count, the kids documented that the instructions were at the eleventh-grade reading level. Then they rewrote the passage. The Los Angeles County Registrar of Voters accepted the new version. Now more than 10 million voters are following the rules written by Al Haskvitz's eighth-graders.

• The Haskvitz class lobbied the state legislature for a water-conservation measure, ultimately passed, that called for planting drought-tolerant shrubs and flowers as landscaping for public roads and buildings. As a demonstration, the kids planted just such a "xeriscape" garden outside their classroom at Suzanne Middle School. They also raised $4,000 in bake sales to pay for a delegation to fly to Sacramento to testify for the bill.

• In another water-conservation effort, the class distributed 5,000 kits to residents of Walnut to reduce the amount used for flushing toilets. The kits were simple plastic bags, to be filled with water and suspended in toilet tanks. Haskvitz says they save 23 million gallons a year.

• The class has lobbied for antilitter and conservation bills in the legislature, sponsored candidates'-night meetings and passed out voter-registration materials. The students raise money each year to help train a seeing-eye dog and to support a polar bear at the Los Angeles zoo.

• The kids have collected oral history statements for the Walnut city archives and assembled a curriculum on local history suitable for use in Walnut's elementary schools. The class also offers to help translate official documents for the benefit of the city's burgeoning population of Hispanic and Asian immigrants. With a $1,500 grant from the Bicentennial Commission, the 1991–92 class worked to translate the Bill of Rights into Spanish, with questions and answers explaining it, on audio tapes for distribution to non-English-speaking families.

There's more, and it adds up to an impressive record since 1985, when Haskvitz came to Suzanne. But as he sees it, the projects themselves are almost incidental—worthy enough, but distinctly secondary. What counts is a style of learning. His kids are to be active, questing, challenging. They are to seek out sources of information, work out problems in teams and come to understand how human events cross the boundaries of history, economics, religion, science and math. "I don't care if they learn history or not," he says. "I don't care if they know the first President of the United States. I couldn't care less. I care that they're organized, that they can solve problems, and that they basically have an appreciation of how they got where they are, the freedoms they have. I'm looking for the big idea." Al Haskvitz sets a high standard: not only does he believe that all kids can learn, he insists that they should be able to think. "I tell them you take the information from this source, and the information from that source, and you're reaching out for an opinion, a conclusion, a hypothesis, and you support it with facts. Support it, support it, support it with facts. My kids think critically. My kids rip apart."

His kids also do well. In the first four years Haskvitz taught at Suzanne Middle School, the school's state scores in social studies rocketed from the 22nd percentile to the 94th percentile. He can't claim full credit for that, since he is only one of eight social studies teachers at the school. But nobody doubts that his example has spurred other teachers to be more challenging and creative. He has twice been voted teacher of the year by his colleagues, and kids from his classes have a reputation for being smart, well prepared and independent. Ken Gunn, principal of Walnut High School just across La Puente Road from Suzanne Middle School, says Haskvitz's students have an immediate impact when they arrive in high school. They have formed environmental and community service clubs and repeatedly taken the initiative in public service projects. "They're a major credit to Al," says

Gunn. In turn, Haskvitz has won some impressive honors. *Learning* magazine gave him its Professional Best award in 1990, with a $19,000 Oldsmobile as his personal prize. Like Jim Thom in Minnesota, he won $5,000 for himself and $10,000 for his program as a *Reader's Digest* hero of education. He has been cited approvingly by the National Council of Social Sciences, California State University, the U.S. Department of Education, NBC, CBS, *Business Week, U.S. News & World Report,* the California Distinguished School Exemplary Program and the National Commission on Social Studies, among many others.

Yet he is not universally admired. Some parents pull their children out of his classes every year, rejecting his liberal iconoclasm and demanding more structure, classroom order and attention to the textbooks. Suzanne students have voted him the school's most popular teacher in five of the past six years, but administrators and his colleagues in the district have repeatedly refused to make him a mentor teacher, a post carrying $4,000 a year in added salary. Haskvitz exists in uneasy truce with his principal, Bryan Cole, who appreciates his energy and the honors he collects for the school but obviously wishes, on the whole, that Haskvitz were almost anywhere else. Reporters on the education beat in the Los Angeles area know him as a good, creative teacher, but groan when they hear his high-pitched voice on the telephone. "I like him," says one of them, "but he has this habit of promoting himself. Just, if he'd sit back and not be so pushy." Haskvitz says it's not himself he's promoting, it's his kids—and he complains that the *Los Angeles Times* has warned him he'll get only one story a year, come what may. "Would they tell that to President Bush?" he demands in all seriousness. Even his friends, however, wish he could be a little less prickly, a little less determined to work against the grain. "If he could only learn to work with the system instead of against it, it would make him a lot more effective," says John Cassato, a former assistant principal at Suzanne who is now the principal of a nearby elementary school.

It's a smoggy morning in February, and a few late commuters and early shoppers are wheeling along La Puente Road, just south of the San Jose Hills and the famed Forest Lawn cemetery. But as they pass

Suzanne Middle School, a sheriff's deputy waves them to the curb. They are trapped, and doomed to be civically improved: Al Haskvitz and his eighth-graders have struck again.

A woman with a resigned expression and two small children in the backseat pulls to a stop. She rolls down her window as Jonathan and Heather, both fourteen, scurry from the waiting line of kids to her car.

"'Scuse me, ma'am," says Jonathan. "We're from Suzanne Middle School. We're conducting a survey of seat belt use. We're reminding people that it's safer to buckle up."

"Here are some cookies for the children, for being buckled up," says Heather. "And a teddy bear." The woman takes them, with a strained trace of smile.

"Here's a bumper sticker. Oh, and a flyer," says Jonathan, handing them through the window. The driver rolls her window shut and squeals away.

So it goes for half an hour. Haskvitz can work with the system when it suits him, and today he has organized this civic action with his friend Frank Girard, the Los Angeles County sheriff's crime prevention officer. There are two deputies, each running a pit stop and keeping the actual log of seat belt usage, and two lines of students waiting their turn to repeat their own variations of Jonathan's spiel. Each team of two students visits a car, picks up another supply of cookies and litera- ture, and rotates to the rear of a line. Haskvitz, short and burly, prowls nervously with Girard. A cameraman from the local cable TV station shoots a lot of videotape. Lylette Lin and Joanne Shin, the class's spokeswomen for the day, talk into a reporter's microphone about seat belts and safety. A newcomer to the class eats four of the cookies, and Haskvitz calls him "Miss Piggy." Another kid gets a little too excited, and has to be sent to the rear of the line to cool off. But the excitement is contagious: by the time they troop back across the lawn to go to their next classes, the whole gang is scuffling and chattering, pumped up with the joy of public service and the thrill of having done something different.

"Their next teachers are really gonna love me," says Haskvitz, back in his own big, cluttered classroom. "I'm gonna hear about this in the teachers' room." But nobody is more excited than he is. This has been a far cry from one of his really big public-service feats, but education, Haskvitz-style, has triumphed again.

The kids have learned about buckling up, for openers. "After today, that'll stay with them all their lives," he promises. And while the brief demonstration took a great deal of organizing, the kids themselves have done all the work—as always in his projects; he's a prime practitioner of that small-bite principle. Students were assigned to write to the National Highway Traffic Safety Administration (NHTSA) for safety belt booklets and sample bumper stickers; then they wrote again and yet again, until they had enough free stickers to give away to all the drivers they meant to stop. The kids sent the booklets to the elementary schools that feed into Suzanne Middle School, so teachers there could pass on the word to the little kids. They watched a videotape on auto safety from the sheriff's office, and Dana Lazneowici and Joanne Shin went to an evening meeting of the City Council to get a letter from the mayor giving official approval for the stunt. Teams of kids were assigned, first to write their own buckle-up flyer, then to translate it into four languages for the Hispanic and Asian immigrants in the area. (The Spanish, Japanese and Tagalog versions got done, but the Korean team's dog ate the translation. When a Korean driver pulled up at the roadblock, Dennis Rhee delivered the message in person.) Each kid thought out a personal speech about buckling up, and practiced reciting it at home. A parent with a commercial bakery connection came up with the cookies, and a team of students rounded up some small dolls and stuffed animals from local merchants. And in the end, more than sixty drivers and whatever children they had in their cars got a practical lesson in safety.

But what's most important, Haskvitz says, is that the kids learned another facet of the great lesson emblazoned over his bulletin board: "Make a Difference." By their combined effort, they actually made some small portion of the world sit up and take notice. "When they came back in, there was a feeling of self-worth in them," he says. "There's a little arrogance, a spunkiness. 'We take no prisoners.' This attitude I love. I love to get kids to talk back in a positive way. Not calling names, but they're ready, they're not gonna sit back and be veggies. The leaders of the world have got to be able to talk and deal. They left today feeling really good. It stays with them, that can-do feeling. I love that. That's my secret sabotage effect, the subversive teacher."

The Haskvitz method isn't reserved for his community-service projects. All his classes are geared to group learning and cross-disciplinary thinking. He doesn't actually ignore the textbook, but he bewilders some parents by running through the material twice, very fast—to give it two chances to sink in, he says. He emphasizes the how and why, not the who, what and when. "You should always teach history in reverse, from now backward," he says. "We never even study the discoverers. What's important is why they came, so we study the economics and religion. Then you know why they'd leave nice comfortable Europe to come over here and make a buck." And he has a bagful of pedagogical tricks to make his lessons memorable—some of them his own, most of them cheerfully copied from mentors or the professional literature, on the small-bite principle that ideas are where you find them.

Rather than teach a chapter of history, he tells his kids to make their own board games based on the chapter. They come up with games that are fun and ingenious: "Colonies R Us," for example, with players moving their tokens across a map as they answer questions about colonial America. Some parents complain that there's too much fun and not enough learning. Haskvitz replies that to produce such a game, a student has to read the chapter, understand it, extract facts and paraphrase them concisely for the questions, relate the questions to the map, organize the whole project and produce it on time, and how much more is a kid supposed to learn from one chapter?

Haskvitz gives both long-and short-term assignments, and kids must learn to stay on top of their long deadlines to avoid last-minute agonies. But many long projects are assigned to teams of students, who can help each other with both organization and creativity. He likes to assign time-lines, for example, in which teams organize the events of a half century and present them in concise and orderly detail. This can be done with illustrations on long strips of paper, or as a playlet or radio talk show, or a home-produced videotape, or a trip in a simulated time machine. "If I were a *teacher*," he says, loading the word with sarcasm, "there would be one way to do a time-line, the way I told them. This way I get four or five." One group presents the second half of the nineteenth century in rhymed couplets. Their signoff on the Chicago fire of 1871: "Dust to dust, ashes to ashes, / Everyone in the city was afraid of matches."

To dramatize economics, Haskvitz assigns each student to draw up a full-page ad for an imaginary product or service. The results are ingenious: one boy offers a magic pencil that knows all the answers to tests; a girl touts a miracle product that keeps hair looking freshly brushed all day. Haskvitz chooses about two-thirds of them as finalists, and the remaining students are given toothpicks as currency and assigned to be consumers. Then the entrepreneurs present their ads to the class, one at a time, with a concise pitch to the consumers. The class becomes a bazaar, with hawking peddlers grabbing and pleading at the cagy shoppers. In the end, the successful sellers have the toothpicks and are dubbed millionaires. The losers grumble: "He only bought Bryan's stupid pencil because he's his friend." Well, says Haskvitz, that's part of economics too; people trade with their friends, and you have to be ready for that. But now they have lost all their money, he tells them; they are poor and homeless; what will they do? They are disconcerted. Two of the millionaires generously offer broken bits of toothpick as charity. Haskvitz assumes the role of government, levying taxes for the general good. In half an hour, democratic capitalism has become an unforgettable reality.

Every year, social studies become an integrated whole as the class produces a massive study of an imaginary island. The island has a geography, a climate, an ecology, a history; its people have one or more religions, an economy, a form of government, a political and social structure. All of these facts of island life have to be thought out and meshed with each other. The project takes shape slowly, over months, with a few daily minutes in class and much committee work at home and by telephone. Haskvitz brings in the skull of a cat, found on the island: what does that imply? Cats eat mice, somebody says, so there must be mice too, and vegetation for the mice to eat. If there was a revolution in the island's history, its causes must be explained and its results reflected in the economy, the dominant religion, the social structure and the current politics. Maps must be drawn and redrawn to show roads, contours, sources of water and natural resources. World commodity markets must be studied and cartel agreements understood to find out what the island's products are worth. Haskvitz suggests, questions, introduces a biological twist here and an economic complication there. The students figure it out. By the end of the year, "The Island" is a two-inch-thick collection of reports, maps, tables, drawings and individual chapters—and the students have learned far more than they realize.

Haskvitz himself is a natural teacher, with enough of the kid in his own makeup to be peculiarly suited to the mercurial middle-school years. He sees his students as emerging people, with homes and parents and siblings, problems and talents and dreams; they are funny and sad, promising and exasperating, veering wildly between childhood and adolescence. He makes a lot of jokes, and his joking is geared to theirs: jocose and heavy-handed, the humor of insult and teasing. He sticks out his foot and trips Judy. She stumbles and shakes a fist at him, and he cowers elaborately. Seeing her later in the day, Haskvitz asks seriously: "Walking better now?" "Huh?" she says. "I saw you stumbling around a while ago," he says. "I'll stumble you," she threatens. "Ooooh," squeals Haskvitz in mock terror. "Quiver, quiver."

Some of Haskvitz's joking seems almost cruel. It is part of his mission to goad his students into active thought, and he can be fairly abrasive about it. A shy Asian girl shows up to transfer into his class, and he wants to know why: "Did they throw you out of the other class?" She laughs, confused and embarrassed. "I knew it, they threw you out," he says. Another girl, assigned to report on the medical pros and cons of auto safety belts, stumbles over her facts and gets some sarcastic ribbing. He needles his kids, he says, until they start fighting back; then he knows they'll be okay. He likes kids with spirit, like Paul Karapetian, dark-eyed and mischievous, drifting around the room after class with a sarcastic, singsong soliloquy for a visitor's benefit: "Gee, it's wonderful being in Mr. Haskvitz's class. He's just a wonderful teacher. He makes learning so much fun. . . ." Haskvitz ignores him, but winks at the visitor. Paul is just completing a history of the city of Walnut, pulled together from widely scattered sources and interviews, to be copied onto computer discs and distributed to all the elementary schools as a local history course.

It isn't surprising that some kids don't take to the Haskvitz treatment, or that some parents prefer not to subject their children to it.

When parents yank their kids out of his classes, that's okay with him, he says, though he feels sorry for the kids. He goes his own way, prowling his big square classroom, his weight-lifter's body balanced on small feet, passing out praise, exhortation and jokes in equal measure. He is a cat walking by himself. His voice rises in pitch as his enthusiasm soars; somebody once called him "that good teacher with the funny voice."

And the classroom is uniquely his turf. It's jumbled, stacked with artifacts: cardboard cartons full of student-made board games, a couple of computers, small cardboard model houses piled helter-skelter on a cabinet, a cow's broken femur, the skull of a dog, stacks of road maps, loose notes in manila folders. The bulletin board is a jumble, too. There are ecological posters: "We lose one species from the earth every day. Gone forever." There's the official procedure for earthquake drill, and the plat of a proposed nearby subdivision that the class is getting ready to evaluate. There's a mock ad, done with care and wit by anonymous students, for a patent medicine guaranteeing high grades: "Haskaminic-A. Gives you a brain even if you don't have one. . . . Caution: Users with a GPA of 3.5 or higher risk severe brain damage." There are a couple of letters from California congressmen, congratulating Haskvitz on his awards. And there's a chart showing the average yearly earnings of workers with varying levels of education, from $13,900 for grade-school graduates to $46,000 for people with a college degree. Money tends to motivate kids, Haskvitz has found: "You can get to them with money." It is Haskvitz's practice, in studied forgetfulness of the school regulations, to leave the door unlocked most of the time. He says nothing ever gets stolen.

Al Haskvitz maintains that he isn't unique. Any teacher, he says, can do what he does. The first secret is to tap into the vast pool of energy churning around in teenagers: "It's just amazing what these kids can come up with, and it makes teaching fun." A teacher does have to work hard for the first few months, he concedes, until the students figure out what's expected of them and discover that they, too, enjoy it. But after that, it's a matter of educating with kids instead of to them, and the teacher will be doing less work as the kids do more. "The less a teacher does, the less he takes part in the learning process, the better it is," says Haskvitz.

So when something needs doing in one of his projects, he spins a little arrow, salvaged from a long-forgotten game, and the kid the arrow points to gets to do the chore. And there is no shortage of things to do. One recent project aimed to document all the features that would interest kids along the length of Interstate 40, from California to North Carolina: rest stops, zoos, bridges, rivers, parks, camping sites, the Grand Canyon, the continental divide. The students used a word processor to write at least 150 letters of inquiry, and they have learned to make creative use of the toll-free telephone book, calling "800" numbers for information and free supplies. All kinds of things can be had for the asking, Haskvitz says. The I-40 project got dozens of free maps, only a year out of date, from the Automobile Association of America. Chambers of commerce in cities along the highway sent reams of material; so did city halls, NHTSA, park departments, railroads, state police and other official agencies. A government computer search produced a printout of every newspaper story ever written about the road since 1965. If some office doesn't respond to two polite letters, the kids complain to the governor's office. "We don't mess around," says Haskvitz.

In any project, the goal is to get the students to be assertive, work together, assemble the information, select what's important and present the results coherently, with opinions supported by facts. But all that is easy, Haskvitz argues: "You can see it doesn't take any money, only postage. You've got to be able to accept a little noise in the classroom. In my class, a behavior problem is a quiet kid. And you've got to use what they like to do. They like to talk on the telephone? Fine, so you let them use it and teach them how to take notes while they're talking and listening." It's all part of making the work interesting. A lot of teachers try to give bright kids more work, Haskvitz says, and what kind of sense does that make? "Is that your reward for being smart, more work?" No, the trick is not to go farther and cram in more subjects, but to go deeper into the subject already there. Anything, he says, is more interesting when studied in depth.

Haskvitz nudges and suggests, and he may help the kids over rough spots: When they were offering help with the city's oral history and a former mayor wouldn't take them seriously, Haskvitz pulled a string and got his attention. But then he turns them loose again, and they get the idea. He doesn't correct them or complain if they misspell a city or mispronounce a name; he doesn't even care when they put an extra syllable in his own name: "Hask-a-vitz." Dates aren't important either. "I'm looking for the big idea," he says, and what he's teaching isn't social studies, it's future leaders who need to be started along the endless road of improving the world. "They know what the Bill of Rights is about, they've studied the Constitution. So they start to see their own rights, and the fact that they haven't got any. Boy, you tell a kid that he doesn't have any rights, and he gets mad about it. Once you wind them up, they're ready to attack anything. They keep going and going, and they'll never take no. They're not afraid anymore."

Nor are they overly reverent of authority: In the world according to Haskvitz, respect is something to be earned. In the aftermath of the Panama invasion, for instance, the class wrote to the imprisoned dictator Manuel Noriega as an object lesson in trying to understand both sides of a case. When Noriega sent back a hand-written recitation of his grievances against the United States, the kids wrote George Bush asking for a point-by-point rebuttal. But when the White House letter arrived, it turned out to be a standard boast about the achievements of the war. Haskvitz recalls, "I handed it to one of the kids, not one of the top achievers, and he read it to the class. And he looked at me and said, 'He didn't answer any of our questions. This is really stupid.' And I knew I was a successful teacher." Not because he encourages disrespect, but because the students had learned that even the President of the United States ought to back up his opinions with facts. "They were able to go right to the core and see it for what it was, a political letter," he says.

Like the Noriega letter, some civic improvement projects spring naturally from the headlines. It can be a galvanizing national event: when schoolchildren everywhere were shaken by the explosion of the *Challenger* shuttle and the death of its seven astronauts in 1986, Haskvitz's class took the initiative in raising money for a memorial stone wall in front of the school. But projects can just as easily start with a casual observation. It was after Haskvitz noticed one day that all freeway exits look the same that he started the I-40 project, aiming to find the real country beyond the federal landscaping.

Almost always, it is Haskvitz who has the initial idea, and he's resigned to that. Kids don't read newspapers, he says, and they don't watch much news on TV either. For all their energy and interest, they tend to accept the world pretty much as it comes to them, and they don't know where to start poking at it: "You have to wind them up." So he was the one who saw the needlessly complicated voting machine instructions and started that project. It was Haskvitz, too, who set the kids off on a long battle against the toy balloon industry. They are trying to persuade the legislature to ban mass launchings of balloons, which some conservationists blame for killing birds and animals that eat the balloons when they fall to earth. So far, Haskvitz has been outgeneraled by the industry, in league with pageant sponsors and merchants who capitalize on the joyous pizzazz of rising clouds of multicolored balloons. But he keeps trying, and his bulletin board displays one trophy of victory: a letter from Disneyland promising no more balloon launches at the Magic Kingdom.

Win or lose, the kids learn valuable lessons from all the projects. Phillip Wener and Erbie Phillips, for instance, were shock troops in the early stages of the balloon war; they have since gone on to high school, but they remember the dogged research they did to winkle out facts about the balloon industry and what it would cost to make balloons biodegradable. A local California legislator, Frank Hill, backed the industry, arguing that biodegradable balloons would be prohibitively expensive. The kids had to call one manufacturer after another, getting facts like pulling teeth, until they finally got the full story. In truth, balloons begin life already biodegradable; they have to get an extra treatment, some sort of preservative bath, to keep the rubber from breaking down in air and sunlight. What makes that expense worthwhile is that if the balloons weren't treated, they might have to be dated, like milk, and the manufacturers might have to accept returns. The class was a huge amount of work, Erbie recalls; Haskvitz made them do a lot of weird things and he was stingy with an A, but it was worth every minute. And when Phillip and Erbie grow up, Haskvitz predicts with glee, "Guys like Frank Hill will really have to look out."

It's part of the Haskvitz lesson that not all the projects end in triumph. One day in 1986, when a fire drill interrupted the class, Haskvitz wondered why the instructions had them all standing in the parking lot. The class started probing, and one thing led to another. It turned out that their assigned spot in the parking lot would be occupied by the pumper truck, so it made no sense for them to stand there, and that the fire hydrants were located without regard to where the buildings were. Nobody had any data on dangerous chemicals in the school. The fire extinguisher in their classroom was not the type recommended for paper or electrical fires, the two most likely kinds, and it was too heavy for girls to use. The school had only two phone lines, and if there were a fire, 1,100 sets of parents would be sure to be frantically calling.

The class was assigned another place to stand during fire drills, and the *American Fire Journal* did a story about their research. A local radio station agreed to broadcast reassurances to anxious parents if an emergency came up. But the reforms ended there. It was officially explained that hydrants were placed according to an ordinance, and the extinguisher met the specifications, and that was that, whether it made sense or not. That was okay, Haskvitz told the kids; they would win other battles; civic activism is always a long shot. "I tell them a long shot is me being mistook for Tom Cruise. They understand that," he says. "They know that not everything is successful. They learned a lot, and they'll be safer in life, because they know more about fires. And you'll sometimes hear the kids come up to me and say, 'You look like Tom Cruise today.' Some days I look more like Tom Cruise than others."

Al Haskvitz is a man with a fairly deep store of anger. He doesn't see it that way; in his own eyes he simply craves justice and ethical conduct, a world that lives up to its own standards. But he seems to find injustice, unfair treatment and hypocrisy wherever he goes. He doesn't understand it, he says ruefully. "I just step in stuff. I just have a gift," he says. "I just walk in and this stuff happens."

He was brought up in the Los Angeles area, the son of a now-retired Ford tractor salesman who seems to be his son's opposite number in many ways. To this day, Haskvitz says, the old man can walk onto a used car lot and charm the salesman into a deal twice as good as the one Haskvitz has just negotiated on the same car. Haskvitz himself originally went into the insurance business, but soon got bored. "Why sell insurance?" he says. "If you're in an occupation and you see it's not helping the future, what are you doing there?" Deciding that teaching would be more meaningful, he got a master's degree in English and history at California State University in Los Angeles and started east, heading for the London Institute of Economics. He got as far as St. John's, Newfoundland, and was deflected by the offer of a full fellowship at Memorial University there. He studied folklore and sociology and says he was well on his way to a doctorate when he stepped into a characteristic mess, discovering by chance that the man who was to supervise his dissertation had actually faked some of his own field research. Haskvitz blew the whistle—what else was he going to do?—and the Ph.D. vanished with the friendship.

And that was the pattern. Wherever Haskvitz went, he found controversy. At Cal State he antagonized the head of his department by trying unorthodox methods. When he taught Mohawk Indians in upstate New York, he became their champion and alienated the local white establishment. He taught handicapped children and gifted students with similar results, feuding with principals and parents. He coached a girls' basketball team in Canada and won a championship, but even that was unpopular: Winning, he says, runs agains the Canadian ethos. He left teaching for a while to work as a journalist, a librarian and an archivist, and always managed to rub somebody the wrong way. "Wherever I go," he says, "I have the kids, the parents, the community and the press on my side. But administrators shake and quake."

That needs a little parsing. Beyond doubt, the kids are his to command. They love his energy, his jokes, his quest for truth and justice; they especially love crusading against authority, from the principal's office to the balloon industry. Haskvitz has a drawer full of adoring letters ("You really are my most favorite teacher *ever!*"), and when he spreads the word, half a dozen of his alumni troop over from the high school to tell a visitor what he has meant to them. Most parents also endorse the Haskvitz method, though there are those who can't stand him, and his own relations with parents are ambivalent. He uses the community and its resources for most of his projects, interacting easily with local officials and pulling in help where he finds it. For current events, for instance, senior citizens from a retirement home or community center can be asked to clip stories from newspa-

pers, to be used by the students to write reports; the reports in turn can
be sent back to the old folks for comment and criticism. But Haskvitz
seems to need unchallenged control over his projects, and that may be
why he is leary about enlisting parents. He himself explains that parents
have an "ulterior motive" for helping, and really want only to help
their own kids; after graduation, parents disappear. "By using the parents, you're opening up a can of worms," he says.

As for the press, it generally likes sources who are likely to stir
things up and make news, and education reporters in the Los Angeles
area generally like Haskvitz, with reservations about the frequency of
his calls. They have also learned that he isn't above a little hyperbole
in the cause of promoting his projects and getting his kids noticed. In
his many retellings, for instance, the nonbinding resolution passed by
the legislature to encourage drought-resistant landscaping has long
since become a full-fledged law. Similarly, on actual examination, the
original wording of the voting machine instructions isn't all that different from the amended version. He isn't a source that a reporter can
accept without challenge.

He is surely a trial to administrators. Haskvitz concedes that he has
a "lack of tact, the inability to suffer fools gladly." To people around
him, that can be an almost perverse refusal to see anybody else's
priorities. Laurel Kanthak, who was principal at Suzanne Middle
School until she left in 1989 to become director of middle level education for the National Association of Secondary School Principals, recalls him as a "wonderfully creative, intelligent teacher," but also as a
bomb thrower who was capable of inviting the governor to attend his
class and leaving her to find out about it only when the long black
limo pulled up to the curb, with police sirens wailing and a carload of
press bringing up the rear. "It was a real privilege to work with him,"
she says. "At the same time, I have to say I'm not sure I could stand
it if I had a whole school full of teachers like Al Haskvitz."

Her successor has no doubts at all. Suzanne School is built Califor-
nia-style, a collection of separated classrooms linked by covered walk-
ways like a spiderweb, and Bryan Cole spends most of his time behind
drawn blinds in his office at the center, fending off trouble. Al Haskvitz
often fits in that category. In 1990, for instance, the principal almost
had a visitation far worse than a mere governor: he found out that

Haskvitz's kids had written the White House suggesting that George Bush might visit the school in his congressional campaigning. The idea was apparently being taken seriously. Visualizing the chaos involved—days of Secret Service inspections, security precautions, TV camera crews, a cyclone invading his school—Cole vetoed the invitation.

The principal acknowledges Haskvitz as "a great idea man" who has done fine work in stimulating his students. But some kids need structure, too, he says, and conservative parents need reassurance that all that stuff going on in class is going to result in learning. Al would be a wonderful resource in a think tank, says Cole, or a senior high school where he could have more scope, or perhaps communicating his enthusiasm to fledgling teachers in a school of education—practically anywhere, he stops short of saying, but in Suzanne Middle School. Cole does say that Haskvitz has told him of his unhappiness at not being recognized as a mentor teacher, and has indicated that it's time to think about moving on. Whatever he finds, the principal promises not to stand in his way.

In truth, Haskvitz isn't really comfortable working inside any system. Some of his friends suspect that he simply can't function unless he's swimming against the stream—and that if the current isn't coming fast enough, he'll sabotage the dam. He enjoys cutting against the grain, says Laurel Kanthak, "and that's too bad, because he could accomplish even more if he would just accept that it is a bureaucracy and he has to get along with it." But even among friends, Haskvitz has a puckish compulsion to test the limits. He tells about the time a whole delivery of copying paper was sent to his room by mistake. Before sending it on to the school's supply room, he wrote his own name on every box. Other teachers couldn't get paper, he says gleefully, until he finally went to the supply room and asked innocently, "What? All these for me?"

He flirts with similar limits in his marriage. His wife Irene, a small, neat nurse, wears a skeptical, wary expression behind her oversized glasses, and with reason. On a day when Haskvitz has a date to go out to dinner with her, he passes up a dozen opportunities to call and set the time; he drives a visitor around his neighborhood in the San Gabriel foothills and stops for a lengthening visit with his friend Sam Maloof, the celebrated furniture designer. It's deep in the twilight when Haskvitz gets home, still without having called, to find a tight-lipped Irene feeding supper to Anna, seventeen, and nine-year-old Max. After considerable coaxing, she agrees to go to a restaurant. Even then, Haskvitz can't resist twitting her. He has had lunch at a place she has been wanting to visit. "You should have been there," he says. "You'd really like it." She refrains from throwing something at him.

So it's possible: a lone operator, bucking the whole system, can start and sustain programs that work and make schools better. It's probably more effective to work within a system, accept help, even set up a network of allies to support the cause. But either way, parts of the Haskvitz method will be useful:

• **Tap into the energy of the kids.**   The more they actually run the project, the more effective it will be—and the more they will learn.

• **Projects must be interesting and fun.**   Let the kids do what they like to do: work together, use the telephone, talk a lot, make wisecracks. Reward initiative.

• **The goal is independent thinking.**   Insist on high standards of factual accuracy and logic; never stifle curiosity, skepticism, irreverence.

• **It isn't necessary to spend a lot of money.**   Free and low-cost materials are easily available to teachers with imagination, persistence and a toll-free telephone book.

• **Use the community.**   Local officials, businesses, service clubs, foundations and the Chamber of Commerce can be sources of help— and so can parents, whether Al Haskvitz endorses that or not. In turn, community service programs can speed learning and get kids involved in the world around them.

• **Projects are where you find them.**   Look around: everything is interesting, and the more you know about it, the more interesting it becomes. A project can begin in a fire drill as well as a national disaster. Start anywhere—but start.

8.
The Parsons School of Good Works

Cynthia Parsons is a short, cheerful, determined woman with every bit as much zeal as Al Haskvitz for the educational blessings of community service. She even shares his indignation at the laziness and irresponsibility of the educators, parents and public officials who don't endorse civic activism and can't see the virtue in letting kids do all the good work they can. But unlike Haskvitz, she believes in the old adage that you can catch more flies with honey than with vinegar. Her story illuminates several small-bite principles: that one person can make a difference, that good programs address real problems and make use of kids, that youthful idealism is a powerful force. But most of all, she shows the value in reaching out for help and enlisting all possible allies. She has set herself up as a one-woman crusade to coax, cajole, exhort and, as a last resort, to bribe Vermont's high schools to put their students to work in community service programs. And in the process, she proves another old adage: There's no end to what you can achieve, if you're willing to let somebody else take the credit.

Her bribes can't be called lavish. In 1985 Parsons persuaded Vermont's new governor, Madeleine Kunin, to name her to an unpaid post as the entire staff of a vague new agency called SerVermont. Then she used that flimsy springboard to get the first of a series of small foundation grants to be used as seed money for school programs. She doles it out, $100 to $300 at a time, to help launch students in such projects as building an aquarium for a retirement home, buying equipment to gather the oral history of a town, or planting elm seedlings that are resistant to the Dutch elm disease. And more often than not, she accepts the proposal for a new program and then turns the tables by showing the applicants that they don't need her money after all. Inexhaustibly inventive, she suggests one creative expedient after another. Wonderful idea, she says; by all means, plant flowers at the local day-care center. But you don't need $100 for seedlings. Instead of buying them at the nursery, why not have the biology class grow them from seeds as a class project? Can't the English class compose a letter to a seed company, explaining the project and asking for free seeds? Won't the lumber yard donate some scrap so the woodworking class can make window boxes and planters? And maybe the art class can do a little research on gardens and design the beds.

What she gets is an operation in the old Vermont tradition of frugality and barn-raising neighborliness, pulling in as many people as possible. Like Haskvitz, she achieves education in the process, with cross-disciplinary involvement. But her primary focus is on the service: She aims to improve schools by involving them in their communities and giving students a taste of the pleasure to be had in helping others. And unlike Haskvitz, Parsons is content to make her difference as a catalyst. She stirs things up, gets people started, nudges a project into motion and then drops out, letting others take the bows. In their different ways, Haskvitz and Parsons both show what can be done with a flat minimum of funding and a modest set of goals—if there is also an endless flow of ideas and a tireless source of energy at work.

Cynthia Parsons operates out of her home, a former one-room schoolhouse in the hamlet of Gassetts, which lies on the outskirts of Chester, a classically bucolic village in southern Vermont. She's still a volunteer herself, a mostly retired teacher who uses SerVermont funds only for travel, expenses and phone bills connected with the projects. The bulk of the money goes for the minigrants, for printing pamphlets about her program and for hiring an occasional college intern to do research. In six years, Parsons has spent a grand total of nothing in public funds and $115,000 in foundation grants. Before she started, only a quarter of the high schools in Vermont sponsored any public service at all. Now all sixty-six of them do at least one community service project each year, and many are considerably more active than that.

The benefits, as she sees it, are immeasurable. In part it is a simple matter of doing good for folks who need help. The work also makes communities better places for all who live in them. But beyond that, students learn to integrate their good works with their studies and make their schoolwork part of real life. And most important, community service is a central part of what it means to be a citizen. Parsons can be a bit saccharine in her stories of young folk discovering the rewards of service, but she is surely right that the impulse is there to be tapped— and that we would all be better off if it were. That doesn't mean that George Bush's "thousand points of light" should be expected to take over the legitimate functions of government, but government can't be expected to solve all the problems of the country, either. In a just society, everybody has responsibility.

Parsons knows that people aren't likely to leap into service work as adults if they have never encountered it in the course of their education. So it is the schools that have to train kids to become what she calls *small-d* democrats—neither isolated from the community nor content to pay the bills while a few elite leaders call the shots. A good citizen gets involved in every facet of community life, she argues, and public service should be woven into the fabric of every school. But that doesn't mean it should be required. The Parsons school of good works has to be voluntary; otherwise there's no joy in it. Community work is a privilege, she says. It certainly shouldn't be parceled out as punishment, either for schoolboy truants or for the Ivan Boeskys of the world. Parsons can't imagine a better way of souring kids permanently on public service than to make it a sentence for lousy behavior. She doesn't even hold with giving credits toward graduation for doing community service in school. "I want the doing to be the reward," she says.

That's an old-fashioned vision, but in lots of ways Cynthia Parsons is an old-fashioned lady. She came early to activism: she remembers campaigning hard as a child for her favorite among the three suitors of her widowed mother, and when he won the competition and became her stepfather, she took his name. He was a labor relations executive for General Electric, and taught her to take an interest in civic affairs in the upstate New York towns where the family lived. That was the foundation for her lifelong concern with public service. The family moved often, and Cynthia attended eleven different schools before she went off to the Principia College in Elsah, Illinois, for a degree in physical education. She was "gradually seduced" into academic teaching, she says, starting in 1948 with a job on an island off the Georgia coast, tutoring two rich children who had just returned from a yearlong yacht trip. She taught in several private schools and went to graduate schools at the University of Southern California, the University of California at Los Angeles, Syracuse University and Harvard, but then took off to learn journalism as a gofer at the *Christian Science Monitor*. She became its education writer, serving two stints for a total of fourteen years. Between those sessions, from 1969 to 1974, she went to Washington to be education editor for the World Bank and then a program officer for the National Institute of Education. It was then that she was running around the country with her Cuisenaire rods, trying to explain the New Math to befuddled teachers. Even in retirement, she still gives classes in education and environmental writing at Dartmouth College and the University of Vermont.

But her vision of community service gradually turned into a crusade of its own, and she knew she needed political backing to get it started, preferably at the state level. When Madeleine Kunin started her run for Vermont's statehouse, Parsons sent her a copy of *Seeds*, her book on educational reform, with an offer to help shape an education plank for Kunin's platform. That led to four or five lengthy and not always amicable talks: the two strong-minded women didn't totally agree on goals or the way to get there. But the concept of SerVermont survived. Both Kunin and her state commissioner of education had doubts about the idea. The program sounded wispy at best, and there were obvious risks in turning a private citizen loose to run around the state with her own agenda and the governor's imprimatur. "I just kept saying, 'Let me try it,' " Parsons recalls. "I said, 'I'll get the money, and let's see what happens in ten years.' "

Kunin set up an advisory board for Parsons to report to, and the program was announced early in 1986. The governor wrote an introductory letter to each of the state's sixty-six high schools, but that was the extent of the official blessing. Parsons had no legislation, no state funding and no authority beyond her own considerable power of persuasion. She logged ten thousand miles on Vermont's roads that first year, spreading the word to the high schools and trying, often in vain, to get principals interested. Some sent her off to the social studies department; most found excuses to do nothing; a few, warned in advance about her staying power, scheduled fire drills to cut short their interviews with her. But she got her first grant of $15,000 from the Edwin Gould Foundation for Children and began offering her minigrants. She compiled an exhaustive inventory of community service jobs available to Vermont teenagers, only to find that nobody wanted it. So instead she made a connection with RSVP, the Retired Senior Volunteer Program, which offered to provide local volunteers as liaison between students wanting to work and agencies that could use their help. And gradually she began winning converts in the schools.

These days Cynthia Parsons is a familiar figure all over the state—"that short fat woman," as she mocks herself—bustling from school to school with dogged purpose and determined cheer. She has a strong, mobile face, with a firm mouth and lively green eyes; her greeting on the telephone lilts with good news: "Cynthia *Par*-sons!" And she has friends nearly everywhere. She travels often to spread the community service gospel across the country, and says thirty states now have programs fashioned after hers to greater or less extent.

But it's never an easy sell. Teachers and principals explain patiently that much as they'd love to have public service programs, there isn't enough time in the day to teach the children what they need to know. Kids stare at her blankly or laugh cynically at the thought of working for nothing. Some of her biggest opposition comes from parents, who don't cotton to unpaid labor or else think, in true Vermont fashion, that schools have no business telling children what to do with their own time. City officials, cops, even librarians tell her they have nothing for volunteers to do. When she makes suggestions, she hears only problems: What about liability insurance? How do we get transportation? Where's the money coming from?

When people talk like that, Parsons says, they're just ducking the issue. She is sitting on the couch in her converted schoolhouse, the stove is cranking out waves of heat, and outside is a dreary February thaw: cold rain turning slushy snow into dank puddles over sheets of ice. The room is familiar-looking, big and square, with its high ceiling and milky glass light fixtures dangling; she has left a couple of the old desks in place, screwed to the floor, with old textbooks scattered on the scarred slanting tops. The blackboard is covered with notes on her various projects, and also with a list of U.S. Presidents, the word "SAVE!" scrawled above it and underlined three times. But the place isn't all museum: A tidy modern kitchen stretches across one side of the room, and a computer occupies a prominent place below the roll-down map of the country.

Liability, for example, is hardly ever a real problem. School insurance policies almost always cover more than the principal thinks they do, Parsons says, and if there's a gap, it can probably be filled by the policy of whoever is being helped. Similarly, there are all sorts of ways to solve the transportation problem. If senior citizens are involved, there's usually a van they can use; during school hours, buses are sitting around doing nothing; failing everything else, why not use the driver education class to transport volunteers or make deliveries? The driver-ed car has to cruise around town anyway, and might as well have destinations. Money can usually be found if it's really needed, and there are SerVermont minigrants as a last resort.

The other obstacles are just as flimsy. What do you mean, there's no time? she demands. Don't the typing classes have to practice? Why not have them practice by typing up documents for the city clerk, or transcribing tape cassettes dictated by old folks who can no longer write letters to their friends? Don't the French classes have to do translations? Well, why can't they translate something real, like oral histories dictated by Canadian-born Vermonters in retirement homes? And what do you mean, the librarian has nothing for young people to do? Wouldn't she welcome a puppet show for the Saturday story hour? Couldn't the parks department use help in cleaning up the riverbank? Why can't the kids help with voter-registration drives, absentee ballots, day-care at the polling places? Why can't they write public service notices, translate welfare regulations into Spanish or write newsletters for the local service club, all integrated with their regular classwork? Don't the school plays have dress rehearsals? Why not invite senior citizens and handicapped kids to be an audience?

The world throbs with good works aching to be done, and Cynthia Parsons bubbles over with examples, illustrations, anecdotes. Children can teach the older generation to be computer-literate. They can make telephone calls to cheer up elderly shut-ins. Older kids can tutor younger ones who are having trouble with their lessons, and just as the San Antonio program proves, both sides can benefit from the exchange. Shop classes can repair small appliances for the poor or elderly, and the gadgets can be picked up and delivered by the driver-ed car. Brochures can be designed and written for community agencies. Students in physical education classes can work, one on one, with handicapped kids training for the Special Olympics. Students can cut out and maintain hiking trails, adopt a local stream or stretch of highway to be kept clean, volunteer for work in soup kitchens or homeless shelters.

The Parsons kind of community service has nothing to do with kids riding bicycles in marathons to raise money that they never see being spent. She thinks community service has to be hands-on, and the more personal contact with the people being helped, the better. She likes projects that are a little out of the ordinary, with a touch of unexpected imagination. There are lots of elementary glee clubs singing at retirement homes, but the one that got a Parsons minigrant planned to use it to buy sheet music for the vintage songs that the old folks really wanted to hear. And when the kids at the Lyndon Institute got a minigrant to put on a "Break the Winter Blues" lunch for local senior citizens, she was particularly delighted with two ideas the kids came up with. First, when the teachers wanted to make a rule on how old people had to be to attend, the students said no: A senior citizen was anybody who wanted to opt in. Even better, the kids said nobody would be served lunch before filling out a form listing chores that the students could help them with—stacking firewood, organizing a closet, cleaning a cellar, anything.

She likes best just that kind of project: one that perpetuates itself, or leads on to further good works. In Woodstock, for instance, the chemistry class regularly monitors the purity of the Ottaquechee

River, and the work is an important part of a continuing state survey of water quality. "I think that's Nirvana," Parsons says—a real job that students can do, one that must be done regularly and makes a real difference in the world. "And they didn't need any SerVermont money, either." In the village of Townshend, students from Leland and Gray High School used a $300 minigrant to design and build aviaries and aquariums for two retirement homes. The original plan was to test a social studies theory that pets improve the quality of old folks' lives. "They couldn't come back in six months asking, 'Are you less senile?' " Parsons says. "So they had to keep visiting and observing." That led to friendships, dictation of letters, games of checkers and chess. The shop class constructed oversize boards and chessmen that arthritic hands could grasp. Some of the retired people taught students to knit afghans and play harmonicas. "The quality is highest when the service is two-way," Parsons says. A bridge had been built between the school and the senior citizens, and the community was that much stronger.

Even without such synergy, there's always something worth doing. Parsons likes to tell about Orestes, a fourth-grader with a reputation for troublemaking who volunteered to find something to do for the local library. The librarian took one look at him and shook her head: no, nothing here, not even putting the books back on the shelves or sweeping the floor. Frustrated, Orestes sat outside on the steps. He noticed a car driving past again and again, searching vainly for a parking space. He flagged it down: Was the driver trying to return a book? She was, and Orestes took it in for her. Then he put up a sign: Return Books Here. A community service had been born. And before long, synergy developed: Orestes was doing chores inside.

There's an element of the goody-goody in all this, which probably goes with the territory. The very label, community service, conjures up images of Junior League volunteers with candy stripes on their nurses' caps, passing out cookies to hospital patients. But anyone who has seen children respond to the experience of helping people in need knows how real their feeling is. Part of it is pure altruism; kids are truly idealistic, and resonate to the idea of being able to help. But in part, too, the fact that they can provide real help makes them important in a way children seldom are. Being needed is a kind of power, as rare and pleasurable an experience for kids in Vermont as it is for the students helping each other in skills tutorial at Parkway North. Like Juan Gonzales and his friends in the Valued Youth Program, the Vermonters respond by becoming responsible—by growing up a little.

In practice, Parsons sees herself as a catalyst in the process: She puts the ingredients together in the laboratory beaker, tries to get a reaction going, then leaves it for others to carry on. She may run workshops for interested teachers, students and school authorities, for instance, and invite applications for minigrants. She may call a meeting of all the people in a community who might take a hand, and throw out suggestions for projects they might like to try. And as a wedge to get community service started in a school, she has learned to accept whatever ideas a community sees as desirable.

By her lights, for instance, Project Graduation is only dubiously a community service at all. It's a national model, used in schools across the country, that aims to make sure graduation parties are drug- and alcohol-free. Typically, a school will join the effort by planning its party at an isolated location where coming and going is difficult (a riverboat, for instance, or a mountaintop ski lodge) and scheduling attractive events at frequent intervals to keep kids on the premises. There are refinements on the technique, too. It's a good idea to get as many kids as possible involved in committees, and the guy most likely to smuggle in liquor should be put in charge of making sure nobody does.

That's all worthy enough, but is it community service? "Well, Project Graduation saves lives," Parsons says. "But it also helps pull the community together to get something done, and that can be the start of bigger things." And above all, it's a foot in the door. It was Project Graduation that finally persuaded the last holdout high school in the state to sign up for public service.

But such expedient compromises soon reach their limits. Parsons has done a good deal of thinking about what it takes to run community service programs, and her rules are both hard headed and realistic. Among them:

• **The program can begin as an experiment.** Parsons will accept almost any idea that gets the camel's nose under the tent. But sooner or later, if it is to survive, the community must be persuaded that service is part of the fabric of education and an essential factor in civilizing kids. This isn't as hard a sell as it sounds, she maintains: "Think about football. Schools spend thousands of dollars, turn their schedules inside out, build huge facilities, all so that young people can collide with each other at high speed as violently as possible. Why do they do it? It's all justified by building in some perceived benefit—the need to develop leadership, teamwork, school spirit. Community service does all that without even maiming anybody. We just have to sell it half as effectively."

• **From the beginning of any project, the principal of the school has to be on board.** She doesn't necessarily have to be enthusiastic, as long as a teacher or two will carry the ball, but she has to be willing to go along. In time a sound program will persuade her it's worthwhile, but she can kill it easily in the early stages if she isn't at least resigned to having it around.

• **Somebody has to be clearly in charge.** It can be a staff volunteer from the school, who gets a reduced teaching load or extra pay for the job; it can be a parent, who is given office space, a telephone and the principal's mandate. Community service can also be run through the social studies department, as part of its curriculum. A program can even be delegated to local service clubs such as Rotary International, the Junior League or the local chapter of the American Association of University Women. But if there isn't somebody in charge, a regular, prominent presence, few students will volunteer and few requests for help will be received.

• **Community service must be more than a one-shot exposure to the world of need.** Parsons has only scorn for programs in which Junior League ladies in station wagons pick up a gaggle of unprepared teens to visit a local hospital for an afternoon, with a report to be turned in next day on "What My Community Service Meant to Me." She has seen students rebel at such perfunctory contacts, knowing instinctively that something more meaningful must be possible. In Vergennes, for instance, high-schoolers who were rehabilitating a shelter for the homeless persuaded their teacher to let them meet and actually work alongside the men and women they were helping.

• **Service tasks can be fairly menial, especially for younger children:** picking up litter, washing dishes, doing gofer chores. But a good program also has room for advancement to more challenging work. An eleventh-grader who is still folding napkins at the senior center, says Parsons, "is not a happy camper." The more responsibility and initiative students are allowed, the better they will respond. And like Al Haskvitz, she insists that whatever the chore, it must be fun as well as worthwhile. A student who would gladly work with a group cleaning up the riverbank simply won't spend hours alone scraping paint, no matter how worthy the cause.

• **Recognition and rewards must be built into the program for the kids taking part.** Notices on bulletin boards, public address announcements, honors at assemblies and certificates of service are all good ideas. Breakfasts or dinners are useful. If the school has a display case for athletic trophies, there should be a matching display of academic achievements and community service awards.

• **While remaining essentially voluntary, community service should be integrated with academic work whenever possible.** If math, science, writing and social studies assignments can be used in service projects, the students are doing no more work than they would do anyway; but the academic work becomes more meaningful and the service is a means to learning. At its best, community service is a kind of team teaching.

• **Good service programs make use of brokers**—those special citizens, found in most communities, who have a talent for seeing what needs to be done, twisting arms, matching students with particular chores, smoothing out problems and making sure recognition is forthcoming. If the person running a school's program doesn't match this description, he should find a broker and let her volunteer. Brokers, like ideas, are where you find them. They are usually delighted to be of use.

Cynthia Parsons, of course, is a broker herself. But her business is wholesale. She starts things up and moves on; in the ideal world, the schools would be making their public service connections without her, and she's happy to fade into the sunset as soon as somebody will take the initiative. "It's fine with me if the schools never heard of SerVermont, or even if we put up a minigrant and they don't realize it came from me," she says.

Thus she counts as a major success the program at Bennington High School, where she had a hand only in the first organizing meeting back in 1989. Memories differ on how it came about; no matter, says Parsons. The important thing is that for the first time, all the major people who could get things done were sitting in one room, talking about community service and how to get a program started. There was the new principal of the high school; the junior high principal, a man who had received one of Parsons' minigrants in an earlier posting; the United Way president; a liaison person from Bennington College; a representative of the Chamber of Commerce; and Dorothy Sullivan, the president of the local RSVP. It was Sullivan who had conspired with Cynthia Parsons to set up the meeting.

At first, nothing seemed to happen. "While I was making suggestions," says Parsons, "the high school principal was taking no notes at all." But the catalyst never knows which button will start the current flowing through the laboratory beaker. In this case, it seemed to be her suggestion that the high school's advanced placement classes might play a role. The principal, Tony Krulikowski, was teaching an AP class in history, and he saw a chance for his seniors to have a public service internship in the summer before going off to college. The Bennington College representative reacted to the idea of mentors for troubled youth. Then it turned out that RSVP had a new member, Millie Katz, who had just moved in from the Midwest, where she had been the spark plug of a full-fledged community service effort. She sounded like a natural broker. At that point Parsons left; the beaker was boiling, and she knows enough to move aside when the reaction becomes self-sustaining. These people wouldn't need any SerVermont minigrants to nudge them into action. Since then she has followed the program from a distance.

In fact, says Krulikowski, the high school did have one service program at that point: a project called PALS, pairing about fifty high school students as mentors for sixth-graders considered at risk in three elementary schools. He wanted to expand from there. And sure enough, Millie Katz turned out to be the key player; her Midwest experience had left her with an encyclopedic knowledge of how to run a multifaceted service program, and she even had samples of the forms she had used. The RSVP program was a great source of energy and volunteers, including a senior citizen who handles files for the school program. The Board of Education approved an expanded program, the Rotary club put up $500 in seed money and promised an annual breakfast to honor the service workers, and Katz set out to recruit them from the school's twelve hundred students.

There were the usual problems and nonproblems. There was no great rush of student volunteers, and Katz had been given a desk in the school's guidance department—a location that wasn't likely to draw much traffic. So she launched a media blitz and set up a table with a sign in the cafeteria at lunchtime. That produced fifteen volunteers in the first week. She found jobs for them in the day-care room and the gift shop at the local hospital, in retirement and nursing homes, working with retarded and Special Olympics children and helping in the animal shelter. A senior English class took on a special assignment, collecting letters to Santa Claus that came to the Bennington post office and writing an answer to each one. A survey of the school turned up an unexpected finding: more than a hundred students were already involved on their own in community projects of one kind and another, ranging from Little League coaching to tutoring preschoolers and visiting retirement homes. Many of them got started through their churches or their parents' volunteer work.

Krulikowski had worried about liability, which turned out to be covered. But logistics were a problem. Katz recruited volunteers from the community to drive students to their after-school activities, and sometimes took the wheel herself. The program has grown; after a year and a half, about 170 Bennington students were actively involved in community service. And behind the figures are the individual stories of learning and growth. Two girls collecting oral histories at a retirement home got so involved in the project that they kept at it all summer. A boy doing volunteer work at the library was good enough at it to be given a part-time paid job. A girl teaching calligraphy to senior citizens discovered a new assurance and self-confidence.

It isn't easy. "The whole concept of service is alien to some kids," says Krulikowski, a tall, bearded man behind a tidy desk. "Most adolescents are very materialistic. So the point is to show them that they can get more than they give. They can lose their big bundle of insecurities and discover things about themselves. If you can just get them started on it, they discover a whole new emotion they never felt before. You get a look from them—'Wow, this feels good!' Then they start to communicate that to other kids, and you get pairs coming in to volunteer together." Even then, the principal says, the students need a lot of training, direction and support. "They have to take the initiative and learn a lot of skills that grown-ups take for granted." Adults tend to forget the years when they didn't know how to organize and plan their time, how to anticipate small problems and handle them, how to find a solution if something goes awry. Yes, he agrees, the greatest untapped resource in education is the kids themselves, "but we have to help them tap all their own resources." Krulikowski aims to expand his program and enlist other schools in the Bennington system to take part, and he hopes that the next round of volunteer work will involve more cross-pollination with the school's curriculum. Perhaps the kids can help in a day-care center, he muses. That way the human services class and the child development class, from the vocational side of the high school, can get practical lessons in nutrition and hygiene.

So there's not much for Cynthia Parsons to do in Bennington, and she feels fine about that. There's more than enough to do elsewhere. And Bennington helps reassure her that the idea of community service is contagious enough to get along without her. "If I stopped doing this, would it stop?" she asks herself, staring at the old tintype of Abraham Lincoln just below the schoolhouse clock. "Well, there might be a little less push. But it's getting some national initiative, and it's got some momentum going here." The idea that's beginning to sink in, she hopes, is both simple and revolutionary: "Children could really improve the way we live—if we'd only let them." And if people can figure that out, she doesn't care at all who takes the credit for it.

9.
To Fill the Schools with Parents

It's one of the great pieties of public education that parents ought to get involved in schools. Over and over, research proves that children do better if their parents take an active interest in their schooling, and teachers and principals repeat like a mantra that "Schools filled with parents are just better schools." On some level, they may even believe it. But in their hearts, most educators seem to have reservations; if they don't see parents as outright obstacles to be overcome, they agree with Beth Muntzinger in Hamilton, Indiana, that once the kids are safely in school, parents ought to stick to nurturing and "let teachers do the teaching." In practice, most parent-involvement programs have a perfunctory air about them. In Indianapolis, however, William Douglas really means it—and with a staff of three bright, funny, unconventional women, he has put together one of the most ambitious and arguably most effective parent programs in the country. Parents in Touch (PIT) shows what can be done to reach out to parents, even in the chaotic conditions of the inner city, if a system is really willing to make the effort.

It was fifteen years ago that Bill Douglas became convinced that the schools had to change. He's a bear of a man who could pass for a former football pro, a onetime high school principal with the X-ray eyes and no-nonsense tone to prove it. Right through the '50s, he says, it didn't matter that half the kids dropped out before they finished high school; they were going to get jobs and have a life anyway. But the world has changed, and "We can't afford anymore to lose a single kid, because we haven't given them the skills they need to compete." And since the schools haven't been redesigned to meet the new needs, educators must reach out for help from parents, the business community and anyone else who can lend a hand. "We simply can't do the job alone. We need everybody," he says. An assistant superintendent who worked his way up through the Indianapolis system, Douglas persuaded the school board to launch PIT in 1979. It was an uphill battle from the start. Both the city and the schools were in decline, and the children's problems reflected what was going on in their homes. In a dozen years, the program has had ups and downs, progress followed by retrenchment. It has certainly not started any grass-roots stampede of parents into the schools. But it keeps stubbornly trying to pull parents in and, failing that, to get them involved in their children's education in their own homes and even at work. The major successes:

• **Parent conferencing.** The annual visit to school to talk over a student's progress with the teacher is the beginning of what parents can do, and it's routine for middle-class families. But many inner-city parents, unable to cope or intimidated by their own school experience, never show up. PIT's first project was an elaborately planned, rehearsed and choreographed effort to get parents to come to conferences. It was an instant success: in its first year, fully half the elementary kids were represented by parents. Recently the rate in elementary schools rose to an astonishing 83 percent, and representation in secondary schools climbed past 60 percent. In all, 30,000 parents a year show up for conferences.

• **Continuing involvement.** At the conference, teachers invite parents and their children to sign a formal contract. The students promise to work hard and take learning seriously; the teachers promise to make it interesting, to communicate with parents and to give homework assignments, and the parents promise to monitor their children, to support the teachers and to provide a home atmosphere that makes learning possible. It is a ceremonial commitment, and kids and parents alike take it surprisingly seriously. PIT also set up Parent Line, a phone number that lets parents choose among 140 tape-recorded messages. The subjects range from magnet schools and special programs to parenting skills, drug and alcohol prevention and teen suicide. The line gets as many as three thousand calls a month.

• **Help with homework.** Both parents and children tap into Dial-a-Teacher, a PIT service in which teachers answer telephoned pleas for help on homework assignments. It's open for business from 5 P.M. to 8 P.M. four nights a week, with four teachers on duty, not to provide answers but to lead the way through the problems and explain methods. They take as many as 15,000 calls a year. On a separate cable television show, Homework Hotline, two teachers field the same kind of calls as a sort of educational TV game show. The two cable networks carrying the show have a total of 150,000 subscribers.

• **Homework for parents.** Four elementary schools have piloted TIPS (Teachers Involve Parents in Schoolwork), giving homework assignments that require a parent to check whether students understand the work and to provide feedback to the teacher. A similar reading program, BEAR (Be Excited About Reading), asks a parent to send in a certificate each time a student reads a book outside of class. Small prizes are given for two or more books per month, and at the end of BEAR's first year, more than one thousand parents and children were honored for having read twenty or more books in the year.

• **Reaching parents at work.** PIT has enlisted thirty-seven Indianapolis employers to give monthly "brown-bag seminars," lunch-hour gatherings where workers who are parents can join discussions of such topics as parenting skills, homework, self-esteem, responsibility in children and how to live with an adolescent. PIT provides guidance counselors, psychologists, educators and social workers to give brief talks and lead the discussions. In its second year, the program averaged seventeen seminars a month during the school year, with about five hundred parents attending each month.

From the beginning, Douglas operated on familiar small-bite principles. He borrowed ideas: the conferencing structure from a program in Houston, the parent contract from Chicago, anything that seemed likely to work from wherever he found it. He laid a solid political groundwork for each new program, and then made sure the world knew about it. "Marketing ideas is very important," he says. "Madison Avenue does it all the time. You've got to do it over and over again." And he found every dollar he could outside the school board's budget. In fact, as the board's expert on outside funding, Douglas brings in $21 million a year in federal and state grants, foundation money and funds from business. PIT has never cost the school board a dime. But Douglas's best move was finding the three tough, clever women who run the show for him: Izona Warner, Frances Richey and Trili Smith. With two secretaries, they are all there is of PIT.

It is a marvel of disorganization, breaking every Parkinsonian principle of bureaucracy. The women have no appetite for ever-growing layers of assistants. None of them has a title more impressive than "counselor." They operate out of nondescript offices in a converted Coca-Cola bottling plant. They have a free hand from Douglas, known affectionately around the office as "Mr. D.," but their authority stems mainly from their own brains, good intentions, political savvy and the alliances they have forged over the years with people of good will in the Indianapolis system. Parents in Touch is arguably the most comprehensive effort in any inner city to raise parental involvement, but it looks and operates like a guerrilla movement.

It is also a funny, affectionate, fast-talking and constantly bickering partnership. "There's only three of us," says Izona Warner, "so there can't be any cliques. What we've got is always two against one, and the lineup keeps changing." Brisk, cheerful and chronically distracted, she's the den mother of PIT, with round, dark brown cheeks and deep laugh creases, a great-grandmother who looks considerably younger than her sixty-six years. Her title is counselor, and she says her job is "to drive the other two crazy. I get things done, but I do them my way." Frances Richey and Trili Smith are the deputies, with official titles calculated to baffle outsiders: Richey a "dissemination specialist" and Smith a "Chapter 1 parent/staff development teacher."

Richey is really a specialist in everything. She comes from the hill country of western North Carolina, and she has the pleasantly weary expression of a woman who can't be surprised by anything: she has worked in projects under the Elementary and Secondary Education

Act ever since it was passed by Congress in 1965. She is slight, graying and inconspicuous, apart from her bright blue plastic raincoat. But she drives a muscular van with flair and authority, and Izona Warner says Frances Richey can solve any problem that PIT runs into, from finding a way around a hostile bureaucrat to producing a professional-quality videotape for a conference keynote. Trili Smith joined PIT three years ago, the youngest of the three and the only one who has actually taught school; she is versed in the intricate lore of federal educational policy and regulations. She is also the one who nudges, cajoles, makes schedules and keeps the operation somewhere near them: "Izona, you got to go now. Mr. D. is waiting." Arched eyebrows give her a quizzical expression, and she is a sharp and effective public speaker. Addressing a workshop on self-esteem, she begins: "You can't give what you ain't got. So get your act together."

The old building is one of those monuments to capitalism that midwest industrialists put up by the score in the '20s and '30s: a handsome, block-long, two-story plant for the bottling and shipping of Coke, with the regional sales office out front. The white limestone art deco façade has "Coca-Cola" carved into it, the flowing script still bright with gold leaf. The building is a designated landmark, a relic of Indianapolis's heyday as an industrial boomtown. Now the city is part of the rust belt, and its downtown section of factories and warehouses is struggling to rise from the dead. Some of the old buildings have been gentrified into office blocks or condominiums, others razed or abandoned. Large tracts of land are vacant, waiting to be redeveloped. Some have sprouted modern hotels, office plazas and shopping arcades. The old Coke plant is now SCIPS, the Service Center of the Indianapolis Public Schools, housing the overflow from the monumental new IPS building a mile away.

The jumble of old and new is fitting. Indianapolis is border country, smack on the Mason-Dixon line and caught between worlds. It is the nation's thirteenth largest city, yet it is small enough to retain much of the heartland's basic decency. Crime, drugs, gangs and pornography haven't made as many inroads as in other cities. Perhaps as a result, it is a popular site for conventions, including a lot of religious gatherings, and of course it has the annual auto race, the Indy 500. But at least in muted fashion, Indianapolis has all the usual urban woes. It has never had a race riot, and old civilities survive, but the courtesies paper over festering resentments between the races that have broken into the open in other cities. The school system reflects the tensions. As fertility rates dropped and white flight to private schools speeded up, the public school population plummeted in the past decade, from 102,000 to only 48,000—an astonishingly small figure in a city of nearly 750,000. The schools are 51 percent black and 48 percent white, with the tiny balance Asian and Hispanic, and in 1991 the school board, voting along racial lines, narrowly elected the city's first black superintendent, Dr. Shirl Edward Gilbert. During school hours, the big parking lot around the SCIPS building is filled with some of the 250 yellow buses that make sure each school reflects the racial mix, carrying kids back and forth from distant neighborhoods.

From the parking lot, a visitor enters the door beside the old loading dock, twists through a couple of corridors, climbs the back stairs and emerges in what was once the shipping department, a huge empty pillared bullpen with a shiny terrazzo floor surrounded by the cubicles of long-departed junior executives. The old Coke brass had the fancier offices in the front of the building, the section with the Art Deco staircase, paneled walls and molded plaster ceilings. But in the rough IPS democracy, it doesn't seem to signify who sits where. The women of PIT occupy three large, equally shabby offices along one side of the bullpen, with their secretaries in a fourth office that doubles as a reception area. It's a kind of railroad flat: To get from one end to the other, they can either traipse through each other's rooms or go out into the bullpen. The office furniture is a hodgepodge of ancient and relatively new pieces, and the place is cluttered with pamphlets, books, bureaucratic folders, relics of former projects, a carton of psychedelic shoelaces meant as prizes for BEAR readers, and the notes from last week's conference. But the disorder falls well short of chaos. Trili Smith knows where everything is, Frances Richey knows what to do with it and Izona Warner makes it all work.

Douglas started PIT with the conviction that parent involvement is both more and less than joining the PTA or helping with a candy sale. "It's anything a parent does to help educate a child," he says in his soft, resonant voice. "It can begin with just lap time, simple things like asking a kid questions about what he did that day. The kid realizes, 'Hey, my parent really does care,' and that's the beginning." These days, too many parents have themselves been deprived of parenting, and have to be taught how to go about it and then how to help their children with the substantive business of schooling. But while most school boards proclaim that they want parents involved, a lot of that is lip service; and when parents do take part, the first few often construct a close organization that freezes out dissent and soon gets co-opted by the school administration. Meaningful parental involvement had to begin, Douglas said, with better contact between parents and schools. The school board went along, and so did the Eli Lilly Endowment, with a three-year grant for $400,000 to back up the program.

But if PIT were to work, people had to know it was available. So it was launched in 1979 with a media blitz, backed up by billboards and local advertising, and a chunk of that first $400,000 went to hire a public relations firm and produce a public service announcement for local TV stations. The idea was ingenious. To symbolize the competition children face in life, a classful of kids were shown racing their desks around the Indy 500 track. It was catchy and effective. But the videotaping symbolized another truth about PIT: It was going to be tedious, laborious work. The tape was shot one frame at a time, moving each desk with its small driver a foot or so forward between frames to simulate the race.

Izona Warner and Frances Richey got a taste of what would be involved with PIT's first major project, the parent conferences. Before PIT there had been open houses in the schools, but they tended to be perfunctory and never drew more than a small fraction of the parents. Some parents were intimidated by schools and teachers, but there were also teachers who were afraid of parents; at the open houses, parents had to stand in line to talk to their child's teacher in a brief, guarded and inevitably unsatisfactory public chat. And the parents who came were usually those who already knew the schools and had kids who were doing well.

The new effort was widely publicized in radio, TV and newspaper stories, and repeated invitations to the parents were sent home with students. Douglas, Warner and Richey took pains to get the teachers' union on board before the project was launched. They hired two staffers of the union to help work out details. Then the union officials persuaded members from each of the sixty-eight elementary schools to go to workshops for training in how to talk straight but diplomatically to parents—to make criticism of a child impersonal, leavening it with praise when possible; not to make assumptions about what parents knew or didn't know; not to imply criticism of the parents or the home. The delegates passed on their training to their colleagues in each school. School administrators were persuaded to conduct classes during the conferences, so that teachers would be free to talk to parents, and some schools even set up evening conferences. After months of effort, there was an enormous glitch when a teachers' strike erupted and dragged on for five weeks, ending just before the first conferences were scheduled and leaving a legacy of bitterness. "We were really afraid it was going to fall apart," Warner recalls. But the patient diplomacy paid off: That first year, parents of more than half the children showed up, and the lines of communication were opened.

Since then, the main effort has been to keep the lines open and make them multiply. PIT has tried more than a dozen individual experiments: remedial reading, family mathematics, workshops on parenting, leadership training and community organizing. Every school in the city puts out some form of newsletter for its parents, and there are elaborate point systems to honor participation with tangible rewards. For attending any teacher conference, orientation meeting or parent workshop, for instance, a parent gets a point and turns in a "participation deposit slip." Four points earn a coffee mug. It isn't much, says Trili Smith, but "those mugs are really cherished." And parent volunteers in the schools take obvious pride in their official identification badges, kept on hooks in the school offices just like the badges of regular staffers.

Some of PIT's efforts have fizzled. The citywide Superintendent's Advisory Council, which was supposed to have delegates chosen by a Parents Advisory Committee (PAC) in each school, has been largely inactive, and the PACs themselves all but vestigial. PIT maintains a separate advisory council for parents from Chapter 1 schools, forty schools in the system that qualify for remedial funds under Chapter 1 of Title 1 of the Elementary and Secondary Education Act (ESEA). Chapter 1 provides the biggest single chunk of federal funding in most city systems, and schools qualify by having high percentages of children on the federal lunch program—a crude but reasonably effective way to define disadvantaged areas. There are also federal subsidies for parents' groups in Chapter 1 schools. But Smith's monthly meetings seldom draw more than sixty parents, even though PIT provides child care, refreshments and transportation for delegates. Other PIT experiments have worked for a while, but then run into problems. When some schools got full-time community liaison people to stay in touch with parents and help solve such practical problems as getting to and from meetings, parental involvement invariably soared. But most of these workers were cut from funding in recent years. Douglas is working for a reversal, and also exploring ways to tuck the cost of community liaison into other accounts.

PIT's best efforts build on the connection first made at the parent conferences. Once in the school, a parent can be offered the contract and asked to sign it, in token of continued involvement. And the parent can take home a folder packed with information: a detailed calendar of the events that will affect her child all year, a list of the spelling words to be learned each week of the year, information about standardized tests and special programs for handicapped or disabled children. When the Parent Line telephone was opened, the take-home folders were printed with instructions for calling and a menu of tapes that could be selected. The folders are also designed to be used as a personal file for each child's papers from the school—the signed contract, teachers' notes, official communications, report cards, awards and certificates. There's no way to tell how many folders are actually maintained as they were intended to be. But the volume of calls to the Parent Line, as high as three thousand a month, suggests that a good many Indianapolis parents know where to find the number and how to use it.

Dial-a-Teacher and the Homework Hotline program have also been clear successes. In large part, that's because they are simply good ideas. Parents feel responsible for their children's homework and want to help them with it, but often don't know what to do when a kid gets stumped. Dial-a-Teacher was modeled on a Philadelphia program that aimed to leap that hurdle by providing help at that key moment. Whether it's the parent or the student who actually picks up the phone, the result is the same: The work gets done, and the parent is encouraged to keep pushing. But the success of the two programs also reflects Douglas's media campaigns at the launchings. For Dial-a-Teacher, for instance, there were features in local newspapers and on TV. The new service was discussed on talk shows, high school journalists were called in to interview the teachers manning the lines, and the governor of Indiana showed up to answer some homework calls himself—an everybody-wins stunt that publicized the program while showing off the governor's zeal for education. Local disc jockeys joined in, answering calls on the air for their own shows, cheerfully stumbling through questions on math and history in the space between records. Within a couple of months, hardly anybody in the city hadn't heard of the service.

After that, though, Dial-a-Teacher has survived on the quality and dedication of the teachers who take the calls. They work every other day for three hours, in shifts of four, being paid at their regular hourly rates. There's a specialist in math and science every day, but most of the regulars can back him up if he's on another call. Teachers love the work. Robert Zetzl, head of the science department at George Washington High School and a regular on the phones for more than seven years, says the best thing about it is "working with kids who care. These kids who call want to find help, to get it right. The ones who don't care, I see them every day." For Sue Cooper, a vivacious second-grade teacher from Elementary School 31, the fascination is talking to the parents: "They say, 'I haven't done this in years, and my kid says things are different now. Is it really different?' Then we work it out, and maybe the method is a little different, but we come to the same answer." Kids call in the midst of family fights crashing around their ears, or from pay phones, repeatedly dropping coins. One suburban boy called so often that his mother, seeing the number on the toll-call bill, dialed it herself to find out who the new girlfriend might be.

"They are as patient as Job," says Frances Richey, and they are: good teachers at work, trying to nudge kids to an understanding of the whole world of learning. As always, some students just scream for the answers, and the saddest of all, says biology teacher Dave Gish from Arlington High, are the ones who know nothing at all, desperate to do the right thing but starting from ground zero. But most of the callers can be reached. Plump, white-haired Terry South, a regular on the phones and also the star of Homework Hotline, smoothly guides a third-grader through the intricacies of four times eight: "Well, four times eight just means four eights, doesn't it? So let's take it in order, Kevin, shall we? What would two eights be? Eight and eight . . . right, sixteen. Now add another eight, that's three . . . right, twenty-four. Now add eight to twenty-four? . . . Good work, Kevin, thirty-two, and that's four eights, isn't it? Four times eight, thirty-two." He adds some quick advice on making flash cards and practicing, and hangs up: mission accomplished.

PIT tries to make sure that parents are welcome in the city's schools anytime. For the most part, they really are, but there are always teachers who send hostile signals—and secretaries can be particularly nasty. Trili Smith recalls a parent complaining that when she stopped by the principal's office and tried to leave a message, a secretary told her that if she needed a pencil, she should have brought one. A few parents actually work regularly as volunteers, helping in classrooms and playgrounds and sometimes earning extra dollars as crossing guards. To lure more visitors, Douglas likes the suggestion of the new Indianapolis superintendent, Dr. Gilbert, that each classroom should have two chairs, painted red, reserved for parents.

But PIT has had to face the reality that most parents aren't going to visit more often than once a year, if that. Most people these days have both children and jobs; many are single parents, and many of those are schoolchildren themselves. And many parents recall their own schooling as unpleasant and intimidating. So the schools must reach out to them, and that's where the new TIPS and BEAR programs come in, letting parents take part in the homework and take pride in what their children do. TIPS was another outside idea, developed by Joyce Epstein, a researcher at Johns Hopkins University. "The parents know they have to sign the work, and they really take it seriously," says Susan Stiffey, a young second-grade teacher at School 74 on the dilapidated near east side of the city. "On the regular homework, I get papers with every single answer wrong. When the parents are looking it over, I never see one like that." And parents are quite realistic in judging whether their kids understand the work, she says.

Another outreach success is the brown-bag seminar program, meant to reach parents through their employers. It began with just fifteen participating corporations and the Indianapolis campus of Purdue University, and has grown to thirty-seven. As many as five hundred parents per month have attended, many of them probably repeaters; at a guess, the program has reached fifteen hundred to two thousand parents a year. In part, the PIT staff likes it as a way to reach men as well as women. Fathers are a relative rarity in school, but actually outnumber women in some workplace seminars. In part, too, the parents at the seminars learn to interact, answering each other's questions and thus gaining confidence and a sense of community. But mainly the seminars are a chance to broaden parents' skills and knowledge of child development. "I can help them respond to their kids," says Tom Bonjour, a behavior specialist with the school system and a frequent star of the seminars. "I get forty-five to fifty minutes, and that's enough to make some impact. I can use some art therapy, play therapy. I can teach them, not tell them, how to spend time with kids. How to interact when they're in trouble. How to respect who the child is. I can teach them how to set limits for kids, how to list and prioritize their problems." The payoff, he says, is that groups often ask him to come back for another session, so he knows they're getting something from it. And if parents can learn to do their job better, he will be seeing fewer kids in deep trouble.

All told, PIT's record is a remarkable return on the investment of its tiny staff. In fact, Bill Douglas has probably found the limit of what they can do. That came late in 1990, when he decided to host a national conference on parent involvement, with seven hundred people and four days of speeches, discussions and workshops. It was hailed as a great success and a milestone in the effort to get national attention for PIT, but it took a great deal out of Izona Warner, Frances Richey and Trili Smith, who put the whole thing together. That took increasing amounts of their time all fall, with a monthlong crescendo leading up to the conference, and the rest of PIT's program suffered for it.

They had to line up speakers, get out invitations and log in replies, make schedules and organize workshops around knowledgeable people. They had to find a place for the conference, reserve hotel spaces, hire caterers and discuss menus, arrange for transportation to and from hotels, correspond with speakers, make backup plans for emergencies, solve crises. They had to design a program, sell ads in it and arrange for printing it. Smith set up all the exhibits in the main hall. Douglas had seen a video introduction at an IBM conference and thought it would be a good idea to introduce this gathering with a video on Indianapolis. A professional filmmaker wanted $20,000 to do the job, so Richey laughed and produced it herself, directing some new footage, using clips from existing material and editing the tape in the educational TV center. It came out fine. But all told, the three of them put in weeks of overtime work, far into the nights for the final month and nearly round-the-clock during the conference, trouble-shooting all the things that can go wrong when seven hundred people get together for four days.

Somehow, there weren't as many brown bag seminars that year. The number of calls to Dial-a-Teacher fell off, too, probably because the PR effort was neglected. "You've just got to keep telling people it's there," says Warner. There wasn't enough time to document properly the number of parents taking part in TIPS. The Parents Advisory Committees got even wispier. There was a falloff in the number of parent contracts signed, though nobody actually counted them. Some principals may have figured that the TIPS and BEAR programs were replacements for the contracts, so they never got distributed. Such things happen, Douglas says, and it isn't necessarily a tragedy. The important thing isn't the contracts as such, but that one way or another, a principal makes parental involvement work. But all in all, the general decline was undeniable. There are limits to what any three people can do, no matter how smart they are or how hard they work. PIT had reached its realistic ceiling.

So the organization is changing. As Douglas sees it, the trend to more autonomy for individual schools is both sound and sweeping: "Site-based decision making," in the trendy jargon, is coming to Indianapolis. PIT aims to be in the forefront. The staff no longer looks for new centralized programs, but works to strengthen efforts at the school level. Recently, teachers and administrators at a few schools tried a new way of reaching out to parents in the distant neighborhoods that provide bused students. The educators announced well in advance that they planned to walk around those neighborhoods on a Saturday morning, and that they would be available to talk to any parents who wanted to chat along the route. A gratifying number of parents took them up on it, and other schools will be encouraged to do likewise. Similarly, Trili Smith is thinking of holding some of her Chapter 1 PAC meetings not at the usual downtown site, but in local schools, with local parents taking turns as hosts. "The local school and its faculty have to reach out to the parents," Douglas says. "It's even more important now for people at the building level to be out front beating the drums."

And Douglas has launched a new pilot program to speed that along. The stress is on training for teachers to help them work effectively with parents, and the program focuses on seven elementary schools that feed into one junior high, in hopes that parents will remain involved as their children move up. The individual schools are trying their own variations, in the spirit of local empowerment, but all of them start with the idea of reaching parents who don't necessarily want to come to school but are willing to participate at home. One school is developing a reader-friendly handbook for parents, telling them about the schools and about how children develop and learn. Another is creating home activities for parents and their children, and a third plans its own comprehensive homework folders for each child.

The new emphasis differs only slightly from what PIT has been doing all along. As in all systems, some principals are more willing to cooperate than others, and PIT has forged strong bonds with principals like Marsha Foley at School 44, Phyllis Imel at School 46 and Rosena Johnson at School 74. And PIT's best stories are of individual successes—people like Arlene Shoffner, a mother of five who found meaning in her life as a parent volunteer at School 44, or Fannie Bunch, who went to school to keep her son out of mischief and stayed to become statewide chairman of the Chapter 1 Parents Steering Committee. Parental involvement is always one parent at a time, one school at a time, which is why it's so hard.

Fannie Bunch shows how far a parent can go, once inertia is overcome. "I worked nights, and I used to make excuses not to go to any meetings," she recalls. She is short, round and beamish, with big spectacles and a rich, infectious laugh. Her son Walter, bright and mischievous, kept getting into trouble at School 42, and a social worker kept telling Bunch that she should do something about it, so she went to a meeting of the parents' group, and "I got stuck. It was the first time I ever knew of a government program where the people it served were allowed to have any input. Most programs, people talk to you, not with you. Your opinion doesn't count for anything." She joined the Chapter 1 PAC at School 42 and helped raise funds by selling supplies at the bookstore. They had to sell five pencils to make a profit of one penny. But Walter kept on getting into trouble, and when he got to junior high, she followed him to school every day and sat with him in class to keep his nose to the grindstone. He didn't like it, she says, but he took it; and by the time he was through school, his mother was a permanent fixture in the PIT structure. That was years ago. She has become chairman of the board of the Indiana State Chapter 1 Parents Steering Committee, and she organized and ran a state conference that drew three hundred participants. She was also chairperson for the even larger 1990 regional conference in Indianapolis of the National Coalition of Title 1, Chapter 1 Parents. "I'm the IPS fossil," she says with her bubbling laugh. "I went to some conferences and I read a lot, and I grew." Frances Richey amends that: "You're a leader now."

What does it take to get parents involved in a school? The PIT staff has never tried to codify it, and in practice the formula is going to vary dramatically from one school or system to the next. The first crucial need is to make sure the system really wants parental involvement. After that, find out what works and do it. But within that broad outline, some rules are useful:

  • **Start small.**   Don't try to put together a whole network of projects at once; start with one school and a focused effort, such as conferencing or the student-parent-teacher contract, and build from there.
  • **Build on established strengths.**   If there is already an effective PTA, try to broaden its appeal; if the principal is well liked and charismatic, use her as the nucleus.

- **Mend political fences.** Make sure that all power bases are covered, and that nobody has reason to oppose parental involvement. The school board, teachers' union and principal must be on board. If there are existing parents' groups with narrower interests, such as a football booster club or parents of disabled children, they must be reassured that their turf will be respected.
- **Reach out.** Most parents can't or won't come to school regularly. They must be contacted at home or at work with regular communications, and must be made to feel involved in their children's education. Send them information about the school and its programs and events. Recorded telephone messages work well. If money can be found for it, a more elaborate voice-mail system can work even better. Work-based seminars for parents are a good idea. A program like Dial-a-Teacher works to support parents in insisting that homework get done and helping children do it. But it must be remembered that the telephone also has limits. In some sections of Indianapolis, as many as half the families either have no phones or are disconnected from time to time. Old-fashioned notes from the teacher still have a place.
- **Look for outside funding.** Federal and state funds can be tapped for a surprising array of programs if you know where to look, and the teachers' union probably has an expert on call. Major foundations are approachable. Often, however, local foundations are easier to deal with and eager to find worthy projects in their own area. Corporations also like to do their good works close to home. But most corporate and foundation spending is short-term, to try out pilot projects; don't count on continuing support once a program is up and running.
- **Recognize and reward involvement.** Identify parents in schools with special ribbons, badges or other symbols. Maintain a bulletin board recording parent activities, and a newsletter if possible. Small tangible rewards like the PIT coffee mug can be valued trophies.
- **Publicize.** Parents must be reminded frequently what services are available and how they can help their children learn. New programs should be announced loudly and repeatedly, and achievements must be trumpeted. The job never ends, but that, too, comes with the territory.

The women of PIT are driving a visitor across town to lunch, Trili Smith at the wheel, Izona Warner navigating from the backseat, the two of them bickering amiably over the route.

"Well all right, Izona, if you say so," says Smith. "it's just, I never heard of getting *there* by going *here*."

"It's a shortcut," says Warner.

"It's all around the barn, is what it is," says Smith.

Warner and Frances Richey are talking about retiring—especially, they say, if Mr. D. ever thinks about another national conference. Smith scoffs at the idea: "You ain't goin' nowhere. You'll be here when *I* come to retire, Izona."

Warner shakes her head: "I mean it. There's got to be a limit." Just as there's a limit on the number of late nights per month, she says, and she never works more than two.

The visitor points out that she has used up the month's quota in the past two nights, and on that schedule she is probably halfway through 1996 already. She gets snappish. That little meeting last night doesn't count, she argues. It wasn't even one of PIT's projects; she just went because she thought it was an interesting program, adult literacy for parents of kids at risk.

Just so; she thinks it's interesting. The visitor bets that Smith is right: Izona Warner isn't about to pack it in.

But the visitor is wrong. A few months later, Warner announces that she's leaving PIT—not to retire, but to take a new job as consultant for a parent-involvement program operating in four outlying districts around Indianapolis. On hearing that, Richey too decides to hang up her mortarboard and go home to the hills of North Carolina. It's a "tremendous blow," Bill Douglas says; "I don't know what we're going to do without them." Fortunately, they have agreed to help with the transition when he finds replacements, and fortunately Trili will stay on the job. It remains to be seen whether PIT can maintain its vitality. But come what may, says Douglas, "We'll keep it going. We have to. It's too good to let it die."

10.
Lighting Up
Helena's Eyes

When they talk about the boom of the '80s in Helena, Montana, they're not thinking of yuppies in Porsches. Their boom came more than a century ago, when gold miners were carousing in the saloons and brothels of Last Chance Gulch and panning for nuggets in every rivulet of the surrounding mountains. The more recent '80s came and went without much trace; in Helena, as in most of the Pacific Northwest, it was really no boom at all but a decade of slow-motion hard times, with young folks moving out and those who stayed consoling themselves that, after all, they had a good laid-back life in a place that was easy on the eyes. And they did. What they didn't have was two nickels to rub together.

So it is a little surprising that when the Helena Public Schools went looking for a remedial reading program back in 1989, they settled on what may be the Cadillac of the business: HOSTS (Help One Student To Succeed), a commercial venture marketed for profit out of Vancouver, Washington. HOSTS uses volunteer mentors from the community to come into schools and tutor slow learners, one on one, with individualized lessons produced for each pupil from a computerized data base. The program costs as much as $19,900 to set up in a single school, and another $3,990 a year to run. But in this case at least, the combination of outside professionals, computers and volunteers from the community proved to be a winning idea—a little like calling in management experts to set up a computerized payroll system. After two years of operations, with the program installed in six elementary schools, the hardheaded Helena educators were insisting that they got a bargain. The program has been solidly effective with problem readers. After start-up expenses, it actually costs less to run than the program it replaced. And what's even better, the model may point the way to new approaches to teaching in all the Helena schools and a sounder, broader base of political support for the whole system.

The tutors start drifting in a quarter of an hour ahead of the bell. They have their own room here in Central elementary school, a converted classroom with adult-size tables and chairs and a coffee urn going, and they sit chatting comfortably, waiting for the little kids. Three of them are retired teachers, a kind of club, and they joke that they'll have to find another place to meet during the school holidays. There's an editor from the *Helena Independent-Record* and a clerk from the Office of Public Instruction in the nearby statehouse. There's burly Greg Broadway, a senior at Carroll College. And there are three fifth-graders, Anne Adams, Kelly Burningham and Nicholas Gailushas, who are filling in today for grown-ups who can't make it.

The tutors work one on one with kids from Central's first, second and third grades. They spend half an hour with each child. Some of them work just one half-hour session a week, others more; they're all volunteers. But this is no haphazard enterprise with do-gooders reading aloud to bored kids. The lessons are tightly scripted and individually designed for each child, and the children get lessons four days a week. The class teacher, Gloria Gabaldon-Lesueur, monitors each student's progress and uses a computerized data base of texts and educational materials to construct the customized lessons. Most of the tutors work regularly with their students, but even if the tutor is a substitute and has never met the student, the lessons are easy to give and just right for each child. Now the tutors stroll into the classroom, next door to their lounge, and each picks a folder from a box on the counter. The folder is labeled with a student's name and contains the lesson for today.

A glance at the lesson is enough to orient the tutor. The half-hour session always begins with a batch of vocabulary words, to be pronounced, defined and used correctly in a sentence—perhaps five minutes' work. Another ten minutes goes to mastering a particular skill: Little Randi, for instance, will work on the long vowel O today, practicing the sound with her tutor Greg Broadway and learning to recognize it in words and sentences ("The mole lives in a ——— [hop, hole, hide]"). Then the pair will spend the last fifteen minutes of the session taking turns reading aloud from a story, again chosen by Gabaldon-Lesueur to match Randi's reading level.

The children arrive, a bright shrill stream into the room. Each pairs off with a tutor, and there are a few minutes of small talk to feed the friendship: Did you and your family go skiing last weekend? Where did you go? Was it fun? But the lesson soon starts, and the classroom is a concentrated buzz of quiet talk. There are pairs all over the room, with Gabaldon-Lesueur and her assistant, Bonnie Noble, moving from one to the next. The teachers may put in a word, correct an emphasis or give a quick quiz to gauge a child's readiness for the next week's lessons. The noise level picks up a notch when the reading begins, but nobody is confused or distracted. When the half hour is over, there's another round of small talk, and then the students head back to their regular classes. The tutors start filling out comments for the teacher on each section of the lesson: "No trouble at all. Too easy for him." "She didn't understand antonyms. Move back a step?"

Gabaldon-Lesueur is preparing her quarterly reports to the children's parents. She will type about a paragraph on each student, and the four tutors who work regularly with the child may chip in comments of their own: "Getting phonemes very well," or "Could use more help in sounding out new words." Today the teacher keeps young Ryan after class; she wants to tell him what his report is going to say. "You're doing fine," she says, brisk and straightforward. "The only thing is, Ryan, you actually read a lot better than you sound, and that's because you're not confident about it. When you start getting confident, you'll be fine. You're already a good reader. What you're going to learn now is how to be an interesting reader. Okay? Good work, Ryan." He nods seriously and leaves smiling.

Helena started looking for a remedial reading program in 1989, when the district found out that its federal funding under Chapter 1 of the Elementary and Secondary Education Act (ESEA) was going to be cut back. Chapter 1 had been funding remedial programs in five city schools, and the cuts came as a surprise. The district had been expecting an increase, but at the last minute, for reasons that still haven't been satisfactorily explained, the allocation from Washington was reduced. So the district needed a way to reach at least as many kids with less money.

Marion Evenson led a delegation of a dozen teachers and administrators to the national convention of the International Reading Association in New Orleans. There were about two hundred programs being hawked there, and she wanted enough colleagues on the scene to be able to give them all more than a cursory glance. And she knew the outlines of what she was looking for. It couldn't be a major departure from the methods and curriculum that Helena was already using. The program must offer training for teachers as part of its package. It should already be set up in a town that she and her people could visit, to check out how the program worked in real life. And it had to be cost-effective, reaching the maximum number of kids with the most help for the buck.

Marion Evenson is a quiet, motherly person, whose low voice and even keel tend to mask a quick wit and a gambler's sense of what to risk. She favors sensible shoes and a short, businesslike cut for her blond hair; she has level gray eyes and a wide, amused smile. Her own teaching career has stretched from ordinary classrooms to Chapter 1 remedial work and special education for handicapped kids. What she liked best was being a principal, running a school and knowing every person in it inside out, and maybe, she hopes, she will get to do that again someday. For now, she works out of a basement office in the small converted school that serves as Helena's district offices. She has the deliberately hazy title of director of student services, and when Superintendent Jim Turner has a problem-child project and needs to be sure it's done right, she gets it.

Evenson is quick and decisive, and she has a talent for finding bright, dedicated people and giving them just enough help to do a job. And if anything intimidates her, it isn't change. She is even creating a major upheaval in her own life: With her daughter off to college, she's had it with conventional three-bedroom life. She couldn't quite persuade her lawyer husband to sell most of their furniture and buy into a condo, but she won her main point. They sold their big house and will build a small new one, in a foothill neighborhood with a splendid view of the little city and its surrounding peaks. The floor plan is no bigger than a condo. "If he wants a four thousand-foot garage, fine," she says. "If he wants to leave out the kitchen, even better. It's probably a stage I'm going through."

In New Orleans, she was intrigued by the HOSTS program as soon as she saw it. The program was computer-based, in a way that fit in with what she had been reading on how computers ought to be used. It would fit into the Helena system, and it would have community volunteers as mentors, a formula that promised maximum efficiency in using teachers and the reduced federal funds to pay them. Training for teachers was definitely part of the package, and HOSTS was already up and running in Billings, just two hundred miles from Helena and easy enough to check out. The problem was the price. "That bothered me a lot," Evenson says. "But I knew I would be buying things I couldn't reproduce in this district in a short time. And I will not discount that all of us were influenced by the salesmanship. Bill Gibbons is a very effective salesman."

That he is. William C. Gibbons is an educational visionary with a hypnotic delivery and absolute conviction ringing in every word. He developed HOSTS starting as an experimental program with federal money in Vancouver, Washington, but ultimately as a commercial product now operating in nearly five hundred school districts across the country. Its origins, he says, trace to his first teaching job back in the '60s, in a district of Yakima, Washington, where the kids were mostly black, Hispanic and native American. Most of his sixth-graders were reading only at second-grade level, and that launched him on a career of trying to understand why they were failing and how to help them. He decided early on that motivation was the key to achievement, and like Burton White at Harvard, he reasoned that parents should be the key to motivation. But needy parents didn't have the resources to give much help; realistically, they couldn't be the answer.

That meant the teacher had to take up the slack. But Gibbons asked the right question, and found the key problem, when he wondered how much real time a teacher has for each child in the class. In a whole day, he found, a student may get less than a minute of a teacher's undivided attention. If motivation was the key to achievement, the teachers couldn't help much, either. That led him to the idea of providing a mentor for each needy student, and finding a way to do it "so members of the community could get involved in a meaningful way, come in and carry out a program themselves without being educators." But how could amateurs do all that—especially if, as Gibbons decided next, lessons should be individually tailored to give each child exactly what was needed every day?

What pulled it all together was the personal computer. "When Steve Jobs first came out with the Apple," says Gibbons, "I remember seeing that in the news and saying, 'This is it.' " The computer could give a teacher control over a whole array of lesson combinations, he reasoned, and help her put together custom-tailored lessons for every student. That in turn would make it possible for amateur tutors to give the lessons. But the first step was to get a menu of teaching materials into the computer. Most schools have a hodgepodge of texts, workbooks and the like, ordered by individual teachers from one year to the next, without even a centralized index of what's available somewhere else in the system. Gibbons developed his own computerized data base of teaching materials on the market, sifting through thousands of books, pamphlets, educational games, classroom exercises and other resources to find the ones he and his colleagues judged acceptable. Ultimately they chose four thousand teaching materials, broken down into 38,000 individual segments that can be called up in any combination for a child's custom-fit lesson every day.

In practice, most districts using HOSTS don't have all 38,000 lessons in their own repertoire. Instead, using the HOSTS matrix, they begin by making a data base of the materials they already have and then order new ones to fill the gaps. Gibbons says most districts going through this process discover that they lack resources for 20 percent to 40 percent of the lessons they actually want to give. Once the holes are filled and the data base is in place, he says, the system "eliminates about 80 percent of the time it takes a teacher to design individual lessons. It becomes cost-effective for them." Some districts want to buy the data base alone, but they miss the point: Computers are just a tool that can pave the way for the truly important ingredient, one-on-one mentoring.

In part, the program works because the lessons are designed to be clear and practically foolproof. But HOSTS partisans argue that there is also a special magic in one-on-one teaching that dates back to Socrates: as surely as in the Valued Youth Partnership or Fannie Mae's Futures 500, it's a relationship that profits both parties. "People make the difference in the lives of the children, not the computer," Gibbons says. "These kids need that human interaction." And given the made-to-order lessons, the fact of the interaction counts for far more than what the tutors actually know. In fact, they don't need to know much more than how to read. The system works equally well using retirees, businessmen, trained teachers, housewives or other kids as tutors. What counts is the personal attention a child receives, with the tutor reinforcing the lesson, correcting mistakes and helping to understand basic concepts.

Certainly the mentors enjoy their work, trying hard not to miss a day and often volunteering for multiple sessions. Their reward comes in feeling that they have made a difference and helped a child; in their most frequent explanation, what counts is seeing eyes light up with the joy of a new idea. Gibbons likes to tell of a retired chemical company executive, a man who had been in charge of building plants around the world, who said his tutoring was "the most important thing I've ever done."

HOSTS has no lack either of zeal or testimonials. But when Gibbons and his team went to Helena to make their pitch to the planning committee, they brought more than snake oil. HOSTS was a solid program by then, with a record of success since 1972; it had been proved on 150,000 students in more than four hundred communities and had won praise from the Secretary of Education, the National Center for Dropout Prevention, Johns Hopkins University, the National Council of Teachers of English and half a dozen other prestigious authorities. It was soon to be selected by the U.S. Department of Education as a national model program for in-school mentoring. And Gibbons offered a final incentive, a solid guarantee: If the children in the program didn't make a minimum average gain in reading levels, HOSTS would give the money back or continue training, free of charge, until the target was hit.

The gains were to be measured in units called NCE, one of education's bewildering array of acronyms, standing in this case for national curve equivalents. An NCE gain of zero means that a child is keeping up with his schoolmates and learning satisfactorily; with a gain of seven points, a student has jumped ahead a full year in reading ability. HOSTS tailors its warranty to the local circumstances, frankly aiming to lowball the promise. "A school is excited when we promise a gain of seven points," says HOSTS president Jerald L. Willbur. "When it actually comes in at ten, they're ecstatic." Montana state standards call for gains of zero or better, and HOSTS was willing to guarantee seven points a year for the remedial students in Helena, who were already far behind their classmates.

There was still the sticky issue of price, and the dickering was intense and hard-nosed, with Marion Evenson carrying the ball for Helena. She argued for a major cut in the start-up fee of $19,900 per school, on the grounds that Helena had avoided the national fad of building large schools, and its elementary buildings average only 296 pupils. On the same logic, she said, the running fee should be less than the standard $3,990 per school. And since Helena planned to use each team of a teacher and teacher's aide in two schools rather than one, the training cost per school should be even lower. Gibbons conceded that his price sounded high, but he argued that his program was efficient. Most remedial programs, he said, cost $1,000 to $2,000 for a single NCE point gained by a single student. But if you divided HOSTS' total fee by the total NCE points gained by all the remedial students, HOSTS cost as little as $100 per point. "We serve more students in less time and get better results," he says.

Evenson still thinks the price is too high. Gibbons denies that he's trying to profiteer from his program, and says he has turned down investment from venture capitalists looking for speedy returns in favor of local investors who would settle for modest gains. But by his own reckoning, he is doing pretty well for them. As a private company,

HOSTS doesn't have to report financial figures. But Gibbons estimated that in 1991 the company would earn about $500,000 on revenues of $2.5 million. That's a profit margin of 20 percent.

In any case, Evenson wangled a substantial discount. The program was put into two schools the first year at a start-up fee of $15,400 for Central School and $13,300 for Broadwater, with four schools to be added the next year at an average fee of $9,885 each. Running fees would be only $1,990 per school after its first year. There was also a good deal of flexibility in applying the program. HOSTS recommended installing it in all of the district's twelve elementary schools, phasing it in over a three-year period. But Turner and Evenson wanted both a quicker and a more cautious introduction, and got their way: HOSTS went into the first two schools in just one year. Each school would train one teacher and one teacher's aide that first year, with each team teaching three half-hour sessions four days a week. In the second year's expansion, the two teams would handle two schools each, and a third team would be trained to take on a fifth and sixth school.

The speedy introduction meant, among other things, that Gloria Gabaldon-Lesueur at Central School and the Broadwater teacher, Laurie Wiedmann, had to work flat-out all that first summer. They had been teaching the Chapter 1 remedial program, and now they had to learn the new system and get it up and running. They got just three days of training from the HOSTS coordinator in Billings; then they started indexing the district's educational resources into a data base, dividing the materials into segments for use in individual lessons, ordering new materials to fill the gaps, and practicing actual lessons. Each of them wrote a handbook, reflecting her individual teaching style and preferences, for use by her tutors. The first group of mentors signed on, responding to a burst of publicity and some small-town personal recruiting, and the volunteers were given the handbooks and a ninety-minute training session. Bernie Hartman, the principal at Broadwater, worried that Wiedmann was overdoing it. She was doing three years' work in a single summer, working late nearly every day, and he finally ordered her to take some vacation.

That first year went astonishingly well. The reading gains spoke for themselves: Marion Evenson calculated NCE gains averaging 12.48 points per child in the program, more than five points higher than

HOSTS had promised. The two schools were actually gaining ground on the basic problem. Each of them had twenty-five slow readers the first year, but so many had been brought back to grade level that neither school had more than twenty kids in HOSTS the second year. And long before the numbers came in, teachers and principals could tell that the program was working. Classroom teachers were enthusiastic, problem kids were improving in attendance and behavior, and there was a general change in the atmosphere. The Hawthorne effect was already at work.

Wiedmann and Gabaldon-Lesueur had some advantages from the beginning. They had both been familiar figures in their schools, working in the Chapter 1 program. Classroom teachers are often possessive about their students and reluctant to send them off for somebody else's help in unproved programs, but the two remedial teachers had proved themselves and won the trust of the children and their homeroom teachers. Even so, they ran into some resistance, and they had to make small compromises to adjust the program to the teachers they were working with. At Central School, for instance, Gabaldon-Lesueur could use fifth-graders to fill in for absent adult tutors. At her second school, Lincoln, the fifth grade teacher didn't approve of that much missed class time, so adult substitutes had to be found. "It's a juggling act," she says. "Our goal is to get the whole school excited about HOSTS, and we do that any way we can."

But HOSTS has changed Wiedmann and Gabaldon-Lesueur, too. In effect, they are no longer basically teachers, passing on ideas and information to children. They have had to learn to delegate that function to the tutors while they have become planners, supervisors and facilitators—in a real sense, management executives. It's a kind of trade-off that makes the whole teaching process more efficient. "It takes extra planning to use the volunteers, but this program lets us do it," says Wiedmann. In the four days of tutoring classes, she keeps testing each child's progress and gets feedback from the tutors on each session; then on Friday she uses that data to plan the next week's lessons for as many as fifty students at Broadwater and Bryant schools—in all, up to two hundred individual lessons every week. "I love it," she says. "In Chapter One, I was all by myself with maybe thirty kids, all at different levels with different needs, and I wasn't able to meet them all. It was frustrating. Now I can use the computer to make the plans and let the tutors do the work. It's real teamwork, and it feels great."

Almost everyone in the program had misgivings at first about using four tutors for each student. It seemed likely to be both confusing to the kids and wasteful of volunteers. In practice, however, it has worked out fine. Since the lessons are individually targeted, daily continuity for the children isn't a problem; and after a couple of weeks, the children get to know the tutors and seem comfortable with all of them. Knowing several new adults helps a child develop social skills, and if one tutor turns out to be less than perfectly effective with a particular child, there are three more each week who may pick up the slack. The volunteers can work with as many students as they like, adjusting their schedules to suit their needs and cutting back if they start to feel pressured or burned out.

The tutors don't get much training, but they don't seem to need much. In the beginning, they are all a bit apprehensive: Will they be able to teach, and really help the children? Superintendent Jim Turner, himself a veteran of thirty-one years in education, confesses to having butterflies after he volunteered to be a tutor that first year. What he found first was a rediscovery, the joy of teaching after years of Olympian authority as principal and head man. "It was just plain fun working with a youngster, helping him, listening to him," he says. "But I also learned that hey, anyone can do this. I had been worried about could we really do it, could we put materials together so that somebody could come in off the street and teach a kid. What I found was that our teachers had put together really good materials that I could work with. It was a good experience."

The lessons do act as a basic road map, and it's hard to get far off the track. In each session, eight to ten pairs of students and tutors are working, usually with both a teacher and her aide to supervise and test. The tutors are told to bring high expectations to each lesson, not to be too willing to concede or excuse failure, and to give the children prompt and honest feedback with no sugarcoating. "There's no point in lying to them," says Gloria Gabaldon-Lesueur. When tutors correct mistakes, they should be matter-of-fact, avoiding personal criticism. But within the bounds of honesty, tutors should be as upbeat as possible, giving praise generously whenever it's earned. (Here too, teaching styles differ. Gabaldon-Lesueur's handbook offers 101 ways to praise a child, including hugs, kisses, "I love you" and "You make me happy." Laurie Wiedmann's list has only sixty-five entries, considerably less effusive: "Exactly right," "Superior work," "Beautiful," "Super.") The tutors learn quickly. "Anybody can stay positive for half an hour," says Rhonda McCarty, the HOSTS teacher in the system's newest outposts, Warren and Jim Darcy schools.

Most tutors worry about maintaining discipline, and there's an elaborate five-step procedure for addressing misbehavior. But in practice, few tutors have ever had to take even the first step, revoking the star given for good behavior. And there's no record of anybody going beyond step two, calling the teacher over for a reinforcing word of authority. There is something in the one-on-one relationship that instills personal respect, on both sides.

Tutors do lack the professionalism of trained teachers; some have a tendency to teach by rote, permitting students to slide through a lesson without grasping its real meaning. But in their role as monitors, the HOSTS teachers usually spot such lapses and intervene. The teachers also know how to check tutors who tend to coach too much. Watching one pair working an educational jigsaw puzzle, Gabaldon-Lesueur says firmly: "There's too many of Harry's fingerprints on that. I want to see Jimmy's hands in there."

And there's no question that the tutors love what they do. What they say most often is that their reward comes in eyes lighting up as ideas sink in; and to hear them tell it, the international energy crisis could be solved by tapping the eyes of the children of Helena. Greg Broadway gets academic credit at Carroll College for his teaching, but he does it to the point of addiction: He regularly tutors twelve kids a week and often substitutes with as many as eight more. Alice Morse, a comfortably upholstered, white-haired retiree, says she tried volunteering in five other programs before she found HOSTS, and "All along, this is what I was looking for." For her, the magic is a combination of the structured program—"The materials make it so easy"—and the sheer joy of helping small people expand their world. She works two days a week in the Bryant school with Laurie Wiedmann, coaching three students each day in thirty-minute sessions. After that she takes a group of five kindergartners off to a corner of the library for half an hour of the special play with blocks, letters and numbers that will help get them ready for the serious business of first grade.

Wiedmann maintains that she's never found anyone who couldn't be a good tutor, given a little help. This is probably an exaggeration; even in Helena, a community small enough that a volunteer is likely to be a known quantity as soon as he walks in the door, one tutor has had to be actively nudged to quit the program. He proved to need a lot of help with his own reading. But most problems of incompatibility, lack of patience or sheer dislike of children are self-correcting. If people haven't got a talent for the work, they tend to find it unrewarding and drop out. Such cases are rare, however. Even when volunteers find themselves with particularly difficult children, those with promise persevere and become successful tutors.

For all its successes, the tutor network started getting strained when the HOSTS program jumped from two schools to six in its second year. In theory, each new student poses a need for four new tutors, and there were almost one hundred new kids. Especially in the outlying Warren and Jim Darcy schools, located six and eight miles out of town in small rural communities, volunteers were hard to find. So Marion Evenson assigned one of the teacher's aides, Bonnie Noble, to take charge of finding and maintaining the corps of tutors for all six schools. Noble has pushed the cause tirelessly in state government offices, senior centers, service clubs and the local media. She even approached a National Guard contingent, many of whom have children at Jim Darcy school, to ask for volunteers. But the best source of recruits turns out to be the existing mentors, who regularly bring in their friends. And much of the strain of the added schools has been taken up as tutors volunteer to work more hours. Laurie Wiedmann needed one hundred volunteers the first year for thirty children; the next year she handled fifty kids with only ninety tutors. All told, the system served 145 students in the second year with 290 tutors, a ratio of two to one. They worked more than five thousand hours. But starting the third year, Noble's list had reserve capacity, with a total of 350 names.

A third of the tutors, ninety-six, were retirees. Another sixty-nine worked in nearby state offices or local businesses, sixty-four were parents and sixty-one were students, many of them from Carroll College. There have been housewives and construction workers, business executives and telephone linemen. The former governor of Montana, Ted Schwinden, has volunteered, and so has Helena Mayor Russ Ritter. Following Jim Turner's lead, most of the principals of the six schools using HOSTS have taken on tutoring chores. The program has used students from the alternative high school, and at Warren School, a dozen girls nearing the end of their sentences at the nearby Mountain View correctional facility were trained as tutors. Five of them came to teach every Tuesday, with a guard to make sure they went back. Their grammar was sometimes dubious, says Rhonda McCarty, but their attitude was fine, they always dressed nicely for the occasion, and the little kids thought they were wonderful.

For most of the people working with HOSTS, the program is an unqualified success. The teachers say custom-tailored lessons are simply an idea whose time has come. "All of us have known how to do this, in principle at least, for years," says Brad Morris, principal at Central School. "But before the computer, we couldn't pull it all together." Even in the Chapter 1 program, says Gabaldon-Lesueur, "We were doing a lot of what HOSTS does. But we needed to know how to use volunteers effectively. They invented the wheel for us."

The gains have continued, though precise figures aren't available; in the second year, the state mandated a change in the complex formula for calculating NCE points, and comparisons became meaningless. But in terms of Evenson's original priorities, the program is certainly cost-effective. Start-up costs totaled $85,800 for the two years. After that, however, the HOSTS fees and miscellaneous costs come to only $16,400 a year for the six schools, and the payroll cost for three teachers and four aides is just $115,000. Thus the annual cost of the program after startup is $131,400. If Helena were to teach 150 students in Chapter 1 remedial classes, it would require at least five full teachers and a payroll of about $150,000, so HOSTS actually saves about $18,600 a year. The cost for each child is about $880 a year. If the average NCE gain had fallen from 12.48 points in the first year to 10 points in the second, the cost would be only $88 per NCE point.

And the Hawthorne effects have been gratifying. Long before the reading scores came in, principal Tom Miller at the Bryant School was seeing "a lot of reluctant learners doing better now." To Lincoln

School principal Dave Pepin, the most spectacular progress was "in the affective area, the way the kids relate to the tutors and see themselves. There's more to this than academic achievement." Teachers, too, have changed as they get more exposure to the tutors and the community attitudes they represent. Alone in their classrooms or talking only to each other, teachers can easily lose sight of parents' and voters' priorities, or dismiss such views as naïve and unprofessional. But with a little more contact, says Jim Turner, the teachers are reminded that "Those are our customers, that's who we work for. Schools belong to people, and we need to remember that."

But the longest-reaching Hawthorne effect is on Helena's attitude toward its schools. From the beginning, the schools made an effort to tell parents about the program and invited them to visit. A fair number have come to watch and stayed to tutor, and that's a gain all by itself. Beyond that, awareness of the program has given the city in general a sense that the schools are trying and that the effort is working. The 290 tutors are witnesses; as Turner says, polls show that people who get involved in schools tend to think the schools are doing well. In turn, they spread that attitude to their neighbors, and that contact helps offset the erosion of interest in public education that has come in recent years with declining birth rates and an aging population. In the end, the taxpayers have to be willing to support their schools, and HOSTS is helping with that.

There are a number of lessons to be learned from Helena's experience:

• **Make the program fit the system.**   In looking for help from a commercial program, keep priorities firmly in mind and work with the supplier to adapt the program to local needs and conditions. No two communities are alike, and schools have individual characters, too. Flexibility is essential.

• **Look for bargains.**   It's possible to cut deals. Bill Gibbons maintains that Helena was the last to get in on any special arrangement, but don't believe it. His own president, Jerry Willbur, says there's a flexible scale of fees depending on the number of students, availability of teachers for training and a district's willingness to showcase the program.

• **Be diplomatic.** Classroom teachers and principals must be brought in early in planning the program, both to get their input and to allay their misgivings about it. In hindsight, Turner and Evenson would have pushed harder to include them. The classroom teachers in particular benefit from firsthand reassurance. At Warren and Jim Darcy schools, Rhonda McCarty has learned to take over a teacher's class for a few minutes to let her go to the HOSTS class and watch what's happening. "It's important for the tutors to see the teachers, too," she says. "It gives everybody a sense of working together."

• **Build in enough training.** Make sure the teachers get frequent, continuing reinforcement. Evenson thinks Laurie Wiedmann and Gloria Gabaldon-Lesueur weren't given enough.

• **Screen the tutors carefully.** Helena has taken no special precautions—but it's a town where neighbors are known, and this casual acceptance has created no major problems. That won't be the case in most communities. Get references and check them out. Contact between tutors and pupils outside the supervised classroom should probably be discouraged.

• **Start small.** Work out bugs in the program with a pilot effort in one or two schools before expanding to full scale. If the program uses community volunteers, do some recruiting in advance, with a list of prospective tutors in hand before expanding.

There's some debate in Helena about where the program goes from here. At Broadwater School, Bernie Hartman thinks HOSTS should be expanded to all twelve elementary schools, even if that means using a lot more of the district's own funds. He thinks every student in every school could benefit from one-on-one tutoring at some point in the educational process, and nothing but good could come of getting the community more involved; if there's a saturation point, he says, it's only in a teacher's willingness to share authority. "Obviously, I'm very positive about the program," he says. "It's not the total answer, but nothing is going to be the total answer. It gives some beautiful options."

Marion Evenson disagrees, at least about the HOSTS program itself. The schools now offering it were chosen because they needed it most, she says, and if it keeps working as well as it has, the number of low achievers in each of those schools will actually decline, so that

HOSTS will be working itself out of a job. Rather than expand the number of schools using HOSTS, she suggests, the solution may be to keep it going in the present six schools, and kids who need help in other schools can be bused to the existing program.

But in the long run, the HOSTS success gives Evenson and Turner an audacious idea: to try to adapt its computer-based flexibility and use of volunteers to other parts of the curriculum and other problems of the schools. Volunteers are already branching out from remedial reading to other areas, as Alice Morse has done with her five kindergartners at Bryant School; similarly, a mother at Broadwater School is chatting to kindergartners in conversational Spanish. Ideally, says Brad Morris at Central School, there's no reason why every teacher in the system couldn't use variations of the computer technique to create at least some individual lessons for every student in every class, with volunteer tutors taking part of the load and teachers functioning increasingly as planners and executives.

What it adds up to is the heady prospect of a new kind of teaching in an evolving school system. Nothing is set in concrete, says Turner, but with careful planning, talent and some luck, there's a possibility for more creative and efficient teaching across the board. The HOSTS experience, he says, "has helped us understand teaching and learning a little better—that there are some other strategies that work, and that teaching doesn't have to be a lonely business, one teacher in one classroom facing all those kids. That you can really share it. That's going to speak to us loud and clear." And it isn't a lesson only for Helena, Montana. What educators are finding out, Turner says, is that "There are a lot of ways to help kids learn, and a lot of people can be involved in that. These are really, truly exciting times."

11.
Cracking Concrete
with Violets

The scene is somewhere between anarchy and chaos. There are fifty or so kids, all but one of them black or Hispanic, and four frazzled white teachers; they are having something resembling a meeting in the third-floor library of the cavernous old Theodore Roosevelt High School. It's a depressing school, shabby, with grates on the grimy windows, guards roaming the hallways and truants taunting their friends through the locked classroom doors. Outside is the desperation of New York City's South Bronx: gaudy storefronts on potholed streets, a swirl of sidewalk vendors, crack vials littering the pavement, furtive men on nameless errands, underage mothers pushing baby carriages.

Tessa, a sophomore from Belize, has the chair and the attention of perhaps a third of the kids, who sprawl in chairs around three sides of an open square. She is trying to run a debate: Should the group vote to set up a community service program, and make it mandatory for all the members? A few kids argue the point, cross-talking and interrupting. Five sullen boys talk steadily in the rear. Kids wander to the sandwich table, chat, scribble in their diaries. A wadded paper napkin is thrown. The volume rises. Tempers flare: "Hey, Tiffany, why you opposed, ya dumb bitch?"

"Who's in favor?" says Tessa.

"Favor of what?" somebody shouts.

"I step down," Tessa declares.

Al Sternberg, a history teacher with the look and mannerisms of a benign Archie Bunker, shouts the tumult down to a minor roar. Community service, he reminds them. Somebody objects that kids have more than enough to do already. Somebody else asks, reasonably enough, won't people hate community service if they're forced to do it? Sternberg explains that sometimes people won't do the right thing until they're made to, but then they find out it's not so bad. Somebody laughs; it may be coincidental.

A motion is made: Have community service, but make it voluntary. It carries, thirty-three to nine. Sternberg pushes plaintively for reconsideration, but a homeboy cuts him off.

"You asked us, we said no, now it's over with," he says.

"Word," agrees a boy across the room.

This is moral education in the South Bronx—a concept that cynics might call an oxymoron. It is a program that aims to help inner-city kids develop ethical reasoning by functioning as a "just community." Roosevelt Community School (RCS) operates as a school within Roosevelt High that makes and enforces rules for itself. In working it out for themselves, students learn by coming to grips with real-life problems of right and wrong. In the violence, exploitation and despair of the inner city, the idea seems bold to the point of recklessness. But for all its obvious shortcomings, RCS has been proving for six years, in effect, that the roots of a violet can crack concrete. Like most urban flowers, it is fragile, gallant, only partly successful, and probably doomed. It is also well worth studying.

RCS is the most audacious of more than a dozen attempts to apply the theories of the late Harvard educator Lawrence Kohlberg. A developmental psychologist and head of Harvard's Center for Moral Education, Kohlberg saw moral development occurring in stages, from infantile self-interest (stage 1) to enlightened principles of justice and fairness (stage 5). He put theory into practice by setting up classes and communities in a series of widely different schools, from mainly blue-collar Cambridge, Massachusetts, to suburban Scarsdale, New York, and inner-city Roosevelt High. The aim was not simply to change students' abstract thinking, but their behavior and attitude as well, by giving them real power to govern themselves, encouraging open discussion of conflicts, and fostering responsibility and a sense of community. By several measurements, the experiments worked. In RCS as in the other schools, students progressed by an average one-half stage in moral reasoning while their classmates in a comparison group advanced only half as far. RCS students showed no gains in scholarship, but their attendance improved—a key factor in a school where absenteeism averages 50 percent. Perhaps most important, teachers and researchers alike continue to see big changes in individual students.

"They really act differently in the second and third semester than they did in the first," says Ann Higgins, one of Kohlberg's associates, who took over his role as observer of RCS after his death in 1987. RCS students, she says, break up fights rather than start them; "they stop other people from doing harm and disrespecting each other. The kids do become more reflective of who they are and how they relate to others." They haven't stopped getting into trouble, but their sins tend to be less frequent and less serious. There is increased self-esteem as the community teaches shy kids to participate and speak out before a group. Fewer kids get pregnant, and Higgins says at least some of the group "are going to college and staying there and doing well, and they tell us that we helped them, that they wouldn't have done it without us." Roosevelt High's principal, Paul Shapiro, uses the eighty students in RCS as a sounding board for new ideas and a route to communicate with the 2,900 or so students in the larger high school. "RCS has good spinoff effects on the entire school," he says.

At Roosevelt, the community meets for just two periods each day, including lunch. On Thursdays, both periods are devoted to a meeting of the full group. On the other four days, one period is spent in academic classes, combining English and social studies in a special curriculum stressing ethical issues. The other period, with lunch, is used for discussion in the four small "core groups" that make up the community, and also for meetings of the three permanent committees: Agenda, to schedule discussions and votes; Fairness, to deal with disputes and disciplinary cases; and Activities, to plan day trips, revenue-raising bake sales and the like. Issues for community discussion may grow out of the curriculum, from an item in the news or an incident in the community itself. After a boy ignored a summons to the Fairness Committee, for instance, the group tried to formulate rules for such cases—a debate that wound down inconclusively with the ending of the school year. New issues are usually brought up first in the core groups, where students can explore ideas and wallflowers find it easier to speak out, and are then taken to the full community for discussion and a vote.

The community is a democracy, with teachers and students casting equal votes, and within the group teachers are addressed by their first names. In practice, however, the teachers are clearly first among equals. They suggest most of the topics for discussion, nudge points onto the table and freely advocate their positions; while they try to step aside when the group is functioning well, they can't abrogate all their authority, especially in a group with such rudimentary communication skills. The students have little grasp of logical thought, let alone parliamentary procedure, and for roughly half of them English is a second language. Al Sternberg, the stocky, balding lead teacher, often has to come to the rescue of the student who is taking a turn as chairperson. Just as often, he finds himself translating a semi-coherent comment or proposal into something resembling English.

The community's autonomy is also something of a pretense. The group doesn't really set all the rules for its members' behavior—it has to follow the code of the larger school and the New York City Board of Education—but it can decide which rules to make part of its own code and discuss why they matter. And it has one fragment of real power: Shapiro lets the Fairness Committee deal with infractions of school rules, such as fighting or stealing, that come up within the community. The committee's decisions can be appealed to the full community.

The group's first task each year is to create and renew its sense of community. Members play trust-building games and practice group problem solving, and every fall there is a daylong community outing to welcome new members and encourage bonding. As it happens, it was RCS's first outing, a daylong visit to an Outward Bound–type program in Westchester County in the fall of 1985, that set up the group's first real lesson in moral education.

The students agreed easily when the teachers proposed that drugs and alcohol should be banned on the outing, and the students themselves volunteered that the ban should be extended to guns and knives. A proposal to outlaw boom-box radios and even radios with earphones was more hotly debated, but in the end the group agreed to leave them behind, too, so that nobody could tune out of the group experience. The outing was a success. But next day one of the teachers, Dorothy, reported that somebody had stolen $20 from her purse. The debate that followed is remembered as a landmark, and a foretaste of RCS at its creative best.

Some students argued that Dorothy was responsible for taking care of her own money and had nobody but herself to blame. (Oversimplifying Kohlberg's complex categories, that was a stage 2 argument. A stage 2 person sees right and wrong in terms of his own interests; others have conflicting interests, but "if you scratch my back, I'll scratch yours.") Most of the group, however, accepted the teachers' suggestion that the theft had violated the community's trust, and that the community as a whole had some responsibility for it. The first solution was that if the money were not voluntarily returned, the community's members should kick in to repay Dorothy. "If everybody puts in twenty-five cents, we'll get the twenty dollars," Sternberg said.

The money was still missing at the next week's meeting, and the debate grew more heated. Most students seemed to accept the idea that the community had a responsibility, but the group split over how far the obligation extended and whether contributions should be compulsory or voluntary. Some said only those who had gone on the trip should be asked to chip in, since those who hadn't gone clearly had nothing to do with the theft. But as Ann Higgins tells it in a research report on RCS, a girl named Diane argued that that wasn't the point: "We are talking about showing Dorothy that we care for her, and it is not only the people who went, it is the whole community." Diane also said people should give voluntarily, "out of their heart . . . I don't want nobody to feel that they have to do it, that they are forced into it."

That was an idealistic argument, and Nelson, a leader in the group, supported it with a point of principle: It would violate people's rights to make them pay if they didn't want to. Diane put the case clearly in the Golden Rule terms of Kohlberg's stage 3 (the level of wanting to be a good person, to follow rules and to care for others): "Put yourself in Dorothy's position. . . . If it was you who were stolen from, how would you feel?" But Harriet retorted that if she were Dorothy, she would look after her own money and not expect to be rewarded for losing it. Harriet added the pragmatic point that if everyone kicked in 25 cents, Dorothy would get more money than had been stolen, which wouldn't be fair. In any case, Harriet and Nelson both doubted that all the people voting for contribution would in fact give anything; if they didn't, that would be unfair, too.

In the end, the decision was for voluntary contribution. A paper bag was passed around and people put money into it. Al Sternberg says some kids put in dollar bills, knowing that others didn't have money to spare. The total came to more than $20, but that wasn't a problem: Dorothy gave the whole fund back to the community, and it became the nucleus of a treasury. The motivation for contributing wasn't entirely clear, Higgins says. Diane's Golden Rule argument wasn't really understood by more than a few students, and RCS wasn't yet really knit together. But the process had begun. There have been no further cases of stealing within the community, and by the spring of that first year, both teachers and students were casually leaving their belongings lying around the RCS classrooms and community meetings. That is a demonstration of trust that is rare indeed at Roosevelt High.

Fifteen miles north of the South Bronx, Scarsdale is a world away— a world of money, privilege and expectations. It is a suburb of strivers and achievers, people determined that their children will have all the advantages, get good marks in good schools and go on to good colleges on their inevitable way to replicating their parents' success. Scarsdale High is known as a fine school, but also a structured and highly competitive place. For students who don't quite fit in, there is a choice: the Scarsdale Alternative School, a classy bastion of relaxed discipline, progressive teaching methods and experiential learning. It is known to everybody as the A-school, and it is built around another of Kohlberg's just communities.

When Kohlberg first visited the A-school in 1978, it was six years old and trying hard to renew its sense of mission. It had been set up as an experiment of about seventy-five students and a staff of five teachers, with its own comfortable building and lush amenities on a campus separate from the high school. But its original impetus had faded, and its students were increasingly skipping the schoolwide meetings designed to make it a democratic community. For his part, Kohlberg saw the A-school as "virtually an ideal situation for exploring the upper limits" of his process of moral development. With their sophistication and advantages, the Scarsdale kids had already reached the "conventional" moral stages, 3 and 4, at which most adults live out their lives. On average, the RCS students come to the school somewhere between stage 2 (self-centered bargaining) and stage 3 (the Golden Rule). Scarsdale students were a full level higher, making the transition to stage 4 (awareness of individual obligations and society's need for rules). They might or might not go on to stage 5, a sense of the whole social contract and a personal commitment to a few absolute values. (In theory, Kohlberg held, there may be a sixth stage for the rarefied likes of Mohandas Gandhi and Martin Luther King Jr.)

Like RCS, the A-school community was set up on the model first tried in Cambridge, at Rindge and Latin High School. The community had core groups, a Fairness Committee to enforce its rules, an ethical-studies curriculum and the weekly community meeting. Because the school was so small, all the students could be included in the community. As at RCS, the first real A-school debate was triggered by the community's fall outing in 1978, a three-day camping trip. The problem was drugs and alcohol. In previous years, the school had taken similar orientation trips, but the group had merely been reminded a bit apologetically that drinking and smoking pot were illegal, and that the A-school would have to comply with the law. The students then blithely ignored the rule, while the teachers, saddled with the impossible task of enforcing it, felt frustrated and impotent. Kohlberg's program provided an excuse to make the new community face up to facts: if the students wouldn't accept the rule as binding, it was unfair to the teachers, who were also members of the community, to leave them holding the bag. The group got that far relatively easily, and voted a real ban on drugs and alcohol during the trip. After the outing, however, it was clear that the rule had been violated. What should be done? Was the whole community responsible for enforcing its own rules?

The debate that followed was a conflict of values. Students conceded that they had a duty to report the violators, but they were stymied by the taboo on informing and betraying friendships. In the end, several violators broke the impasse by confessing and accepting a relatively mild punishment, a week's loss of voting rights in the community. That relieved tension and produced a surge of community feeling, with support and encouragement from the group for the repentant offenders. After that, voluntary confession became the approved way of dealing with similar offenses.

The next step was harder. In 1982, under prodding from the teachers, the students confronted the issue of cheating and ultimately passed a rule against it. In theory, they also agreed that they shared the responsibility of enforcement: There would be an honor code. If a student saw someone cheating, he should confront her, persuade her to confess and if necessary report her to the community. This would be difficult, they all agreed, but a student named Ginny made the clinching argument, a combination of stage 3 and stage 4 reasoning: "I would be able to do it because I would expect her to do it to me. It's not fair to the community because the community would fall apart if people thought they could cheat. . . . You just have to harden yourself and say that you have to do it. The community has to be based on honesty."

The crunch came several weeks later in a core group meeting, when Jenny, a sophomore, confessed that she had cheated on her homework. After considerable discussion of her offense and repeated apologies, she said she felt hypocritical because she knew that someone else in the group had also broken the code, and she didn't want to confront that person. When that didn't prompt a second confession, Jenny indicated that the other cheater was Mary. Weeping, Mary admitted that she had let her best friend, Sally, copy her homework. Then she turned on Jenny: "I feel terrible about what I did, but you know, Jenny, I'm really angry with you. Why didn't you say something to me first? That's our rule." Another student, John, broke in to denounce the honor code: "I believe in the rule, but I don't believe in how we agreed to enforce it. You should never report on a fellow student. We need to be loyal to each other." But Jenny argued that she was doing it for the good of the whole community. "This school has helped me, and I'm going to help make this school a good place," she said. "If that means reporting on a friend who breaks a rule, then that person is not much of a friend anyway. I'm going to report on them. If we don't follow the rules we make, then it's a joke."

The upshot was that Jenny and Mary confronted Sally, they all apologized to the community, the group applauded their contrition and everyone felt better. However painful, it had been a catharsis, leading to "a stronger sense of solidarity" among the whole community.

In the American tradition of individualism, this focus on community values can be a little disquieting; it has echoes of Maoism in its public self-criticism and pressures to conform to group norms. Is the Kohlberg approach akin to brainwashing?

In their book *Lawrence Kohlberg's Approach to Moral Education*, Ann Higgins and F. Clark Power tell the story of Jenny, Mary and Sally and confront that issue directly, arguing that this process is nothing like "big brother" at work. For one thing, the just community's scrutiny focuses on public rules that have been set democratically, not on private and personal matters. "Unlike moral education models in authoritarian and totalitarian countries," they maintain, the just community's public discussion "is not used as a form of humiliation and emotional ostracism; it culminates in a reaffirmation of everyone's worth to the community."

But a Maoist might make the same claim, welcoming a self-accused "capitalist-roader" back to the party cell. It's plain enough that indoctrination is going on here. Kohlberg never pretended to be value-free, and his teachers have always been open advocates in the community discussions. He did claim to be noncoercive, merely leading willing students to loftier ways of thought, and that seems a bit disingenuous. The teachers are sincere enough in trying to help the community arrive at its own sound values. But the kids understand the hidden premise: that some ways of thinking are better than others, and that the teachers know which is which. One former student at the A-school, Edward Zalaznick, wrote an article arguing that the Kohlberg structure was intimidating, since students were being "pushed" by the teachers to arrive at "right" answers and a "higher" stage of reasoning—one that, by definition, they didn't yet understand and therefore couldn't dispute.

Zalaznick himself had no quarrel with the values he had learned, and he prized his new reasoning skills. He just felt manipulated by the process. And in the end, such objections to the program amount to nitpicking. Nearly any thought-provoking discussion of ethics in a school setting has to be a clear gain for the kids. If they are being indoctrinated, they are at least learning to think about the lesson.

Since Kohlberg's death in 1987, the A-school has pared some of his explicit content from its curriculum. A course called Ethical Issues in Decision Making, once a mainstay of the school, is now an elective. A "mini-course" on Kohlberg and Jean Piaget, his predecessor in developmental learning, was dropped from the orientation week. Still, "I don't think any of us are less Kohlbergian," says the A-school's lead teacher, Tony Arenella. The five teachers and two interns still set the tone for the school, focusing the issues to be discussed and, consciously or not, pointing arrows to the "higher" stage of thinking. Arenella concedes that while he doesn't see himself as an authority figure, "Some kids do. They see me as my position, not just as Tony." And when wink comes to nod, he himself portrays the school's freedom of thought as a means to a somewhat authoritarian end. "You can't teach responsibility without freedom," says Arenella. "You have to allow kids to screw up. Then you can tell them how to be responsible."

When moral decisions are discussed, says a student we'll call Susan, "there's never one right way. You just look at the reasoning that went into it." But inevitably, she says, the reasoning the teacher uses looks best, so yes, Zalaznick was right: "Teacher intimidation seems to happen."

Susan, a senior, turned herself in to the Fairness Committee last year, admitting to cutting a day of school and possessing marijuana. "I happened to be at a community meeting where emotions were high and a lot of things were coming up at once," she explains, and so she confessed. "Most people who do that feel stupid afterward. I did."

It was a feeling of being "dorky," she says: uncool, a callow enthusi-ast. She had set herself up for mild but real punishment, a period of "eight to threes" when she wasn't allowed to leave campus all day. "It was like, does this community really mean so much to me that I should do this?"

But the answer turns out to be yes. Susan would certainly do the same again, this time without misgivings "because now I'm more secure." She says the just community has changed her, "expanded my dialogue with many people, made my reasoning more complex." And it's the community, she believes, that gives the A-school its roots. Without that grounding, "It would have fallen apart."

Tony Arenella, an energetic and charismatic teacher, agrees with Susan on that. A good many of the alternative schools founded in the '60s and '70s have long since folded, he says, for lack of rationale, purpose and real community, and "I think the theoretical underpinning that the just community has given us has helped us to survive." He has been with the program from its beginnings, helping to plan it and working as one of the teachers before he became the leader. But he also consulted on the founding of the RCS program and sat in on some of the meetings there. And for all the A-school's amenities, its sophisticated students and the intricacies of the moral reasoning they explore, Arenella confesses to a twitch of envy for the program in the South Bronx. "In some ways, the quality of discussion was less abstract and more dynamic," he says. "If someone was stealing or threatening someone else, they got to the heart of the matter."

RCS has been an uphill battle from the beginning. In the spring of 1985, after a year of planning, Al Sternberg signed up nearly one hundred volunteers to start the program in the fall term—but when school opened, only a quarter of them showed up. The teachers had to ask the students to recruit their friends to get enough kids to form a community. As in the Futures 500 program in Washington, that wispy quality of inner-city commitments has been a permanent problem at RCS: Six years later, English teacher Marlene Warren was complaining to the community that although fifty-seven members had voted for a trip to Philadelphia, only twenty-eight people had brought in consent forms and money for the excursion. "You can't seem to sustain your interest," she scolded. "I say there should be no more trips."

Also from the beginning, the gap between the program's ideals and the reality of the surrounding streets has been a constant obstacle. "You wonder, will they take it with them when they leave school," says Susan Sedlmayer, a social studies teacher who guides the Fairness Committee. "The minute these kids get on the subway, they have to be in a different mode altogether, just for self-preservation."

And given the problems, RCS measures its triumphs on a small scale. The discussion of community service, for instance, seems to be a defeat for the teachers—but in the upshot, a community that hadn't been thinking about service at all had discussed it and voted to set up a program, and that's better than nothing. The annals are made up of such fragile victories. There was the student who was ordered by the Fairness Committee to repaint the halls he had sprayed with graffiti, and went on to discourage other graffiti artists. There was Nelson, the self-assured leader, who actually changed his mind one day as a result of other students' arguments—a milestone in the community's development, and Nelson's as well. There was Isaac, who was given an overly harsh punishment; rather than drop out or boycott the community, he chose to stay, accepting part of the penalty and flouting the rest. There was Diana, who broke up a fight between two hulking boys and later tried to organize a just community in her college dormitory.

In the early years, RCS benefited from a rising tide of interest in Kohlberg's programs. Kohlberg himself monitored RCS until his death in 1987, and there was foundation money to support studies of its effectiveness and promise. New Kohlberg communities were being set up, including two at the elite Bronx High School of Science. For a while, there was even a second community at Roosevelt High: Roosevelt Community Renaissance. RCR was aimed at an even more difficult target group, students who had already failed ninth grade at least once and were at extreme risk of dropping out.

But hard times have come for most of Kohlberg's programs. Shortly after his death, Harvard closed his Center for Moral Education. Ann Higgins, his disciple and fiancée, moved on to Fordham University. Another longtime associate who worked at RCS, Betsy Rulon, has settled in Massachusetts. One by one, the communities he set up expired; RCR died in the New York City budget squeeze of 1990. At this writing, only Scarsdale Alternative School and RCS survive. The Scarsdale community seems secure, though even there Kohlberg's influence is waning and the A-school is focusing on its new role as a member of Theodore Sizer's Coalition of Essential Schools. At RCS, however, it is hard to avoid the conclusion that the program is winding down.

For one thing, despite his avowed enthusiasm for the community, principal Paul Shapiro inherited it from his predecessor and has reforms of his own to cherish. He has decreed two major and possibly crippling changes in RCS, designed to make it fit into his new "house" structure at Roosevelt High. Originally, the program started in sophomore year, after students had made the adjustment to high school and matured accordingly. Now freshmen are included, and the teachers find that it's harder to keep order and the quality of the dialogue has declined. "The ninth-graders just don't know why they are there," says Higgins. Even worse, since the freshmen don't know enough about the program to volunteer for it, a community that used to be purely voluntary now includes students who were simply assigned. Commitment suffers, particularly when a student is called before the Fairness Committee. "The kid will say, 'I didn't choose this,'" says Sternberg. In the old days, community members would actively recruit among the freshmen for promising new members—a process that made the old members clarify their own thinking and cemented their involvement in the community. Now, says Higgins, the illusion of autonomy is further weakened: "When you take away voluntarism, you've lost the basic power to choose." Even though upper classmen can drop out of the community and the ones remaining want to be there, she says, "you still have the dead weight of the freshmen."

The program has also suffered from the waning of outside interest in it. In the first years, the W. T. Grant Foundation put up nearly $400,000 to evaluate RCS and other new communities. The flow of researchers and journalists created its own Hawthorne effect. "Kids feel special when people are taking an interest," says Higgins. "That halo wears off when the program gets old." And the general retrenchment in the program has affected the teachers, who show signs of fatigue and demoralization. After postponing it for three years, Al Sternberg chose to take his sabbatical in the fall of 1991, leaving Marlene Warren in charge of RCS. She had been with the program for years, with enthusiasm and devotion; whether she can lead it remains to be seen. The other teachers insisted—perhaps too emphatically—that she was up to the task.

All told, the future doesn't look promising for RCS. Shapiro says it is in no danger, despite the fact that the program is a drain on his budget: The four RCS teachers must be granted a reduced teaching load to give them time to run the community, and there are no outside funds to meet that cost. It's an open question whether the principal's resolution can weather the city's latest budget crisis, and then whether the program can find a new infusion of spirit.

But the RCS record and the success of the Scarsdale program prove that this model of moral education can help at least some schools improve both themselves and the ethical development of their students. For schools that want to set up similar programs, the first essential is to find teachers who want to try and who are willing to be open and experimental with kids; above all, they must see them as real people who are to be led, not forced, to ethical thinking. Beyond that, these are the minimum requirements to do the job:

- **The students must be old enough.** Elements of Kohlberg's program can work with younger children; programs in Kansas City and New York's Westchester County have recently applied moral education in elementary schools. But to function as a true community with a degree of autonomy, the group must be of high school age.
- **The group must be large enough.** To function as a community, there must be more than one or two classrooms full of kids, and more than one or two teachers to supervise them. Ann Higgins thinks three teachers and their classes are the minimum, with four or five as the ideal, making a community of fifty to one hundred and twenty-five. The lower the student/teacher ratio, the better, but the concept can work with as many as twenty-five students for each teacher.
- **The group must have real power.** Community members must feel that they are not just playacting, that their debates and decisions have a real effect in the world. As with RCS, autonomy will probably be strictly limited; no group of students is going to be allowed to set all its own rules. But the more independence they have, the greater the chances of learning. At a minimum, the principal must

give the group authority to deal with minor offenses without being overruled by the administration.

• **The program must be given financial support.**   Community activities take at least two periods each school day, and the teachers need a third for planning, consultation and review. The third period must be in lieu of another teaching period. If a teacher's regular load is five periods a day, the community teachers will be teaching only four, two in the community and two outside. Thus the basic cost of the program will be one-fifth of the salaries of the teachers involved. If there are three teachers whose salaries average $35,000, the program will cost the school $21,000 a year. If the community includes seventy students, that will be $300 per student.

• **The program must have a special curriculum built around ethics, carrying a credit toward graduation.**   Here again, the principal must approve changes in the regular class work. Teachers in previous just communities have worked out basic instruction plans, and Ann Higgins, Betsy Rulon and Tony Arenella are available for consultation on Kohlberg's theory and its application. Higgins says there have been no problems getting approval for the curriculum changes from state agencies or regional accrediting associations, and if a school really wants the program, there are no insurmountable problems in fitting it into the daily schedule.

• **The community should be made up of volunteers.**   It's true that all the students in the A-school are community members, but that's part of what they have chosen by attending the school. And even if RCS survives in its present draft-army form, it's clear that the original voluntarism was better.

It's the last community meeting of the year at RCS, the day for giving out the RCS scholarship. The prize may be the only one of its kind: a fund, raised by the students, to be given to one or two graduating seniors who have been outstanding members of the just community. The winners are chosen by a committee of underclassmen, who judge the candidates not by their popularity but according to their grades, their leadership and their contribution to the community. "Every year the students pick the scholarship winner," says Al Sternberg, "and every year I agree completely."

This year the fund totals $300, raised in bake sales, candy sales and the like. Rigoberto, poised and cool, a rising power in RCS, has the chair and enjoys it. "You all have to be quiet instead of running your mouths," he announces. "Excuse me, you in the back, for the twentieth time!" The committee has found two winners, Sternberg says, and will give prizes of $125 and $175. Principal Shapiro gives an inspirational speech, concluding: "The future is what comes first." In Miss America style, the runner-up is named first: Atricia Stanley. Cheers and applause. The winner: Millie Talentino. Pandemonium.

It wasn't a controversial choice, says committee member Joyce Matthew; most people came up with the same two names. But there was a reasoned debate in the committee and some changing of minds. Joyce herself originally favored splitting the money evenly, and she voted for Atricia ahead of Millie. But the others persuaded her, she says, that "Millie helped more than Atricia. Every day on her lunch period she comes and helps." That is especially noteworthy since Millie isn't even a current member of the community: She had to drop out this semester because of a conflict in her schedule. Then too, says Joyce, Millie "had better grades, and she chaired more than Atricia. I like the way it turned out. It was easy and it was fair."

Once again, Al Sternberg agrees with the verdict. Another year is history, and justice has been done in the just community.

12.
Who, Me?
Go to College?

Bob Coplan was trying to give away money, and he wasn't finding takers.

The year was 1967, and Coplan was a lawyer in Cleveland. He had just taken on the job of running a small family foundation set up by a local businessman, Roy Markus; among other things, the fund was to provide scholarship money to help inner-city students go to college. But there simply weren't enough kids applying, and the money was going begging.

Coplan could easily have shrugged and used the funds for some other worthy cause. But "God bless him, Bob wouldn't take no for an answer," says an old friend. His first response was logical. On the theory that the scholarship just wasn't well enough known, he tried spreading the word about it. He had already organized a dozen of his friends to establish mentoring relationships with poor black students, and now they sent a message through the network: Help is available; if you want to go to college, just come and apply for it.

But the word that came back was, "Who, me?" Most kids from the inner city simply never thought about going to college. No one in their families had gone and none of their friends were going; and even if they thought college was for them, they wouldn't know how to begin. It was like thinking in a foreign language. They knew vaguely that applications would be complicated and probably expensive, and the cost of tuition, room, board and books would be staggering. Financial aid might be available, but they didn't know where to look for it. The whole idea was just off the scope.

Coplan had identified a real problem, which is the first step in starting any creative project. Then he found a deceptively simple and brilliantly effective solution: the Cleveland Scholarship Program (CSP), a way to provide help and counsel along with financial aid. In its first twenty-three years it helped more than 65,000 men and women go to college. Funded mainly by local foundations and the Cleveland business community, CSP keeps part-time advisers in all the city's high schools to seek out qualified students, encourage them to set their sights on college, help them with the applications and financial aid forms, and if necessary put up the last few dollars needed after all the available tills have been tapped. What's more, CSP stays in touch with its college students to help them through the inevitable crises of campus life. That's part of the reason why more than three-quarters of the program's freshmen actually graduate from college—a figure well above the national average.

All this costs less than $250 for each student applying to college, including the expense of the "last-dollar" grants given to about seven hundred students each year. In terms of bang for the buck, contributors see CSP as a splendid investment. For the students it helps, however, it is a good deal more than that. "If I hadn't known about it, I'd be struggling," says Cornell Jordan, who recently graduated from Cleveland's grim East High School and headed off to Youngstown State University. "Every time a kid comes in and hands in one of those forms, that's a piece of the dream."

When Ethel Adrine holds court at East High, as she has been doing two days a week for the past fifteen years, there is always a crowd of students waiting outside her tiny cubicle. Adrine (pronounced Adrien) is the CSP adviser at the school, a onetime teacher who now spends her time encouraging, counseling, chivying and sometimes bullying students into finding colleges, getting their applications and financial aid forms filled out, and getting their lives organized enough to make the leap from the inner city to a college campus. Buxom and grand-motherly, she sits jammed against a tall filing cabinet; around her small desk there is room for three tightly packed visitors. She is calm, reassuring and comforting, with strong features in a warm brown face.

Craig Wilson is going to be a challenge for her. He's a slight, worried-looking boy who came back to East High after doing badly at the elite private University School, where he was one of only twenty-eight blacks in a student body of four hundred mostly privileged subur-ban kids. Demoralized, Craig didn't work hard enough at East High to make up for his dismal grade point average at the private school, only 1.9 on a four-point scale. But he is obviously smart, with a composite grade of 24 on the ACT college admission test—a score that ties him with East's valedictorian. Craig would like to go to New York University or Case Western Reserve in Cleveland. In spite of the high ACT score, both of them would probably turn him down after their first glance at his transcript.

Adrine asks if Craig can find a teacher at University School, or perhaps an adult friend with some standing in the community, to write a letter for him to the assistant deans in charge of minority affairs at the two colleges. And as she probes his story, it becomes clear what such a letter would say. A 1.9 average at University School is equivalent to 2.5 or even 3.0 at East High, which isn't all that bad. And Craig had been in water way over his head at University School: Because of the long bus ride from his inner-city home, he had to put in a twelve-hour day just to attend classes, work on the yearbook and newspaper and earn a letter in baseball. On top of that, he had been holding down a part-time job as a waiter. There had been no time to study.

Craig tells all this in matter-of-fact tones; he isn't offering it as an excuse. But Denise Roberts, CSP's director of advisory services, is sitting in on the interview and thinks otherwise. She knows somebody at Case who might be able to pull a string, she says; she will put in a call today or tomorrow. Meanwhile, Craig has been accepted at both Central State and Cleveland State universities. In a pinch, he could go to one of those, make a good record and transfer later to NYU or

Case. In any event, says Adrine, the paperwork needs to get done. Will he get his parental income statement filled out, or will she have to climb into her car and chase him down?

Like Indianapolis, Cleveland is a Rust Belt relic of the Midwest's glory days of industry. The central city has been in decline for three decades. When the civil rights movement began stirring emotions and consciences in the early '60s, Bob Coplan and most of his friends were already, as they now say wryly, carpetbaggers: they had fled the city's growing squalor to commute between their downtown offices and such leafy suburbs as Shaker Heights. For years, the city was symbolized by the repeated burning of the Cuyahoga River, a stream so polluted that it would literally catch fire. The old heavy industries were decimated by overseas competition, the woes of the auto industry and the economic restructuring of the '70s and '80s. Cleveland is attempting a comeback these days, with increasing numbers of service businesses, light electronics, a convention center and the like, and the downtown section has two new shopping plazas, several modern hotels and a renovation of its fine old railroad station in token of civic revival.

But revival has yet to come to Cleveland's schools. As in other cities, white flight has left the school system disproportionately poor, black and lacking in political support. African-Americans make up just 50 percent of the city's population, but the schools are 70 percent black, with enrollment of 75,000, only half what it was in the city's prime. Poverty and dropout rates range from above average to appalling. At East High, 75 percent of the students qualify for free or low-cost lunches under the federal program. Each year, 550 to 600 freshmen come to school; half of them leave by sophomore year, and in 1990, only 142 survived to graduate. The schools have their share of dedicated educators, but these people swim against a heavy current: Money is chronically tight, apathy is endemic, and the city school board is prone to patronage and political feuding. Off the record, a local industrialist and CSP director calls the board members "a wretched collection with no interest in education at all—they just hand out contracts." The city got its first black superintendent in the mid-'80s. Within a year his suicide had shaken the system. His successor lasted only a year.

Standard measurements of the Cleveland system are bad enough. By the ninth grade, fewer than 60 percent of the city's students can pass the Ohio proficiency test in reading, and fewer than 20 percent pass the math test. High school dropout rates are officially pegged at 38 percent, and the reality is even worse: The system doesn't start counting until the tenth grade, when large numbers have already left. As in Washington, high grades don't necessarily indicate achievement, and a Cleveland high school diploma isn't much prized by college admissions officers. Given all this, says Paul Patton, executive assistant to Mayor Michael White, "Nobody will ever appreciate the full miracle that CSP accomplishes."

CSP exists mainly to seek out and serve average students. On its face, that seems to conflict with the small-bite doctrine of high expectations, and in fact the charge can be made that the whole program falls a bit short in pursuing excellence. But as Coplan saw it, the straight-A students and star athletes weren't the problem. They were already making their way, and they would probably continue to succeed. The kids who needed help were the "average-letes," who had no goals to work for and nobody to point the way to anything that would be worth a little sweat. Thus, under the program's rules, students need only a 2.0 average grade to put in an application, and the qualifying level for CSP's last-dollar grants is only 2.5. The CSP clientele roughly reflects the racial mix of the schools, with 68 percent black and other minorities. More than half the students—55 percent in a recent year—are the first in their families to attend college. As with many inner-city programs, the gender mix has tipped heavily to the female side, by as much as 70 percent in recent years. But the program is trying hard to get boys up to grade, and recently got back to 40 percent male participation.

It is a vindication of Coplan's vision that, once in the program, students tend to stay in and succeed. CSP had never kept systematic track of its students after they went off to school, but in 1988 a questionnaire was sent to a random sampling of the people CSP had sent to college. It would be a reasonable guess that successful alumni were more likely to respond than failures, and thus that the study is skewed to some extent, but even so the results are impressive. In all, 77 percent of the alumni who answered said they had gone on to get a degree.

Most national samplings have found that fewer than half of all students entering college actually graduate.

All this gets done on a remarkably modest annual budget: $930,000 at last tally. The Cleveland Scholarship Program gets by with a full-time staff of just nine, from executive director Christina Milano to the office receptionist. Its twenty-one high school advisers, working in the city's nineteen public high schools and in twenty-two parochial and suburban schools, get fees of $67 to $100 for each day they work. For that, they help about 3,500 students submit six thousand applications every year to institutions of higher education. If the students can't afford fees for taking tests, applying to college or filling out financial aid forms, the advisers help them apply for waivers. Failing all else, CSP pays the fees. In the end, more than 2,100 of the students are accepted at universities, community colleges or trade schools, and seven hundred of them get last-dollar grants from CSP itself to fill the gap between the student's own resources and the financial aid that can be found.

The advisers know every wrinkle of the standard state and federal grants and loans, and they have found a host of special scholarships, including funds earmarked for Ohio kids who meet a donor's specifications and obscure grants offered only at one college or another. It's a measure of their expertise in milking the system that the average last-dollar grant from CSP is less than $400. In fact, for every dollar the program itself gives, the students collect $10 from other sources. But frugality is still the rule: On any objective scale, the need for money outreaches the supply. Almost 70 percent of the CSP grants go to students with family income below $20,000. Tight budgeting reflects the reality of lives in which small sums can loom desperately large. CSP puts up nearly $30,000 a year to pay application fees that parents can't afford, and its campus representatives often find themselves asking the program to advance such emergency funds as $65 in unexpected lab fees. Nearly all the students must work part-time to make ends meet, often to the detriment of studies and grades.

The CSP students face challenges beyond the chronic financial pinch. Especially for those without a college tradition in their families, there are enormous adjustments to be made in leaping from inner-city neighborhoods to campus life. Few of them have solid study skills or academic standards; many have no notion how to select a major subject, how to distribute required courses, how to deal with instructors or budget their time. So the students get counseling in college life during the summer before they matriculate, and CSP staffers stand ready to help if problems develop. All students are required to visit CSP headquarters every summer for a chat about their grades, their summer jobs and their general progress. And on the eight Ohio campuses where CSP students concentrate, the program maintains campus representatives to offer advice, help and a sympathetic ear.

"That follow-up is the real secret of CSP," says mayoral aide Paul Patton, himself an alumnus of the program. Patton still meets people who recognize him from fifteen years ago as their campus representative at Ohio University at Athens. Since then, the campus rep part of the program has been strengthened and formalized: Representatives are chosen for maturity and knowledge about their schools, and are paid about $1,200 a year to be available to other CSP students. But the principle remains the same. "What we did was try to prevent some problem from becoming a crisis," Patton says. "Aid packages can be very lean, and they can make unreasonable demands for part-time jobs. We could find alternatives or make representations." Clarence Mixon, CSP's long-time executive director, was particularly useful in times of crisis. "If somebody's father suddenly died or got laid off, how do you tell the system that the available income has been cut in half?" says Patton. "There was always a way to handle it, and Clarence knew." Mixon also had a sure touch with troubled kids. He recalls rescuing one girl who had flunked out of Ohio University and didn't know what to do next; she was living in friends' rooms until he put her in his car, weeping, and took her back to Cleveland. He got her into the community college; after a year, she had pulled herself together well enough to return to Ohio University.

CSP's most illustrious alumnus, Mayor Mike White, found his crisis at Ohio State University in 1970: A firebrand in the Afro-American disputes, he got thrown out of school. CSP could have cut him loose, he says now. "They could have said, 'This guy is a troublemaker. Let's cut our losses, let's not put any more dollars into this fella because we're not going to see a return.' But they did just the opposite." CSP found a lawyer who fought the case and got White reinstated. A mercurial, intense man with a flashing smile, the mayor says now, "That left kind of an indelible impression on me. When people who don't really know you are ready to back you up . . . well, the least I could do is the best I can."

And the tradition continues. For Gino Ranieri, problems escalated to the crisis level almost as soon as he matriculated at Cleveland State University in the fall of 1990: Campus officials told him they had lost all his records and could do nothing to help him. He got the impression that this was his problem, not theirs, and he had foolishly kept no copies. His father, a struggling entrepreneur who was trying to keep two pizzerias afloat, couldn't help either; he kept making suggestions that didn't sound terribly useful: File a lawsuit, get a bank loan. But Gino's campus representative called Juanita Storey, the forceful and energetic CSP staffer in charge of the representatives, and her call to the university turned things around. The records were suddenly found and the crisis was over. "CSP is always there, the best thing I've got going," said Gino the following spring. "Looking back over the first year, I think I should give them more credit."

Strictly speaking, Ethel Adrine shouldn't be spending time on this visitor. Iptesam Saleh, an immigrant from Palestine, is East High's valedictorian, with a straight-A transcript that will easily get her into practically any school she wants. But Adrine takes obvious pleasure in her company, and it's easy to see why: Joyous and sparkling, Iptesam is a delight.

She wants to go to Salisbury State College in Maryland, where it seems there's a young man. The story isn't wholly predictable: In the Middle East fashion, it's her father who wants her to marry the boy. The American twist is that the two young people have conveniently fallen for each other. But there's also a case to be made against Salisbury State. Iptesam has piled up $3,200 in a college scholarship program, the Cleveland Initiative for Education. If she goes to Salisbury she will get the money, but if she goes to Case Western Reserve in Cleveland, Case will quadruple the total. Does romance outweigh $9,600?

Adrine isn't pushing her either way. All she says is that whichever choice Iptesam makes, she has to finish her financial aid forms. Adrine has already helped her with the admissions forms and coached her in writing an essay, and she's ready to do more.

A couple of years ago, the East High yearbook was dedicated to Ethel Adrine. "She's only here two days a week," says Iptesam, "and she's the most famous person in the school."

The advisers are the heart of CSP. They coddle, cajole and encourage; they bug students about deadlines, references, official documents and notary stamps. They steer kids to apply to appropriate schools, and discourage them from asking for last-dollar grants if there's enough money available elsewhere. They run interference with the school board's bureaucracy when the main office is slow to produce official grade transcripts or gets them wrong. It takes a number of special qualities to be a good adviser, and CSP has reliably found them. At first, they were resented by the schools' own guidance counselors, who saw them not only as invaders on the turf but rivals who were more knowledgeable, sympathetic and credible with kids than the counselors themselves could be. Those frictions have eased, in part because the counselors have learned to leave much of the college admissions work to CSP and focus their own efforts largely on the myriad social problems confronting Cleveland students. As a class, says Martin Gottfried, the administrative coordinator at Shaw High School in impoverished East Cleveland, the CSP advisers are "the best and the brightest, which the educational system doesn't always get."

In the beginning, CSP recruited mainly former teachers as advisers, people who missed being with kids and wanted to supplement their pensions with part-time work. They were talented, effective and tireless; more than twenty years later, the last of that first crop is about to retire. The new advisers are still dedicated and effective, but also a bit more varied than they used to be. Some former teachers are still being hired, but other recent recruits include a minister, a former college admissions officer and a onetime minority affairs adviser at a university. Denise Roberts, the canny young woman who has done most of the recent interviewing and hiring, says it's not a job many people would find alluring: There are no fringe benefits, per-diem pay never tops $100, and there's not much prospect for advancement. But once hired, the advisers find it addictive. There's little turnover, a reliable flow of applicants and a waiting list for the few openings that come up.

Roberts says she looks first for zest. "Kids can be trying, the conditions aren't beautiful, and a lot gets heaped on you. So you'd better be enthusiastic," she says. Advisers must be assertive enough to push through the bureaucracy and defend their turf, and autonomous enough to work without much supervision. Shy people, incurious people and those who don't show genuine liking for kids all get rejected. And Roberts stays alert to the possibility that some applicants—especially the men—might like kids altogether too much. So far, she says, that has never been a problem, but references are always checked thoroughly. Training is flexible. Some new advisers, like the former admissions officer, can move right into the job with just a few days' work on procedures. Others study for a semester or more, then team with a veteran for the first months of actual work with students. The biggest challenge for advisers is always the special situations, says Roberts: "You get the kid who's been thrown out of his house, but doesn't earn enough to qualify as an independent, and you have to figure out how to handle that. But if you know how to talk to kids, the rest comes naturally."

The advisers start registering their presence and advertising their services when eighth-graders make their first get-acquainted visits to high schools, the year before they actually enter. For the next four years the advisers keep reminding the kids that they are there. They make regular appearances at assemblies and award ceremonies. They hold daytime and evening financial aid workshops for parents, explaining the system and the need to fill out the intrusive forms, and these sessions are so well organized and publicized that they draw as many as one hundred parents at a time. But the serious work begins in senior year, when applications start flowing. The advisers apply for fee waivers for students who can't afford to pay for SAT or ACT tests, or to put up $25 or so to apply for admission or financial aid.

Sympathetic teachers can be a big help to the advisers in getting kids to think about college: At Shaw High, CSP adviser Carol Keske says some teachers give their students extra credit for attending her annual financial aid assembly. But it's Keske who exhorts them to apply, calms their examination nerves, helps fill out their forms and persuades their parents to cooperate. She found a special scholarship for native Americans and helped Anthony Hoges get the papers to prove his 25 percent Indian heritage. Without her, says Marc Graham, "I probably wouldn't have been able to apply to half the colleges I did." Marc is smart and accomplished enough to have a realistic shot at getting into MIT, but he says: "I know I couldn't have done it all by myself."

Ethel Adrine is going through the thickets of the FAF, the federal financial aid form, with the shy, silent eighteen-year-old we'll call Latisha. The form is four pages of forbidding questions ("Interest rate of your most recent Stafford loan or GSL. *Mark only one box*"), and eight pages of equally forbidding instructions on how to answer them ("If section B instructed you to complete the *gray* and *white* areas of the form, give information for all family members included in question 20"). Adrine is filling out the form and Latisha is watching.

"Having a baby isn't the end of the world," Adrine tells Latisha. "You can make changes and get your life in order." Above all, Latisha shouldn't give up on college and a career. Her mother can look after little Maurice for a while, and Latisha can get help from the federal Aid to Families with Dependent Children and the program called LEAP. She will also have to go to summer school to make up for the time she was out of school in December, having the baby, but she will get her diploma in August, in time to matriculate. She's applying to three local colleges, and she wants to become a social worker.

In filling out the FAF, the baby is actually an advantage. Because she has Maurice, the government now considers Latisha an independent student, so her parents' income doesn't have to be taken into account. But she should also send in an Ohio Instructional Grant Application, which can get her as much as $3,300 a year for a private college or $1,326 for a state school, and that form does require a listing of the parents' income. Latisha must get those figures, and she must get the welfare department to verify that she expects to receive $3,288 from AFDC next year. She can also apply for a CHOICE grant of $500 from the state, but that's simple, Adrine says. She just has to sign a statement of residency.

Latisha ought to make $400 or $500 over the summer, but she

thinks that may be a problem: She might not be hired, since she got fired from her last job. Adrine coaxes the story out. Latisha had been working for a day-care center, which told her to get inoculated against measles to protect the children. Since she was already pregnant, her doctor refused.

"Well, that's simple enough, isn't it?" says Adrine. "There's a legitimate explanation, and your doctor can back you up. Nobody will hold that against you." Latisha nods, with a tentative smile.

Does she think, a visitor asks later, that she could handle all this without Mrs. Adrine's help?

"Uh-uh," says Latisha.

For the advisers, ethical dilemmas come with the territory. Some of them are familiar to any social worker: the problems of reconciling poor people's lives with the official fictions of laws and printed forms. An adviser may well discover, for instance, that the income she is listing as a parent's really belongs to a grandparent. It's a benign deception, since it reflects the family truth: The grandparents are raising this student, whose parents are no longer around. But unless there's a legal adoption, the form cares only about parents. What's an adviser to do? Similarly, many mothers have stable relationships with men who would be willing to help with their children's education, while the real father won't put up a dime. The forms have no room for such arrangements.

Some advisers fall into tacit conspiracies with the students they help. For one example, they routinely try to maximize grants and minimize loans to their clients, not wanting to see them come out of college with huge debts hanging over their heads. In other cases, the advisers often wink at statements on the FAF that are plainly ridiculous. "When somebody says she's bringing up three kids on a total income of $7,230," says one adviser, "and she comes in better dressed than you are, you know there's more income somewhere. Is there a boyfriend? Is there drug money? Is she a hooker? Who knows? I never, never ask. My job is to facilitate this form, not to be a cop. Somebody else can find out if it's true." In all probability, nobody will; most colleges make very little effort to verify the forms.

But the basic dilemma is more troubling, and it was built into CSP in Bob Coplan's original vision. Is CSP really setting its standards high enough? Is Ethel Adrine doing too much for Latisha, Craig and Iptesam? Shouldn't the kids be made to take a little more initiative, learn the ropes for themselves? At bottom, should the Latishas of the world be going to college at all? Is Ethel Adrine helping the country by milking the system of every last taxpayer's dollar in order to send a barely literate unwed mother to get a piece of paper that might be her meal ticket as a social worker, keeping her on the public payroll all her life?

Those are sensitive questions, and none of them are easy. There's no doubt that the advisers go beyond their instructions: They aren't supposed to fill out forms, merely to coach students through them. It's clearly easier for both parties when the adviser actually puts pencil to paper, but Lily Drayton, twelfth-grade guidance counselor at Shaw, worries about a generation raised to be dependent for help of all kinds. Richard Boyd, a longtime CSP supporter and head of the Martha Holden Jennings Foundation, tends to agree. "There's too much hand-holding," says Boyd, a former state superintendent for the Mississippi school system. "At some point along the line, people are going to be asked to do practical things. Maybe you have to say, 'If you can't fill out the forms, you don't belong here.'"

That touches a very sore point. The forms are certainly difficult. "I can just see some kid from a disadvantaged home," says Howard Steindler, current president of CSP and a partner in Bob Coplan's old law firm, "coming home with thirty or forty pages of information and forms, and asking his or her mother, who's just worked all day and who has difficulty reading, to fill all this out. And then give the kid seventy-five dollars to mail it in. It's a tragedy." Others see the forms in even darker terms. "This document is institutionally racist," says Shaw's Martin Gottlieb, brandishing an FAF application. "It may not be intended that way, but there's just no need for it to be this cumbersome and punitive." But the forms are not impenetrable; like IRS income tax instructions, they are designed to guide people through the process whether they understand it or not. "The truth is, if you sit down and read the directions, you can figure it out," says Lily Drayton. "Perhaps they feel inadequate or uncertain, and that's understandable. But I don't always feel I've helped somebody if I just do it for them."

It's also understandable that Drayton is not universally popular among the kids. But she means to be their friend when she says, "When you get to the college situation, there are things you have to do to help yourself."

Beyond doubt, talented kids take advantage of the advisers' willingness to help. Kellie Edwards, who has applied to four good schools with Carol Keske's help, argues fiercely that higher education should be free to everybody, and it's unfair to make some people pay more than others just because their parents happen to have money. She's clearly as bright as she is militant, but she says she never even looked at her own financial aid forms; she simply handed them first to her mother, then to Keske.

But that process seems entirely natural to many people. "I've never filled out a ten-forty form in my life," argues Paul Patton. "There's nothing wrong with having experts to do chores for you. It's just practical." And in the end, he's right. There's little educational purpose to be served by forcing students to struggle through the forms, which they will never again face after college. Tina Milano, the poised and professional executive director of the program, shrugs off the debate about the intricacy of the forms as so much mystique. "That's not really what it's about," she says; sure, it's supposed to be a self-help program, but if she were in the adviser's shoes, "I really don't know what I'd do." What makes CSP work, she says, is a bunch of caring people who take trouble with kids and keep them focused on important goals. As long as the advisers take pleasure in helping with the forms— and they do—that will be part of the relationship.

The Latisha question is more troubling, and at least some CSP people say privately that it bothers them. But it's probably not for CSP to resolve anyway. The educational system is what it is, with elementary and secondary schools that don't educate kids and colleges that are willing to function as trade schools. If Latisha can get a degree and learn to be a social worker, she'll be independent, productive and ahead of the game—and so will the rest of us, Bob Coplan argues. Now retired and living in Florida, he remains fiercely proud of his program as an efficient and highly pragmatic way to bootstrap potential failures into good citizens. "Our mission isn't to reform the system," he says, but to work within it. College is simply a good thing, giving people a chance to escape dependency, make decent lives for themselves and get their own children out of the poverty cycle. The CSP faith is that over the years, whatever investment that takes will be repaid many times over. It's hard to argue with that.

And in those terms, says Coplan, CSP is an even better bargain than it seems. Of the two thousand kids sent to school by CSP every year, perhaps seven hundred would have made it on their own. But because of the program, two-thirds of the crop have been moved from low-end jobs into the middle class, he argues; and the fact that they aren't looking for entry-level work makes openings for thirteen hundred kids who never participated in CSP. "So when you help two thousand kids, you're really helping thirty-three hundred. I can't prove that, but it has to be so."

As long ago as 1983, the Cleveland Scholarship Program began replicating itself. Having set up in all the city's nineteen public high schools, CSP started offering its services to parochial and suburban schools, charging fees that would cover its costs and help to carry the central program. That operation has expanded to twenty-two schools in and around Cleveland. In addition, fourteen independent programs modeled on CSP have been started in cities across the eastern part of the country, from Boston to Miami. The latest is in Lorain County, just outside CSP's home territory in Cleveland. The clones vary widely in many details, but all of them have learned from CSP's experience:

• **Build a broad base of support.** A scholarship program must have the backing of the school system, and must maintain cordial relations with the bureaucracy. It should have an umbrella organization with a board representing local foundations, the business community, educators and any other significant political groups. Without such support, the program can't attract continuing funding or a professional staff.

• **Offer benefits to everybody.** The program must not be seen as an affirmative action plan benefiting any single segment of the population. "There were a lot of programs with white people helping black people, and they all died," says Coplan. CSP scholars reflect the mix in Cleveland.

- **Squeeze every nickel.** From the start, CSP budgeted for a lean operation and has kept it that way, with small permanent staff and part-time advisers. "We run it like a profit-making operation," says president Steindler. "We hire the best people we can find and expect a lot from them. We have a real good grasp on our numbers, and we haven't done more than we could afford. Our financial projections always come out within five percent of the targets." As part of its management, CSP insists that board members take an active role and do real work, not merely ratify staff decisions.
- **Scholarships are good, but not essential.** Money adds credence to the advice being given, and CSP's last-dollar grants to needy students may make the difference to their success. The lure of funds also helps publicize the program as a whole. However, most CSP officials believe the program could succeed if it offered no direct financial aid of its own, but merely encouraged students to apply for colleges and helped them get outside scholarship funds.
- **Provide continuing support for the students.** Once in college, students can't be left to fend for themselves. CSP students are required to maintain their summer contacts with the office, and they know help is available from CSP staffers in any kind of crisis. The mechanism can be flexible. On campuses where there aren't enough CSP students to warrant a paid campus representative, they may form informal support groups.
- **Advisers are the key.** Recruiting them calls for judgment, sensitivity and the best kind of personnel sense—and references must always be checked.
- **Start small.** "We've always taken small bites," says Steindler. Even after a quarter of a century, in adding new features to CSP, the first step is to make sure the problem being addressed is the real issue; then the proposed solution gets tried in a pilot program before moving to full-scale operations.

And it's clear that starting small can stretch to the scholarship program itself. It needn't be city-wide, with a million-dollar budget and a full staff. The CSP structure and principles could be applied in a single school by anybody who likes kids, wants to help them and will take the trouble to learn the ropes of college applications and financial entry forms. If there's an existing staff of counselors, it may be possible to work with them: They will almost surely complain of overwork, so they can't very well refuse help. What you do from there depends on your diplomatic skills—including, if necessary, your willingness to let others take the credit, at least for a while. If you can line up some outside financing, it will make your program visible and credible. But that's not essential to begin with. A CSP could grow from the efforts of a single volunteer parent.

CSP has had a bumpy transition from its early successes to its present status as a mature, continuing program. Like many such projects, it lived for years on the energy, enthusiasm and dedication of its first generation of leadership. But after Coplan's retirement, some of the directors began to feel that CSP was losing focus. There were complaints that Clarence Mixon, the charismatic and much-loved executive director, was paying too much attention to starting up replicas of CSP in distant cities, and not enough to what was happening in Cleveland. In one of its periodic crises, the Cleveland school system had challenged the business community to set up a second scholarship program, the Cleveland Initiative for Education (CIE), as a token of business commitment to the schools; and while there was no ostensible rivalry between the two plans, there was uneasiness about their overlapping coexistence. There was also some feeling among CSP directors that the CIE program was cutting into fund-raising. An outside management study recommended some changes, mostly minor ones, but the director reportedly resisted. Finally Mixon left.

Some bitterness remains. Mixon himself is still in Cleveland, as an assistant principal in one of the high schools. None of the directors is entirely happy about the symbolism of replacing a black man, who had served for eighteen years, with a blue-eyed blonde woman, no matter how sound Tina Milano's credentials as a career manager of nonprofit organizations. But the consensus is that she is getting the program back on track, reassuring the major backers and starting a couple of promising initiatives.

Nobody foresees major growth for the program, and what growth there is won't be fast: the small-bite principle is firmly in place at CSP. There are two pilot programs now being tried, one focusing on providing mentors in business for CSP students after college, the other on helping "nontraditional" (read "older") students through the college admissions process. Both seem to solve real problems: There are increasing numbers of older people who feel a need for college, and CSP graduates can profit from the kind of networking connections that middle-class alumni take for granted in starting careers. And both ventures seem promising in their early stages. If it succeeds, Tina Milano hopes the mentoring program could help solve another problem: Thus far, CSP alumni have been notably slow to contribute to the program that helped them, even though growing numbers are entering the high-wage phase of their careers. Mentoring could be a way to spark their interest.

Perhaps the most obvious direction for CSP to branch out would be to extend its reach to younger students. By the time they reach senior year in high school, where CSP contact becomes intense, only determined survivors are left in school at all. Some staffers and backers think the program could easily expand into dropout prevention, starting at the middle school level or even earlier. But others see dangers in overreaching CSP's expertise, diluting its efforts and losing focus. "I'd look at that very carefully," says Howard Steindler. "When the great shirtmaker decides to branch into neckties, it's a logical idea and it might work. But he might also end up with great shirts and lousy ties. It might even cut into the quality of the shirts, and then where is he?" In the end, says Milano, one secret of CSP's success may well be that "our students are motivated enough to come to us." A new and expanded wave of kids who have to be coaxed to stay in school might raise the failure rate in college dramatically.

And as a mature program, the Cleveland Scholarship Program feels little pressure to branch out in any direction. Stagnation is bad, the directors agree, but overreaching is deadly; as Richard Boyd puts it, "The woods are full of failures that should have stuck to their original mission." CSP's mission is still clear and still being met—and if the program does nothing more than that for the next several decades, it will be a blessing.

13.

The Catchers
in the Rye

Dennis Littky no longer remembers just where the idea for the advisory program came from. It was in the air in those days, part of the yeasty middle-school reform movement of the late 1960s and early '70s, when earnest young educators with tie-dyed shirts and sandals were trying to create a whole new kind of school that would help kids through the agonies of early adolescence. Littky was one of those pioneers, and he got his big chance when an adventurous board of education hired him as the founding principal of a middle school for the communities of Shoreham and Wading River, on the east end of Long Island. The advisory program became the cornerstone of the Shoreham–Wading River Middle School: a way of making sure no kid in the school can get lost—that every child, every day, is getting close attention from at least one adult.

Two decades later, Shoreham–Wading River is among the tiny handful of American middle schools that are recognized as genuine pearls of the educational system. It was cited as exemplary in the Carnegie Corporation report *Turning Points,* and singled out as one of four *Successful Schools for Young Adolescents,* a book by North Carolina educator Joan Lipsitz. The school plays host to a steady stream of educators from schools across the country hoping to adapt its methods and copy its success. It is a plain delight to visit: a pleasant, happy place, full of bright-eyed children, gifted teachers and smart administrators. Kids arrive as average students and leave well above their grade level. They go on long field trips, explore careers, perform community service and produce remarkable art, literature and music. They roam the halls on the honor system, without passes, and most of their lockers have no locks. Perhaps even more remarkable, the system that Dennis Littky created survived his passing. A dozen years after he moved on, Shoreham–Wading River's advisory program is even stronger than he left it. It is a tribute to the power of his vision, the talent of the staff he assembled and the creative dedication of his successors. It is also a lesson for anyone who wants to keep a good thing going.

In hindsight, the advisory idea looks obvious, particularly for children in the hormonal tumult of grades six to eight. In most middle schools and junior high schools, students make an abrupt passage from the cocoon of the elementary homeroom to a fragmented day of one class after another, seeing six or eight teachers, each of whom in turn sees perhaps 150 students a day. The bright kids, the natural leaders and the troublemakers get attention. A quiet student who doesn't stand out drifts from teacher to teacher, each of them assuming that somebody else must be close to the kid—but if there's a problem, the student has nowhere to turn and no advocate in the system. The remedy came easily to Littky and his colleagues. Their generation was brought up on J. D. Salinger, and they resonated to Holden Caulfield's vision: There are children at play in a vast field of grain, heedless of a precipice at the edge of the field; Holden's job is to save them, to catch them before they fall over the cliff. Littky's people too would be catchers in the rye. At Shoreham–Wading River, says principal Cary E. Bell, "Nobody falls through the cracks. Every student has someone who knows that student extremely well."

The program is clearly a success, all but universally praised by teachers, students and parents. But despite its long record and the explicit endorsement of the Carnegie report, the advisory program is still a rarity. Nobody knows for sure how many of the nation's 110,000 public schools have adopted some form of advisory, but the high estimates run in the dozens, not the hundreds. To anyone who has seen what goes on at Shoreham–Wading River, that's hard to understand.

"I've got this trouble getting organized," says Matt. "I always say I'll write down what I have to do, but then I never get around to it."

Matt is an eighth-grader, reserved and dark-haired, a quietly intense kid in sneakers, dark corduroy pants and a plaid flannel shirt buttoned right up to the throat. He's having his advisory session, one on one, with Ross Burkhardt, the social studies teacher who has been his mentor, ombudsman, advocate, teacher and friend for the past four months. The two are sitting in a corner of Burkhardt's classroom, with its furniture jumbled from the last class and its walls and ceilings festooned with hundreds of posters, cartoons, maxims, mottoes and exhortations: If not us, who? If not now, when? Life's tough, ain't it. Seize the Day. Expect the unexpected. Follow Instructions. How many real teachers have you had in your entire life? Mr. Burkhardt is a dweeb.

Matt says he bought a notebook to write down what he has to do, but he forgets to use it—"or else I write it down and then there's too much to do."

Burkhardt is sympathetic. Maybe you could ask a buddy to discuss your schedule with you, he suggests, and bug you when you get behind. He tells Matt he's just written a book (*Men Our Age*, a compilation of Studs Terkel–like talks with classmates at his twenty-fifth Dartmouth reunion), "and I made targets for myself. I had to finish fifteen pages before I let myself see a movie. And I had someone who checked me out on that." Matt nods seriously.

"You know what the word *discipline* means?" says Burkhardt.

"Following up on what you have to do?" asks Matt.

"Pretty good definition," says Burkhardt. "You might want to prioritize things. Like, if you have five things to do, which is the most important?"

Matt says he tries, but time runs out. That's okay, says Burkhardt, keep trying; you've got your mind on it now, and if you want to get organized, you'll do it. It's just a matter of being realistic about how much time things take and how much time there is, he says. "You've been fooling yourself. Stop fooling yourself, that's all."

That was what Matt wanted to talk about, and both of them seem content to let it go at that: subject covered. Burkhardt moves on. He has asked Matt to list his accomplishments of the past year and his goals for the next one. Matt pulls out his list, scrawled in pencil on a much-folded piece of paper. He's had a good year: he made the tennis team, got five A's and two B's on his last report card, raised his own money for family birthday presents instead of mooching from his mother, and made it all the way down the toughest trail at the ski resort without falling.

"Good job, Matt. What else? Got a girlfriend?" No, but Matt was named MVP on the baseball team and made a good friend, Joe.

This year, besides getting organized, Matt wants (not *wants*, Burkhardt corrects, he *intends*, and Matt accepts that) to get six A's on his next report card, to move up from doubles to singles in tennis, to stop losing things, to build stronger relationships with his friends and to go to France on the school's language exchange program. He also plans to take lessons in scuba diving and to get a little dog for his brother Dave, since the dog they have now seems to like Matt best and that makes Dave unhappy.

"Good list. Good job," says Burkhardt. Advisory is over.

What's important, Burkhardt says later, is building confidence. "Kids respond to a large extent to how they're treated," he says. "The basic idea that we all agree with is that the kids are going to need support. There will be crises, and you need to develop the trust before the crisis. You don't develop the trust in the middle of the crisis." Matt had been due for a conference anyway, but he had wanted to talk about getting organized, and that was fine: He was ready to deal with that problem, and Burkhardt would follow it up as the year went along. The listing of goals and achievements is just a device Burkhardt finds useful once a year, a way of helping the kids to get some perspective on their lives.

Why had Burkhardt simply accepted Matt's agenda, without suggesting any larger goals? "I don't have any right to set up his agenda. I'm just interested in them looking at the idea that they can list accomplishments and declare intentions," says Burkhardt. "Look, this is the fourth or fifth conference I've had with Matt, and there's a lot of information I bring to it. What you saw was not anything but the Matt

I know. He was not off his center. That's the kid I know, so there was not much need for me to steer him back to reality." But shouldn't Burkhardt at least have suggested that Matt might want to find out whether his parents were up to having another dog around the house? "I should have done that," he says. "Sometimes I'm not very fast on my feet. I will do that."

It's hard to imagine Ross Burkhardt not being fast on his feet. He's a teacher most kids adore, tall and lean in his sneakers, dark slacks and rolled-up sleeves, with piercing eyes, vast energy and only a minor thinning of his sandy hair to show his years. His clear tenor voice can stop a dozen simultaneous adolescent conversations, and he is comfortably at home in the bewildering fast-forward world of the pre-teen, which crams the emotions of a whole Italian opera into the attention span of a gerbil. In class, he is part showman, part ringmaster, part oracle and all awareness; he flicks from one subject to the next, keeping even a roomful of thirteen-year-olds straining to follow. But he is tuned uncannily to the twitch or uncertain monosyllable that hints that a wallflower may be about to blossom, and he will stop a whole class dead to wait for that thought and celebrate its arrival.

He is tolerant, friendly and interested, but candid and straightforward to the point of roughness. A boy we'll call Kevin has complained about getting downgraded for turning in a report on notepaper instead of three-by-five cards, as instructed. Burkhardt explains it, for Kevin and the class. You're a good kid, he tells Kevin, and one bad mark isn't going to ruin your record. But he pulls no punches: "Here's the thing, Kevin. The world doesn't care about you. Just like a bus is gonna hit you if you walk in front of it, the world is gonna step on you if you don't do the right thing. You have to take responsibility. There are penalties for what you don't do, and you have to start learning to take care of yourself." He points to the sign, Follow Instructions. The instructions were to use cards. If Kevin had lost his cards, Burkhardt could have given him more. And what about the bibliography that was supposed to be handed in with the report? There wasn't any bibliography.

"Okay, Kevin? Anything more to say?" This isn't browbeating; Burkhardt wants to be sure Kevin understands and has no more points to argue. No, says Kevin, not at all sullenly. Another subject is closed.

And Burkhardt has made another deposit in his trust account with the whole class. He doesn't make exceptions and he doesn't deal in cotton candy; they can count on him to tell the truth and be fair.

The teachers at Shoreham–Wading River aren't all like Ross Burkhardt, of course. His wife, Diane, who also teaches eighth grade, is quieter, more intense, a prober, a woman who wears deliberate calm like armor against the surging sea of adolescence around her. Jerry Silverstein, the school's media teacher, is a fast-spieling enthusiast with a core of reflection. Frank Caldorale, who teaches social studies, is a curly-haired punster who treasures his kids for their meteoric unpredictability: Lewis Carroll, he says, had prepubescents in mind when he wrote *Alice in Wonderland*. Bob Coons, who teaches science, is more dry and reserved, with a twist of humor at the mouth and a vast sandbox filling one corner of his classroom—to teach archeological technique, he explains. All of them have their own advisory styles, with varying degrees of closeness. Some advisers take kids out to the bagel shop for their conferences. Some take their whole advisory group, eight to ten kids, to movies or on camping trips, or to New York City to see a play or the Museum of Modern Art. Some never leave the school. It doesn't matter. The point is to stay in touch, really know the students, make sure somebody is there when there's a problem.

At Shoreham–Wading River, a middle-class school in a semirural community seventy miles from the urban woes of New York City, the problems that advisers face are seldom life-threatening. Weapons and hard drugs have come up only three or four times in the school's history; there have been some drug- and sex-abuse problems involving families or older kids, but the most common crises are with kids who feel friendless, students at odds with teachers or other kids, or children trying to cope with a divorce or death in the family. Advisory systems have worked in schools where the problems can be a good deal more serious; Cary Bell came to his principal's office from a job teaching homeless and troubled adolescents at Boys Town, which also had an advisory program. As he says dryly, "We were doing similar things with a very different population." But a problem needn't be life-threatening to be serious. As parents know, even minor crises can be overwhelming to children who haven't yet developed their own identity and sense of perspective, and a trivial mistake can sometimes lead to a permanent wrong turn for a sensitive adolescent. That's where the advisers can make a difference.

It isn't only teachers who are advisers. Each advisory group should be as small as possible, to make sure the kids get maximum attention and to encourage them to bond as a group, so the school recruits administrators, coaches, the librarian, nearly every adult in the school to function as advisers. Cary Bell takes a group most years; so does his assistant principal, Bonne Sue Adams; so does Joanne Urgese, who runs the community service program and explains the school to its many visitors. With most of the adults pitching in, the advisory groups are no larger than eight to ten students.

The forty-minute, one-on-one conferences are the heart of the advisory system, but the glue that holds it together is the fact that each advisory group meets twice a day: for twelve minutes to begin each morning, and again for fifteen minutes to eat lunch together in the adviser's classroom or office. It doesn't sound like much time, but teachers and pupils alike testify to the importance of these daily gatherings. Each group becomes a small family in the school community, with a closeness that tends to last even when the students move on to new groups and new advisers. The morning meeting is like a mini-homeroom, with attendance taken, announcements made and a salute to the flag. But there is also the exchange of gossip and quick, glancing discussion of school, local and even world events. If a student is absent, a "homework partner" will call her that evening to pass on the assignments for the day. The brown-bag lunches involve sharing food and confidences; each group backs up its members in the small daily crises and victories of school life. Advisers see each student in all the roles that child is exploring, and the group excursions out of school or projects inside the walls serve to bond students together in learning experiences.

Students like advisory. Like kids everywhere, accepting whatever comes their way, most of them think this is just the way school is; a few, who have transferred to Shoreham–Wading River from conventional schools, are bowled over by the school's freedom, tolerance and openness. Over the years, the school's literature has quoted kids praising their advisers and their groups: "I can trust him." "You can hang out and relax there." "It sets the mood for the day and even the year." "With the kids in your advisory, you always have somebody you can talk to." "The best part is knowing that you can talk to your adviser on your level and he can relate to your problems." Or, as Joan Lipsitz quoted a seventh-grader in her book, "They absolutely know me here." Advisory group becomes a kind of safe haven in the school, a secure base camp for the assault on new peaks. Complaints about the system are rare; as a seventh-grade girl named Chris told a visitor, "I never heard of an adviser who wasn't fair. My friend had an adviser she didn't really like last year, and that wasn't as nice, but it was okay. And she got a better one this year."

Advisers are matched with kids in a long consultative process, taking into account personalities, interests and recent history ("No, not John. I flunked his brother, and his parents don't like me; it wouldn't work"). In the course of the year, each adviser has seven or eight forty-minute conferences with each student in the group, and the adviser meets with each kid's parents at least twice. The adviser is a student's main link to the school. If there's a discipline problem, for instance, a teacher or administrator takes it to the adviser; the adviser consults on any punishment, deals it out to the student and explains the situation to the parents. If a student feels badly treated by the school or another teacher, the adviser serves as advocate, interceding for the student and pleading her cause. Each adviser is constantly switching hats, but nobody seems to mind. "Everybody has gone to bat for a kid against another teacher," says Jerry Silverstein. "So there are no hard feelings." Sometimes, in the heat of a crisis, kids just can't explain what has happened. One of Joanne Urgese's charges was thrown out of class for kicking another boy. What he didn't manage to tell the teacher was that the kick was in retaliation for one that she hadn't seen—and when Urgese explained that, the case was reopened and punishment was spread out more equitably.

New advisers often find the role uncomfortable. "New teachers say, 'Well, what am I going to do, face to face with a single kid for forty minutes?' " says Cary Bell. So the school provides a nine-page "Advisory Handbook," laying out minimum standards, suggesting topics of conversation and possible group projects, and issuing a few cautions. Advisers are warned against trying to be psychologists or getting overly involved in a child's family life, and they are told to call in the principal, the school psychologist or a guidance counselor when needed. In the beginning, most advisers follow the book. But they grow into the role, fitting it to their own personalities. "It's not my style to get too close to the kids," says Bob Coons. "They need their own space, and I respect their privacy." Diane Burkhardt, in contrast, is known as a strong, involved adviser. And most of them have their own slant on what the role demands, differing in degree but not in essentials. "The essential part of advisory is being an advocate for your kids, an intermediary," says Diane Wikstrom, a French teacher. Frank Caldorale thinks some teachers get too close to their kids. "I'm not here to be their friend," he says. "If a friendship develops, that's fine, but I'm a teacher first." But as Ross Burkhardt sees it, what advisers need at bottom "is the attitude that there's these eight kids out there who are very special to me. Look, I walk down the hall and look into a classroom and there's Robin. She looks up and I wave. It takes an eighth of a second, and nobody else notices, and we go back to our work. I'm doing advisory when I do that. She knows there's somebody who cares about her."

The new girl—call her Jill—has been having trouble fitting in. After six weeks in the eighth grade she still has no real friends, not even in Diane Burkhardt's advisory group. Burkhardt discusses it with other members of her teaching team, in their regular Friday morning meeting, and then more guardedly in the Monday morning staff meeting for all fifty-five adults in the school.

"We brainstormed activities she might be part of," she recalls. "It wouldn't work to try to force-feed her into things." Since Jill is a reader, perhaps out of lonely necessity, she is introduced to the yearbook staff and the people who run *Contemplations*, the prize winning literary magazine. She is also encouraged to sign up for community service: It often happens that low achievers and wallflowers turn out to be good at helping other people. They can outshine the academic stars when they're dealing with old folks or handicapped children.

But a big part of Jill's problem is her hair—unkempt, dirty, a shame and a handicap. Other kids shun her and snicker, with that sure childhood instinct for the wrong kind of difference, and she is self-conscious and ashamed, but seemingly unable to do anything about it. "So we brought in the social worker and the school nurse," says Burkhardt, "to find out if there was a health problem and to check out the home situation." Their findings aren't encouraging: The family seems barely functional, but there is no real ground for interfering. Instead, Diane encourages Jill to come to school on the early bus, the one that brings kids for advisory conferences, band practice, preschool gym and club activities. Diane will keep a bottle of shampoo and some rinse in her desk. Jill can shower in the locker room and wash her hair before advisory group starts the day at 8:30.

All of Jill's problems haven't been solved. But she has a poem coming out in *Contemplations*, she's working well with a brain-damaged child, and she's fitting into the group a little better these days.

There's nothing exceptional about the Shoreham—Wading River community. It's middle-class, mostly blue-collar territory, overwhelmingly white and heavily Roman Catholic, two hours out of New York and well past commuting range. It isn't the kind of community that demands intellectual excellence, or complains when its kids don't make the Ivy League. The population includes a few farm families, some workers from the aerospace plants and small factories closer to the city, numerous shopkeepers, policemen and local government workers, a few scientists and technicians from the nearby Brookhaven Laboratories. There are quite a few teachers from other communities who know the school's reputation and want their own kids to go there. And of course there are some people from the Lilco plant, the nuclear fiasco that has shaped the school's destiny.

Long Island Lighting Co.'s Shoreham nuclear plant was just a $506 million plan in 1972. But partly in anticipation of the plant and its payroll, the area was growing fast enough that nearby Port Jefferson, which had been taking kids from Shoreham and Wading River in its junior and senior high schools, had notified the two towns that they would have to build their own schools. That set off several years of turbulence. The Shoreham school board, introduced to the progressive reform movement by a district principal, started thinking about a middle school instead of a conventional junior high school. The board's first significant move was to reject an architect's proposal for an egg-crate classroom building in favor of the newly fashionable open classroom concept.

But the board's biggest gamble was Dennis Littky, a professor at the Stony Brook campus of the State University of New York who was crusading for liberal change in the schools. Littky was only twenty-seven, with a flaming red beard, radical ideas about schools and a casual way of dressing; alarmed parents instantly labeled him a hippie. But the district principal recommended him, and the board took a chance. For two years, while the middle school and high school were being built, Littky installed his ideas while presiding over a messy and sometimes chaotic set of improvised arrangements. He had his backers, vigorous and hardworking, but there was open warfare between them and the traditionalist parents who demanded order, discipline and the three R's. Littky fought, often brilliantly, to win over the critics. He refused to compromise on curriculum, but defused the hippie image by keeping the school immaculate. He organized a cell-like network of neighborhood representatives to spike rumors, respond to complaints and educate their neighbors about the new methods. He set up orientation meetings to explain the school, and he had parents reading John Dewey on basic philosophy and Fritz Redl and Charity James on the needs of young adolescents. In the end, he prevailed; the school was simply too good to be denied. The academic record speaks for itself: At last reading, Shoreham–Wading River's kids, whose IQ averaged an unremarkable 112, were scoring two years above grade level in math, and three years above grade in English, on the Stanford Achievement Test in the seventh grade. Perhaps as much to the point, the school was obviously a wonderful place to be. Parents actually complained that they couldn't get their kids to come home at the end of the day.

Littky's greatest achievement was his staff. He recruited a set of young, idealistic teachers already imbued with his zeal for child-centered schools; then he gave them a loose rein and backed them fiercely. They recall him with something close to worship, as an inspired leader who could lift them to heights of creativity and endless hours of work for the cause. "His charisma made you want to try things," says Diane Wikstrom. "If it didn't work, that was okay. You'd try something else." Nobody was picky about punching clocks. If an evening meeting was called, nobody even asked if he would be paid for attending. They were outsiders in the community, knowing only each other, living their lives in the school, bound together by the hostility of the angry parents and the excitement of their common work.

They recall it now as old soldiers savor a long-gone campaign, finding the present stale and pedestrian by contrast. There is a degree of grumbling about the new regime and its changes, and the old-timers struggle to keep things in perspective. "We used to talk about becoming old farts who can talk about nothing but how it was in my day," says Jerry Silverstein, "and that has happened to some extent." He was present at the creation, and so was Ross Burkhardt. "I don't have a complaint. Why wouldn't I be happy here?" says Burkhardt, not sounding altogether sure. "For Christ's sake, I can do what I want. I work in a place filled with professionals where I get all sorts of support, and I'm acknowledged for what I do. What am I looking for? What is anybody looking for? My God, people who are bitching or complaining about this, they should spend just one day anywhere else." Teachers at Shoreham–Wading River have autonomy and responsibility, he concludes. If that sounds a lame, anticlimactic note, how could it be otherwise? What are autonomy and responsibility compared to youth, and the glory of building something new and fine?

From the beginning, advisory was the core of Littky's vision, the heart of a school designed not to fill passive kids with information but to help questing youngsters past the perilous shoals of pubescence. There was also to be team teaching, to make lessons flexible and maximize the time each teacher spent with a child, and cross-disciplinary teaching, integrating studies in the four core subjects of English, social studies, math and science. There would be extensive field trips to provide experiential learning and expose children to the real world. Community service would teach them the joys of helping others and being part of the world they lived in. There would be real art and music classes, good drama, a sports program not just for jocks but for everyone. The school would be open, responsive to new ideas, ready to experiment. It would be a happy place.

It was the staff that made all that happen. But there was help from an unlikely corner: Lilco's Shoreham plant was growing too, nowhere near as successfully as the school. Costs multiplied tenfold and deadlines slipped. Antinuclear activists kept up a drumroll of protests about pollution and safety factors. As the plant grew, the utility paid huge taxes based on its swelling investment, and the school system got its share; by 1990, when the plant was providing 90 percent of the community's property taxes, the middle school was spending more than $11,000 for each of its 452 students—nearly two and a half times the national average. Teacher salaries averaged $49,062. Field trips stretched to four or five days spent wandering the battlefield at Gettysburg, four weeks studying the ecology of the seashore and the mountains. The school acquired an added gymnasium, carpeted hallways, two sets of bus runs every day. The twelve-acre campus, dotted with scrub oak and pine, sprouted a small farm, complete with livestock, barn and greenhouse, to be used as a teaching resource and maintained by the students themselves. The school filled with computers, audiovisual devices, TV editing equipment, music synthesizers. The community service program burgeoned. Kids sallied out on yet more field trips to explore career options. A new foreign language exchange program began sending students on trips to France and Spain.

Some people started saying that if anything symbolized Shoreham–Wading River Middle School, it was money. But the golden goose is dying. By 1991, the antinuke protesters seemed to have won their crusade. Lilco announced that it was abandoning the Shoreham plant, after a decade of building and $5.5 billion down the drain. The utility would continue to make payments in lieu of taxes, but they would be phased out over ten years. The hard times haven't yet arrived for the school, but they are on the way. Can Shoreham–Wading River survive with its spirit intact? Cary Bell says the answer is yes—that the character of the school was set before the funds started rolling in, and that what matters is ideas and people, not money. Whatever happens, he says, the advisory system will never be abandoned. "It's part of the fabric of the school," he says. "It would be difficult to imagine the school without it. I can't picture the board or anyone else thinking of eliminating advisory."

Shoreham–Wading River has already survived a crisis, more traumatic in its way than losing funding: It lost Dennis Littky. Restless and burned out, he left town in 1978 to recharge his batteries in a mountaintop cabin in New Hampshire, where he would go on to wage new battles and duplicate his triumphs as the reforming principal of Thayer High School in the hardscrabble mill town of Winchester. But his going left a huge hole and a permanent sense of loss. Littky's successor, Cary Bell, knows that he will always be measured against a memory considerably larger than life; even though the pioneers recruited by Littky are now a minority of the staff, they set a tone, and there's a faction that will always find Bell wanting. Diane Burkhardt, for instance, complains about "unilateral" decisions. But she concedes ruefully that the pioneers "think we own the place, and we still think we ought to be calling the shots." She credits Bell with good intentions and a solid record of his own innovations. But "Dennis is a rare person, someone who empowers people," she says. And as she sees it, "Cary and Bonne Sue Adams are not inspired leaders. It frustrates me sometimes. . . . What's missing is a sense of vision. We should be able to count on them to call us to the next level."

"I have no illusions," says Bell. "I'm not the sort of person Dennis was. At first, I might have felt badly that I wasn't. But it doesn't mean you can't be a good leader and an effective person and run a good school." In fact, Bell says, "Had Dennis stayed, people tell me he could not have lasted another year. It would have been a mess, because he's very good at creating things, but in terms of sustaining, he's not."

Beyond dispute, Cary Bell is good at sustaining. He is a calm, even-handed, measured and measuring man, remarkably open and candid, an innovator who can also compromise. He is soft-spoken and self-assured, if a bit defensive about his no-win position as Littky's replacement. Though Bell is black, a surprising choice to head a school with only six black students, this fact seems truly irrelevant in the context of Shoreham–Wading River; whatever quarrels people have with him, they aren't about race. What strikes a visitor is that Bell gets credit only in passing for his own remarkable record: keeping the best of Littky's vision, actually improving some features of it and adding new programs of his own. Working in Littky's permanent shadow, he has made it Cary Bell's school.

Bell wasn't the first in the line of succession. He was a finalist for the job when Littky left, but the staff argued strongly that Littky's assistant principal, Jane Wittmore, should get the job, and the board went along. Her two-year rule has been called a caretaker administration devoted mainly to keeping the flame alive. When she resigned, she went back to teaching in the school, and this time Bell got the job. He came to it from a career in private education, ending at Boys Town. And from the beginning, he understood the rare quality of the system he was taking over.

"I felt it was almost like a sacred thing, to keep this school," he says. The problem remains to know what to keep, what to replace, what has served its purpose: the school must be a living thing, not a shrine. If the Hawthorne effect is to keep working, there must be new programs from time to time to keep alive the school's excitement and sense of adventure. But the staff has changed too, as both Bell and the pioneers observe. As the years have passed, youthful dedication has ebbed, and tie-dyed T-shirts and granny glasses have given way to teenage children and station wagons. There isn't the old automatic willingness to give up perks and work overtime; the union has become a bigger force. The pendulum of academic reform has swung back to basics, and some teachers who used to push openness and self-esteem now favor shorter field trips and more academic rigor.

The sum of Bell's changes is impressive. Shortly after his accession, he moved to bring order out of chaos in the school's daily life. Littky had run the school on a different schedule every day, a source of endless confusion; Bell unified the schedule, to almost universal relief. In the process, he changed the sacred advisory system by inaugurating the advisory lunch. Previously, large classes had eaten lunch together—as Ross Burkhardt observes dryly, "Not a good idea"—and this innovation too was unanimously judged an improvement. Gone and all but forgotten is the onetime institution of "sustained silent reading," or SSR, in which students used to begin the day with twenty-five minutes of recreational reading. But Bell has greatly expanded Littky's community service program. To bring a touch of diversity to his monochrome district, he has recruited three black teachers, stressed human-rights studies and begun exchange programs with inner-city schools. He encourages such academic eccentricities as Bob Coons's archeological sandbox, along with countless projects in multimedia presentation, unconventional music and the like. And it is Cary Bell who gets credit for the language exchange programs, in which several dozen students a year spend two weeks or more visiting schools in Quebec, France and Spain.

Bell has some of Littky's touch at public relations. He puts out a stream of memos, letters and brochures to keep the community informed about his school, and he has set up a visitors' program, complete with a lunch prepared and hosted by the kids, for the dozen or so curious educators who troop through every month. And in the vital area of recruiting and hiring, he has found staffer after staffer who responds to the school's spirit and basic premise. Assistant principal Bonne Sue Adams, for instance, was a runner-up in the second search for a new principal, but leaped at the chance to be second in command because "This is where I want to be. These people really believe in what they're doing." She is large and tousled, with red hair fringing her face and a voice full of West Virginia; she also has a vast fund of energy, warmth and humor, and her own hearty commitment to children. "Look at 'em," she says, waving at the corridor teeming with kids outside her office window. They are gawky, lovely, shrieking, hangdog, sullen and endearing by turns, self-important and shy. They are middle-school kids, a vast lode of promise just about halfway to civilization. "*Somebody's* got to love 'em," she says.

But it is never easy to maintain a vision. Bell fights a constant rearguard action against the traditionalists who still don't see the benefits of child-centered schools. There is the state, with its new push for stringent testing; there are the parents who move into the district because they have heard it's a good school, but are then horrified to find it isn't their old parochial straitjacket. And there are always staffers who get tired of the effort, or who lose the faith. Bell sometimes winds up fighting Littky's own partisans: "I find myself defending what I think they should be defending, because they've moved into some other place."

A couple of years ago, there was something approaching a schism in the school, with some teachers and parents urging major reforms to stress discipline and academic content rather than make students feel good about themselves. In a penetrating article about the conflict in the *Phi Delta Kappan*, the magazine of the national teachers' society, educational writer Gene I. Maeroff came down on the side of "exuberance," but concluded basically that the school was a good one by any measurement. The schism is subsiding these days, with the resolution largely in the Littky tradition. There are more field trips of a single day, fewer of four or five; on the other hand, more visiting speakers are being scheduled to bring the world to Shoreham–Wading River instead of the other way around. The staff has voted to stop giving the Stanford Achievement Test, and has asked the state's permission to experiment with a new grading system, based on students' portfolios of their own work and evaluations of classes by visiting experts. The important thing, says Bell, is to keep the school child-centered, and for all the talk of schism, the truth about Shoreham–Wading River is that "even the people you'd call tough academicians have a child-centered approach. Even for those people, the kid is more important than the content of the course."

Maeroff put his finger on another special quality of Shoreham–Wading River: its concern for every child works to benefit the vast bulk of kids who are neither superstars nor in need of special help. Bowing to parental agitation and the real needs of a few kids, Bell has installed a program for gifted and talented youngsters to match its special education program for handicapped children. "The school can't deny that there are special needs, and we see special at both ends of the spectrum," says Bonne Sue Adams. But the school refuses to expand the gifted program beyond 1 or 2 percent of the students, she says; just as with kids who are educationally challenged, most of the talented children will be mainstreamed in heterogeneous classes, as middle school reformers have always urged.

For the woman we'll call Mary Andrews and her husband, it was a major financial strain to move into the Shoreham–Wading River district. But they are glad they did. Their younger son, Harry, a special education student, hadn't been doing well in his old school. There was hardly any mainstreaming for special ed kids, and there were a lot of putdowns from teachers and other students. Harry has blossomed in the Shoreham–Wading River system, doing well in his mainstream classes and becoming a team manager; his mother chokes up a little when she tells about going to a game and watching Harry, earnestly and carefully keeping his records.

But in a way, the older boy, Carl, has done even better. He was a quiet, inconspicuous kid, one who never made the honors list or got picked for special projects at the other school. "They were really big on the gifted and talented program," she says. "That meant, every time you went to the school for a play or an honors program, you saw all the same kids up there." At Shoreham–Wading River, Carl's adviser got to know him and recommended him for the accelerated math program, and "he really came out of his shell."

In fact, she was a little appalled at Carl's effrontery the time he called his adviser at home, at night, to talk about a trip he was supposed to take with a boy he didn't much like. She wasn't at all sure it was okay to bother the adviser—"I was like, Whooo"—but the adviser wasn't bothered at all. "He just told him, 'It'll be fine, Carl, we'll work it out in the morning,' and they did." She also worried that Carl would get too far behind in his work when he went off for three weeks on the Spanish exchange program, but that worked out too: He came back and caught right up.

Mary Andrews isn't taking anything for granted. After her boys are safely through the school, she says, "I'll kiss the ground here." Until then, she's ready for trouble. But she likes the school's attitude. She remembers a parents' meeting where the traditionalists were complaining that the gifted and talented program is too small, and that there isn't even an honor roll. She quotes Cary Bell's answer with quiet approval: "We have to serve *all* the children."

What would it take to set up an advisory program in an ordinary school? As Dennis Littky sees it, the idea can work anywhere and in almost any kind of formal structure. In fact, he says, it probably exists to some extent already: "If a school is truly kid-oriented, whether they formally adopt an advisory system or not, you'll find something like it in that school."

Littky is coming up on fifty now, with a good deal of gray in his red hair and beard, and his forehead has expanded past his ears. But the eyes under the wire-rimmed glasses still flash impatiently, and he still dresses like a hippie, in two-tone black sweatshirt, gray chinos and sneakers. His dog pads around his office in the Thayer school, with its shabby old desk piled high with unreturned phone messages. Littky still forgets appointments, schmoozes in hallways when he should be meeting important people and raises conventional hackles: It set off a three-year community war in Winchester when the school board tried to get rid of him back in the '80s, mainly because they didn't like his style. In the end, the voters threw the school board out instead.

Winchester is a dirt-poor town, with nothing like the Shoreham nuclear plant to support luxuries. So the advisory program Littky has now can't afford, as Shoreham–Wading River does, to count advisory time as a formal teaching period. That means less time spent face to face, less time for advisers to confer with each other, less structure to the whole program. What makes it work, he says, is the advisers' conviction that it's important: "You just have to believe in the system, that there will be an advocate for every kid." Like Shoreham–Wading River, Thayer starts the day with a short advisory group meeting. Littky finds ways to compensate teachers for time spent in individual conferences. These meetings aren't as frequent as at Shoreham–Wading River, but kids are encouraged to keep journals, which give advisers added insights. Advisers keep in touch with their students' parents, and they stay with a kid for the full four years of high school instead of switching off every year. That has pluses and minuses, Littky says; both sides gain in depth and intensity of the relationship, but lose some diversity and breadth of acquaintance in the school. It all works, he says, because nobody thinks the advisory system is a frill. "You should simply demand that every kid has an adult mentor."

Beyond that, Cary Bell and his colleagues agree on several desirable features for any advisory program:

• **Keep the group small.** Eight to ten students is probably the optimum number; Jerry Silverstein thinks the maximum would be about fifteen.

• **Daily meetings of the advisory groups are essential.**

• **Don't limit advisers to teachers.** Reach out to recruit all the adults in the building, down to the janitor if he wants to take part. The Hawthorne spinoffs in building morale and unifying the school are enormous.

• **Advisers need support.** They can get by with a minimum of formal training, but they should have a written handbook and informal guidance from experienced colleagues who are on call. They must be backed up with professional help in a real crisis.

• **Advisers must know the limits of their role.** They are teachers, not counselors, psychiatrists or best friends. They may be tempted to be surrogate parents, and in some cases, says Bell, that may be the right thing to do. But in most cases advisers should avoid too much closeness, intruding on a parent's territory or setting up as a rival for affection or loyalty.

• **A student's adviser should be his main contact with the school.** If there is a disciplinary problem, the adviser should be consulted, and should notify the student of the penalty. Advisers must also be ombudsmen, interceding for their students in any conflict with other teachers or staff.

• **Be alert to the danger of unhealthy relationships.** There has never been a hint of sexual abuse at Shoreham–Wading River, Bell says, but it's always possible. The main safeguard, says Ross Burkhardt, is merely a good teacher's sense of professionalism and responsibility. But everybody is human.

There will probably be resistance from some teachers to a new advisory system, Ross Burkhardt says. Not all teachers are dedicated enough to make the effort involved; some are burned out, and some have never accepted the basic idea of child-centered education. But even if a fifth of the advisers are dragging their feet, says Burkhardt, the kids will be better served with an advisory system than without one, and in time the resisters will either be converted or leave. What's important is to establish human relationships. Just as doctors shouldn't see their patients merely as a damaged heart, a ruptured appendix or a broken arm, so educators must see children, all the children, as human beings. At bottom, that's all it takes—but it's a lot.

It's harder to codify the school's success in making the transition from Dennis Littky to Cary Bell. Bell himself deserves a large helping of credit: Without his understanding and enthusiasm for Littky's vision, it would surely have withered. His innovations have been both ingenious and faithful to the spirit of the original. Even his compromises, like the gifted and talented program, have been minimal, and they are in tune with the changing times: no principal can afford to ignore political realities, and the educational trend toward academic achievement and accountability is becoming just that.

The program has bowed to another reality, adjusting to a lower level of intensity. As no less a critic than Diane Burkhardt remarks, nothing stays the same for twenty years, and the young zealots who founded the school have lost some of their own drive while their new colleagues arrive with a cooler view. It's symbolic that Diane Burkhardt and Diane Wikstrom are both representatives for the teachers' union now; they are hardly militants, but they do look to the contract to make sure that teachers get their due, and that time freely given doesn't turn into time stolen. Some teachers are even talking about being paid for field trips. What with one thing and another, the trips get shorter and formalities are taken more seriously. "We're doing the same thing different ways," says Bonne Sue Adams.

But even if the zeal has dwindled, none of Bell's moves would have worked without the talent, dedication and intelligence of the Shoreham–Wading River staff. They are a remarkable group of people. In an outsider's view, in fact, the tensions among the staff are themselves a token that creative ferment is alive and well. It's only when people care deeply about what they are doing that they bother to argue principles, and the staff carries on a permanent impassioned debate about everything from the merits of testing to the fundamental premises of teaching. Here again Bell deserves credit for his hiring talent—but then, the quality of the applicants also reflects the school's reputation and the brilliance of the founding rebels. Whether it was the chicken or the egg that came first, its name was Littky.

In the shabby old office in Winchester, Dennis Littky is being gracious. He knows Cary could have killed off the whole vision, he says; it takes a big man to do what Cary has done, and it's too bad he has to be defensive about following somebody else's act.

Well, says a visitor, you throw a big shadow.

"Yes," says Littky, unsmiling. "I do."

14.
Putting Kids
First

Despair drives the call for revolution. It's only when people decide that the system is past saving that they are willing to consider dynamiting the schools and starting over. And despair is understandable; across the country, the educational structure often seems frozen and immovable, a dead weight stifling change.

But these twelve stories prove that despair is not warranted. The cynics are wrong: We can make our schools better. We don't have to destroy the system or wait for radical reforms on a national scale, with all the cost, delay and disruption they will bring. These twelve programs, chosen almost at random from hundreds of similar efforts around the country, prove that educators and parents can find their own ways to make schools that help children learn. Money helps, and money is available, but it needn't take a million dollars to improve a school. Educational theory is important, but it isn't necessary to graft on a whole new system of teaching.

What *is* needed is a way of thinking about children—an attitude that all these programs have in common. It has nothing to do with sentimentality. "*Somebody's* got to love 'em," said Bonne Sue Adams at Shoreham–Wading River, and it's true that children need love, but not necessarily from their schools. What they need from their schools is respect: respect for all the children, the bright students and the slow learners and all the kids in between. Children are people in progress whose business is learning. They have needs, and they have responsibilities. They must be understood as individuals, challenged to their limits, held accountable for their work and helped as they need help.

It is all too easy for schools to lose that focus on children. Systems develop their own imperatives. Progress is measured in test scores, lesson plans filed, pages covered in the book, assignments passed out and papers graded. Faces blur. A child becomes a set of numbers on a file card. In a whole day, as William Gibbons of HOSTS discovered, a student may get less than one minute of a teacher's undivided attention. Kids who fail or just don't fit get shunted off with the other goats to the remedial class, on the assumption that they are defective— damaged merchandise. The overall message is that the kids don't matter, and it is a deadly message. William Glasser, a psychiatrist and school reformer, writes in *The Quality School* that children do badly in class mainly because they don't work hard, and they stop working because they believe that no one in the system cares about them or what they do. Caring means simply respect: recognition that they exist and matter.

Teachers who begin as idealists can learn to ignore and even despise children who fail or misbehave. Carol Kolar recalls that when she was teaching traditional remedial classes at Parkway North, "When the kids made trouble I really disliked them." They had become a threat and a challenge, rejecting her and making it harder for her to teach other children who had a right to learn. That's a process that can happen in any school; most people can recall from their own school days escalating wars between teachers and classroom rebels. The breakdown is worst and most corrosive in inner-city schools, where the teacher's reaction may be colored by cultural differences or outright racism. Teachers begin to look through the kids, take their failures for granted, dismiss them as already lost to the civilized world and not worth caring about. There is a telling verb in the language of the ghetto: to *diss*, which means, quite literally, to disrespect. Slum dwellers go through life being dissed, by everyone in authority—bosses, policemen, social workers, desk clerks in hospital emergency rooms. It stokes a rage that can become homicidal. In the inner city, a person can get killed for dissing somebody. Kids get their first taste of it in school.

When the system is changed, however, even teachers who have begun to despair can relearn respect for children. "Just from working in a smaller group, you find out they're people," Kolar says. "You recognize their low self-esteem. Then you can handle an incident on a personal level. You can take the kid aside and say, 'Hey, why are you doing this to me? I'm on your side, remember?' And that's usually enough." For the student, that personal level acknowledges humanity and personal worth. It is the beginning of learning.

Good schools and good teachers know, with Cary Bell, that "The kid is more important than the content of the course." With Al Haskvitz, they know that the first priority is not learning facts, but learning how to learn, and that children do best when learning is interesting and fun. Like Rosemarie Stocky, they set out to build "a culture where everybody can work together for the benefit of the kids." And the kids get the message, a dozen signals every day that they are important and worth some effort. Juan Gonzales is trusted to be a teacher. Leah sees the scratches on Clarissa's wrist. Ross Burkhardt waves at Robin from the corridor.

But true respect for children also includes holding them to the highest standards they can achieve. Looking at these twelve programs, it's easy to mistake their warmth and caring for permissiveness. Centering education on children doesn't mean approving of everything they do, or lowering goals when students are too lazy to reach higher. Real respect comes with toughness and discipline. These educators know that to let kids think that there are no rules, that nothing much is demanded of them, is a kind of child abuse. Haskvitz is stingy with his A's. Jennifer Matthews gets Kolar's message: shape up or ship out; make something of your life. Ross Burkhardt tells Kevin the truth, that the world will step on him if he doesn't measure up.

The main principles of small-bite programs follow naturally from that central core of respect for children. Given respect, it's a matter of course that all children can learn; naturally, expectations will be set high; obviously, schools work with kids instead of on them, and use the students as active partners in their own education. All that holds true whether the program is community service, helping parents with preschoolers, using underachievers as tutors or harnessing the boundless energy of eighth-graders to lobby the legislature. When educators have respect for kids, kids are the best thing they have going for them.

There's more to good schools than that, of course. Successful innovators won't be distracted by the delusion of the magic bullet that will cure all ills overnight. They know how to spot a real problem and make a practical effort to solve it, one step at a time, on a scale big enough to work but small enough to be manageable. They know how to borrow ideas. They won't permit the best to be the enemy of the good. They watch their budgets and operate on a shoestring if they have to: "You learn to work with what you have," says Mildred Winter of PAT. They welcome ideas and reach out for help; as Jim Turner puts it, "There are a lot of ways to help kids learn, and a lot of people can be involved." Small-bite reform makes use of parents and community volunteers and outside professionals when necessary, and the innovators use that help creatively to bolster their programs and develop political support. Like Dennis Littky and Bill Douglas, they have an eye for selfless and dedicated talent. Like Douglas, Al Haskvitz and Jim Thom, they are horn-blowers with an eye for effective publicity.

Innovators tend to see things that are too obvious for most people to notice. It took Bob Coplan to understand that kids in Cleveland didn't need more scholarship money, but a vision of going to college and a little help in coping with the formalities. Similarly, schools have been penny-pinching operations for so long that teachers themselves tend to take it for granted that they don't have telephones, so it seemed almost revolutionary when PIT started Parent Line and Dial-a-Teacher in Indianapolis.

The examples don't end with this book. At Vanderbilt University, Jerold Bauch has taken the telephone idea even further: He is marketing a program that combines classroom telephones with a computerized message center. That gives teachers the option to send voice messages to selected parents, to record general messages for any parents calling in, and to receive messages in return. Bauch says schools using the system have chalked up increases as high as 580 percent in the number of contacts between parents and teachers. The spinoffs include better attendance, higher homework completion, more parent-school involvement and, ultimately, more learning and higher test scores.

Sometimes the insights for programs come from dogged research. At the University of California at Berkeley in 1979, Uri Treisman was trying to understand why Asian students routinely did well at freshman calculus while blacks had the highest failure rates, even when they came with high SAT scores. After an eighteen-month study, Treisman discounted all the conventional explanations involving poverty, cultural attitudes toward learning, low motivation and the like. The difference turned out to be simple. Black high achievers were self-reliant loners who had succeeded almost in spite of their families and friends; Asians were used to taking advantage of networks, and they formed study groups. When Treisman nudged black students into organizing a study workshop, their failure rate fell from 60 percent to 4 percent. The discovery led to a workshop program that quickly spread through the California system and to thirty other universities.

Perhaps most important, the best programs understand the Hawthorne effect and aim to provoke it. That sense of excitement and involvement is crucial because education is a human transaction, a social enterprise. What makes a school better is not its bricks and mortar, not the money spent per student or the computerized classrooms or the curriculum in use: Those are tools for people to use, and the people are what matter. Educators like Don Hugo, Bill Douglas, Cary Bell and Jim Turner know, as Hugo put it, that "when we begin to think better of ourselves, that belief system permeates the school. It becomes a self-fulfilling prophecy."

At bottom, the Hawthorne effect gives back something bigger than the sum of what's put into a project, and the difference comes from somewhere in the human spirit. The effect shows up in dozens of ways; every innovator in the field of education has stories about people or incidents that suddenly changed the whole nature of whatever was happening. And in isolation, such stories tend to sound romanticized, oversimplified, bathetic: the standard journalistic vignettes chosen to prop up a dubious success with a tear-jerking anecdote.

But the stories are real, and they are to be found in small programs across the country. Hawthorne is Laurie Wiedmann in Montana, working so many hours to prepare her new remedial reading program that her principal has to order her to take some vacation. Hawthorne is the kids from P.S. 126 on the Lower East Side of Manhattan, attending Saturday classes at the posh Brearley School in one of the city's public/private partnerships, and going back to their family shelters and welfare hotels with a taste of what education can be if there is order, purpose and the kind of facilities that make learning fun. Hawthorne is also Fannie Bunch in Indianapolis, following her son to school to keep him working, and going on to become a fixture in the city system. Like hers, most of the Hawthorne stories involve people growing and having epiphanies, large and small. Somebody decides, "Hey, I can do that," and somebody else says, "Well, if she can, I can too."

The Hawthorne effect works best when it comes in one program after another, spreading through a school like ripples in a pond. Thus, when a onetime college professor named W. A. Franklin became principal of the moribund Bowling Green High School in 1982, his first target for improvement seemed modest enough. He set out to raise the school's attendance record, which was in the bottom 10 percent in Kentucky. Franklin challenged a core group of faculty members to come up with a plan that would change the students' behavior. Their answer was a new incentive system: Any student with a perfect attendance record would be exempt from taking final exams. Some parents objected, fearing that the already weak school would lose what remained of its academic standing. So Franklin roped them into his reform structure. He put together a policy review committee including teachers, parents and student representatives. That led to a standing committee on school improvement, and a series of projects including building renovations, advanced placement classes, an antidrug program that won national recognition, and a set of leadership seminars. In attendance, which was the original priority, Bowling Green jumped to the state's top 10 percent, and the number of students permitted to skip their finals has risen from only ten in the first year of the program to more than five hundred with perfect records. But that was only the beginning of the change. Achievement test scores rose. At last count 70 percent of the graduates were going on to college, the school ranked in the top ten in the state in finalists for national merit scholarships, and improvement programs continued to multiply. In honoring Franklin as one of its educational heroes of the year for 1990, the *Reader's Digest* concluded that Bowling Green High School had become a place of pride.

The Hawthorne ripples from an innovation can be elusive and hard to document. Across the country, for example, literally hundreds of schools, from elementary through senior high, have installed conflict-mediation programs to teach children to resolve their own disputes, ranging from squabbles over petty gossip to full-scale gang wars. There are no hard statistics to prove that the programs have any effect on actual fighting, let alone on rates of truancy or disciplinary actions. But teachers and principals offer lavish anecdotal evidence that the programs not only work to keep peace but actually raise attendance, enhance self-esteem and lift a school's spirit. At Junior High School 45 in New York City's Bronx, principal Joseph Solanto was skeptical at first about the program, but then saw his students, most of them black and Hispanic, developing poise, confidence and self-esteem. He concluded that that was because of the program. "I've been won over," he told *The New York Times*.

And quite often, the Hawthorne effect can surprise everybody. When American Express and Shearson Lehman Hutton started the New York Academy of Finance in 1982, their aim was to modernize the city's antiquated vocational education program with a course aimed at training students who weren't college material to be bank tellers and back-office workers for Wall Street firms. In a sense, they succeeded all too well: 95 percent of the program's graduates get so fired up by the course that they go on to college rather than take low-level bank jobs. The program has since expanded to courses in public service and in travel and tourism, with similar early results.

The Hawthorne effect can also spread change from the school where it starts into the surrounding community. The Carnegie Corporation's widely praised 1989 report, *Turning Points*, singled out Louis Armstrong School, a middle school in the New York City borough of Queens, as a learning center for the whole community. The school provides a forty-minute Early Bird program that regularly attracts three hundred of its thirteen hundred students for early morning clubs and classes in sports, music, computers, crafts and foreign languages. After school, volunteers from the community come in to tutor students individually and to offer classes in computers and dance. There are Saturday classes for pupils from surrounding elementary schools, a summer program of workshops for teachers, and adult education in the evening offering English as a second language along with courses leading to the high school equivalency diploma. Finally, students from Louis Armstrong work in nonprofit service agencies at LaGuardia Airport, in TV and radio repair shops, and at the local police precinct.

There's only one problem in aiming for the Hawthorne effect, but it's a major one: Innovators must beware of being too ambitious and failing spectacularly. Small failures aren't necessarily fatal to a school. A modest program can be recognized as a mistake and abandoned without lasting damage, as long as other ventures are soon started. But a really humiliating disaster in a major reform provides the excuse for the enemies of change to say, "I told you so." Volunteers walk away, telling themselves that they won't make the mistake of trying again. And that kind of experience all but guarantees that no more changes will be tried in that school system for years to come.

The lesson in that is by now familiar: Start small. Apart from that, there's a lot of room for maneuver in deciding where to begin changing any school. Educational reform is an idea whose time has come; principals, school boards, even the unions are surprisingly willing to entertain ideas. There's also a lot of money available. Even in a time of federal spending crunch and tight state and local budgets, major experiments are going on with public funding. Foundations large and small provide billions of dollars for elementary and secondary education, much of it to support innovative small programs. And educational involvement is now fashionable for business. Across the country, there are more than 100,000 "partnerships" between corporations and individual schools, with corporate largesse ranging from donated equipment and summer internships to college scholarships and teacher incentives. In New York, Chicago, Miami and Minneapolis, businessmen have persuaded city officials to let them set up whole new experimental schools built around sweeping reforms. According to *Fortune*, business donated $2.1 billion to educational causes in 1988, and the trend is up. More than at any time in the recent past, innovators can probably find the money to try what they want.

But it's vital to remember that school improvement is never a one-shot proposition. Even if the radical reformers could find a nostrum for excellence and spoon it into every school in the country overnight, any school that stopped there would soon become boring and stagnant.

Good schools that keep their edge, like Shoreham–Wading River, are built around a flow of new programs designed to keep the Hawthorne effect going, creating excitement and energy among teachers, students, parents and the whole community. Like a shark that must swim constantly to keep water flowing over its gills, school improvement has to keep moving or die.

You're a principal, a teacher or a group of parents hoping to make a school better. Where do you begin?

Process is more important than product: the fact that a program is alive and working counts for more than its content. Nevertheless, programs must be carefully chosen. Among other things, you have to identify real needs in the school or community, find out about costs and sources of funding, figure out how the new idea meshes with programs that already exist, and mend your political fences.

If there is an idea already on the table, don't take it as given. A little time spent researching similar programs can save a lot of trouble, spot possible problems, turn up unexpected new angles and techniques, and generally help you avoid reinventing the wheel. You may find, as Steve Keeslar did, that somebody else is ahead of you—or that, like Jim Thom, you can't solve one problem without tackling others as well. In the "Sources and Resources" section of this book, you'll find some suggestions on how to locate information and advice; these sources will lead naturally to others as your plans progress. Educational reformers are usually generous with ideas and counsel, and there is a vast amount of information available. Local librarians can be enormously helpful.

The limits of any program are usually set by the amount of money available for it. An idea as ambitious as the Futures 500 scholarships needs a fairy godmother on the scale of Fannie Mae. There are such benefactors to be found, both as individuals and in corporate boardrooms. Since Eugene Lang pioneered the idea in 1981, literally scores of philanthropists have followed him in "adopting" a whole elementary class and promising to finance college for every child who doesn't drop out. That gesture tends to be more dramatic than successful; given the record so far, if you can find another rich person thinking of such an adoption, she might be persuaded to support another program instead.

Big corporations have been remarkably generous, starting with IBM (which gave $58 million for education in 1988 alone), Coca-Cola (pledging $50 million over ten years) and RJR Nabisco ($30 million over five years). Such companies have community relations departments that approve individual donations, but it never hurts to have a contact in the executive suite. Smaller companies can be just as lavish on their own scale, particularly in the communities where they operate. Do some research on local corporations: What's their charitable record? What kind of causes do they favor? Which bigwig has given a speech on education and can be challenged to back it up with money?

Don't ignore foundations. The big national honeypots like Ford and Carnegie can be approached, particularly with a truly novel idea, but the best bet is probably a small local trust with roots in your own community. Start with a list of contributors to your community chest or United Fund drive. And don't overlook local service clubs, which can come up with money, ideas and actual work. In Vermont, Cynthia Parsons found natural allies in local Rotary clubs and the statewide senior group, RSVP.

Even if funds were unlimited, it would be best to start small—particularly if a school is just beginning the effort to improve. Ambitious programs tend to metastasize malignantly, outrunning the time and effort available and producing more frustration than hope. A modest program can be modified in mid-course or even dropped without permanent damage. The innovators learn by doing, and can be more ambitious next time. The essential thing is that there must be a next time. Small bites are part of a continuing meal.

Schools are political, and you have to deal with the politics—or else, like Al Haskvitz, be prepared to do battle with the whole system. First identify friends and foes: What are the factions in your school, and what do they want? Who is likely to favor your idea, and whose ox will be gored? How can the program be changed to bring some opponents on board without cutting the heart out of it? Don't make unnecessary enemies; make sure you don't inadvertently alienate somebody by failing to invite, notify or consult. If there's a parent-teacher group and you're not in it, join, and spend some time planting seeds before springing your proposal. Or find a powerful sponsor in the PTA who will join your group. Make sure everybody who will be affected by the program understands it, especially the kids. If there are objections, try to put them to rest. Accept suggestions. Cultivate the principal; without her backing or at least consent, the program is dead. Sound out the building representative of the teachers' union. If opposition develops, try first to soothe and convert, second to neutralize or outflank. Open conflict is the last resort.

When the first program is up and running, cast around for the next one—and bring it along just as cautiously as the first. With success, you can be more ambitious. Sooner or later, someone will want to try versions of the radical reforms now being proposed on the national stage. If they seem right for your school, why not? In fact, it's worth remembering that if the big reforms prove worthwhile, every school in the country will have to phase them in just as you will grapple with your first program, whatever it is. You'll be in far better shape to make big changes work if you have had a little practice with small ones.

If you weren't an idealist, you wouldn't be trying school reform at all. But you will also need a lot of hard-nosed realism. If you haven't got the energy or political skills to get the job done, you must recruit a leader and be content to follow. If your idea won't fly, you'll have to drop it and try another one. Borrow ideas freely, but adapt them to fit your needs. Be flexible. The program is going to change, and the best you can do is try to keep the changes benign. Don't hide your light. The more the whole community knows about your program, the better, and a public relations effort is a necessity. But remember Cynthia Parsons: There's no limit to what you can do if you let somebody else take credit for it. Make sure credit is spread around liberally.

You're not going to achieve perfection, and you shouldn't try. Remember, the best is the enemy of the good. Remember too the very human people in this book, fighting through obstacles and their own shortcomings to succeed on balance at limited goals. They're no more superhuman than you are. If you fail, admit it openly and move on briskly to the next idea. But don't go dewy-eyed and set your sights too low, either. Sooner or later in any program, somebody is going to say, "If we can get to just one kid, the whole thing is worth it." No, it isn't. In the real world, you've got to do a lot better than that.

Since you *are* an idealist, you are willing to begin the long journey. Good luck, and keep the faith. The enemy is mediocrity, and his allies are indifference, cynicism and despair. Don't give up. Nothing you can do is more important than helping children learn. Nobody can hand you any formula to solve all the problems at once; there isn't any shortcut to making schools better. But that's also the good news: Once you get involved, you get to make one small miracle after another. Who could ask for a better reward?

APPENDIX
Sources and Resources

For readers who want to pursue small-bite reform in general or follow up on the programs in this book:

The best general source is the U.S. Department of Education. Its small pamphlet, "What Works: Research About Teaching and Learning," is an admirable brief summary of recent research and thinking about education, written in English, with a high quotient of common sense. It is surprising and refreshing to find such a book being produced by a government. The pamphlet is no longer in print, but reference copies are available at some liberaries.

The Department of Education also collects specific information about small-bite programs in something called, bafflingly, the National Diffusion Network. The NDN identifies programs, claims to verify that they are effective, selects promising ideas for funding on an experimental basis, and spreads information about successful programs that schools can adopt. The NDN is itself an important resource: It can work with local schools to develop new ideas or help schools identify their problems and adopt suitable programs that already exist. Each year, NDN programs are installed in about 29,000 schools, and 83,000 teachers and administrators receive NDN training. There are NDN facilitators in every state. The central NDN address is National Diffusion Network, Office of Educational Research and Improvement, U.S.

Department of Education, 555 New Jersey Ave. N.W., Washington, DC 20208-5645. Phone: (212) 219-2134.

For the NDN catalogue, *Educational Programs That Work*, a compilation of about 450 successful programs, send $10.95 plus $2.00 for shipping to the publisher, Sopris West Inc., 1140 Boston Ave., Longmont, CO 80501. Each program is described in a page of text, including its goals, tactics, procedures, requirements, costs and a contact for more detailed information.

A similar list of eighty-eight programs, some of which are also covered in the NDN catalogue, is called *The Learning Bank*. It can be had for $10 from the National School Boards Association, 1680 Duke St., Alexandria, VA 22314. Phone: (703) 838-6722.

A more specialized pamphlet is *Education That Works: An Action Plan for the Education of Minorities*. This includes descriptions of dozens of individual projects, all of them specifically targeted at minority students. Single copies are free if you send a 10-by-12-inch envelope, self-addressed, with $2.90 in postage. Write to Project Director, Quality Education for Minorities Project, 1818 N Street N.W., Suite 350, Washington, DC 20036. Phone: (202) 659-1818.

Turning Points, a 1989 report by the Carnegie Corporation's Council on Adolescent Development, is a fine general discussion focused on early adolescence; it includes capsule descriptions of several dozen programs. It is available for $9.95 from the Carnegie Council on Adolescent Development, 11 Dupont Circle N.W., Washington, DC 20036. Phone: (202) 265-9080.

For information on the enriched remedial English program at Parkway North High School, contact Carol Kolar, director, Reading and Writing Center, Parkway North High School, 12860 Fee Fee Road, Creve Coeur, MO 63146. Phone: (314) 851-8349.

Information about the Futures 500 scholarship and mentoring program can be obtained from Lonnie Edmonson, manager, Futures 500 program, Federal National Mortgage Association, 3900 Wisconsin Ave. N.W., Washington, DC 20016-2899. Phone: (202) 752-7850. At Woodson High School, contact Aona Jefferson, director, Futures 500 program, H.D. Woodson High School, 55th and Eads Streets N.E., Washington, DC 20019. Phone: (202) 724-4500.

For San Antonio's peer tutoring program, get in touch with Dr. Maria del Refugio Robledo, director, Partnership for Valued Youth, Intercultural Development Research Association, 5835 Callaghan, Suite 350, San Antonio, TX 78228-1190. Phone: (512) 684-5389.

The National Organization of Student Assistance Programs and Professionals is at 250 Arapahoe, Suite 301, Boulder, CO 80302. Phone: (303) 443-

5696. For the Moorhead High program, contact James A. Thom, director, Student Assistance Program, Moorhead Senior High School, 2300 Fourth Ave. South, Moorhead, MN 56560. Phone: (218) 236-6400.

Information on helping parents with preschool children can be had from Claire Eldredge, dissemination coordinator, National Center for Parents as Teachers, Marillac Hall, University of Missouri–St. Louis, 8001 Natural Bridge Rd., St. Louis, MO 63121-4499. Phone: (314) 553-5738. For the program in Hamilton, contact Steven C. Keeslar, elementary principal, Hamilton Community Schools, R.R. 1 Box 208, Hamilton, IN 46742. Phone: (219) 488-2101.

Alan Haskvitz can be reached at Suzanne Middle School, 525 Suzanne Road, Walnut, CA 91789. Phone: (714) 594-1657.

Cynthia Parsons and SerVermont are at P.O. Box 516, Chester, VT 05143. Phone: (802) 875-2278.

For help in starting parental-involvement programs, contact Ms. Trili Smith, Parents in Touch, 901 N. Carrollton, Indianapolis, IN. 46202. Phone: (317) 226-4134.

For information on the HOSTS remedial program, the source is William E. Gibbons, chief executive officer, HOSTS Corp., 1801 D Street, Suite 2, Vancouver, WA 98663-3332. Phone: (206) 694-1705. In Helena, contact Marion Evenson, director of student services, Helena Public Schools, P.O. Box 5417, Helena, MT 59604. Phone: (406) 442-5773.

Help in starting a Kohlberg-style moral education program can be had from Ann Higgins, consultant, Lawrence Kohlberg Program, Dept. of Psychology, Fordham University, 441 E. Fordham Rd., Bronx, N.Y. 10458. Phone: (212) 579-2175. Advice is also available from Anthony Arenella, lead teacher, Scarsdale Alternative School, Post Road, Scarsdale, NY 10583. Phone: (914) 723-5500 ext. 144. Betsy Rulon, another Kohlberg researcher, is at 17 Channing St., Cambridge, MA 02138. Phone: (617) 354-4862.

For the Cleveland Scholarship Program, get in touch with Christina Milano, executive director, 1380 E. Sixth St., Cleveland, OH 44114-1606. Phone: (216) 241-5587.

In starting a student advisory program, contact Dr. Cary E. Bell, principal, Shoreham–Wading River Middle School, Randall Road, Shoreham, NY 11786-9745. Phone: (516) 929-8500. Dennis Littky is principal of Thayer High School, Winchester, NH 03470. Phone: (603) 239-4381.

There are several excellent programs that I have mentioned, but did not cover in detail since they seemed too ambitious to be called small-bite projects. For information on the Comer model schools, contact Dr. James P. Comer, Yale Child Study Center, P.O. Box 3333, New Haven, CT 06510. Phone:

(203) 785-2548. For the Coalition of Essential Schools, Theodore Sizer, chairman, Department of Education, Brown University, Providence, RI 02901. Phone: (401) 863-3384. For the Accelerated Schools Project, Henry M. Levin, director, Center for Educational Research, Stanford University, CERAS 402, Stanford, CA 94305-3084. Phone: (415) 723-0840.

Information on the Trans*parent* voice-mail system for schools can be had from Dr. Jerold P. Bauch, director, The Betty Phillips Center for Parenthood Education, Box 81, Peabody College of Vanderbilt University, Nashville, TN 37203. Phone: (615) 322-8080.

The National Academy Foundation, the highly successful effort to upgrade vocational education for the financial community, the travel industry and other occupations, is located at 660 Madison Ave., Suite 1804, New York, NY 10021. Phone: (212) 754-0040. Phyllis R. Frankfort is executive director.

An explanation of direct instruction, the behavioral approach to learning, can be had from Prof. Siegfried Englemann, Department of Teacher Education, University of Oregon, P.O. Box 10459, Eugene, OR 97440. Phone: (503) 346-3555.

Dr. Uri Triesman, who developed the study workshop program for black students, can be reached at the University of Texas at Austin, Department of Mathematics 8.100, RLM Building, Austin, TX 78712-1082. Phone: (512) 471-7711.

For information on New York City's Public/Private School Partnerships, get in touch with the Office of School and Business Linkages, New York City Board of Education, 110 Livingston St., Room 628, Brooklyn NY 11201. Phone: (718) 935-3275.

There are many programs teaching conflict resolution techniques and a National Association for Mediation in Education, based at the University of Massachusetts in Amherst. In New York, Effective Alternative in Reconciliation Services (EARS) is at 3013 Webster Ave., Bronx, NY 10458; contact Marcy May. Phone: (212) 920-6313.

For sources of funding, there are several directories available from The Foundation Center, 79 Fifth Ave., Dept. TE, New York, NY 10003. Phone: (212) 620-4320. They are expensive; try the local library first. *The Foundation Directory* ($175) lists 7,500 of the largest national foundations, with detailed information. *The Foundation Directory Part 2* ($140) gives similar data on 4,200 middle-size foundations. The *National Data Book of Foundations* ($125) has little more than addresses, assets and annual expenditures for thirty thousand foundations, nationwide. There is also the *National Directory of Corporate Giving* ($175), offering quite detailed information on twelve hundred corporate foundations and five hundred direct corporate charity programs, and *Corporate Foundation Profiles* ($125), with even more detailed profiles of 250 of the largest corporate programs.

There are far too many good books on education to permit listing. However, for a good summary of current thinking on major reforms for the schools, read *Smart Schools, Smart Kids* by Edward B. Fiske (Simon & Schuster, New York, 1991). For a detailed study of Shoreham–Wading River Middle School and three other exemplary middle schools, all facing widely different challenges, read *Successful Schools for Young Adolescents* by Joan Lipsitz (Transaction Books, New Brunswick, N.J., 1984). For a provocative approach to educational reform, try *The Quality School: Managing Students Without Coercion,* by William Glasser M.D. (Harper & Row, New York, 1990). Glasser is a psychiatrist who applies to education the thinking of W. Edwards Deming, the neglected American prophet who taught the Japanese how to produce quality goods after World War II.

ACKNOWLEDGMENTS

I owe many thanks. At *Newsweek*, editor-in-chief Rick Smith and editor Maynard Parker generously approved the working schedule that made the book possible. Jerry Footlick was an invaluable source of information and perspective; Tom Morganthau, Aric Press and David Alpern all provided counsel and encouragement. Farai Chideya's perceptive reporting was the basis for much of chapter 11, and a brief account of the Kohlberg program appeared in the magazine.

A great many people gave me time and information. I am particularly grateful to Nancy Berla, at the National Committee for Citizens in Education, and Beth Peckham-Jones of the *Reader's Digest*. Jane Glickman at the Department of Education, Barbara Finberg at the Carnegie Corporation, Andrea Taylor of the Ford Foundation and Hugh Price at the Rockefeller Foundation were all helpful. Thanks also to Rosalie Byard of the Brearley School, Laurel Kanthak at the National Association of Secondary School Principals, Kathy Russell of the National PTA, Marcy May at Effective Alternative in Reconciliation Services, and Jacqui Marshall at *The Washington Post*.

For help in reporting on Parkway North, particular thanks to Carol Kolar, Rosemarie Stocky and Don Hugo. I am indebted to John Borsa, Larry Moceri, Jackie Morgan, Don Natale, Fred Schue and Don Senti. Henry Levin provided indispensable background. I learned a great deal from the students, including Felicia Boxley, Darrell Cole, Andre Cotte, Eddie Current, Kevin Frye, Perez Green, Antoine Jones, Lamont Kemper, Lisa Longhi, Kristy Lueck, Jennifer Matthews, Alex Ogniben, Jacquetta Peoples, Laura Rader, Julie Sapit, Mitchell Stovall and Ricky Wood. I am grateful to Rosemarie Stocky for letting me use her doctoral thesis, "The Effects of Integrating Reading and Writing Skills Across the Curriculum: A Senior High School Model," presented to the graduate school of St. Louis University, 1990.

In the Futures 500 program, Lonnie Edmonson, Harriet Ivey, Aona Jefferson and Lucile Christian were indispensable. Special thanks to Janice Daue for her patience and energy. Henry Cooper, Garey Crosson, Caroline Fitzgerald, Ken Friedman, Harrison Hewlett, Jacqueline Lovingood, Donna Purchase and Ingrid Williams were candid and generous with their time. My thanks and best wishes to students Ronald Benson-El, Alicia Doughey, Romia Huggins, Marguerite Smalls, Marlisa Smalls and Natalie Thomas.

At the Partnership for Valued Youth, special thanks to Cuca Robledo, Merci Ramos and Frances Guzman. Dr. Jose Cardenas was indispensable. I am grateful to Manuel Bejarano, Sharon Collums, Maria Ferrer, Louise Gaitanos, Gilbert Garcia, Sylvia Glass, Linda Grimm, Aurelio Montemayor, Victor Ortiz, Roddi Stevens, Annette Taute, Nelda Wiest and Laura Yzaguirre. My admiration and respect to Gilbert Hernandez. Thanks for time spent with Jesse Chavez, Alicia Hernandez, Mike Goff and Laura Longoria.

At Moorhead High School, Jim Thom was tireless and extremely generous. I'm in debt to Toni Bach, Cathy Bjorklund, Kathy Bossart, Jan Childs, Mary Churchill, Donovan Dulski, Lynn Halrast, Russ Henegar, Bill Iverson, Bob Jernberg, Scott Matheson, David Miller, Corrinne Pestes and Lynn Sipe. Students Tracy Bostick, Amy Cermak, Rachel Elofson, Sara Forsythe, Matt Kloeck, Hans Nielsen and Leah Roy were talented and forthcoming.

In the Hamilton Community Schools, my thanks and respects to Steve Keeslar, Beth Muntzinger, Gary Nordmann and Becky Norris. I am grateful to Lynn Bercaw, Cherie Dick, Pam Harger, Sue Hile, Nila Howard, Jill Mason, Ellen Moor, and Pam and Randy Shoemaker. At Parents as Teachers in St. Louis, Sue Trefeisen and Mildred Winter were helpful. I enjoyed meeting Kathie Dick, Charlie and Maggie Howard, Jacob and Libby Moor and Kayla Shoemaker.

It is a treat to know Alan and Irene Haskvitz, and I hope they still consider me a friend. In Walnut, California, thanks also to Judy Arlotti, John Cassato, Brian Cole, Frank Girard, Ken Gunn, Linda Lee, Sam Maloof, Don Skraba, Georgia Titov and Genevieve Vaughn. I profited from talking with Sujee Dissanayake, Maribelle Estrella, Paul Karapetian, Erbie Phillips, Chad Turner, Aaryn Urell and Phillip Wener.

In Vermont, Cynthia Parsons is unique. I am also in debt to Jack Coleman, Tony Krulikowski and Rebecca Warren.

At Parents in Touch in Indianapolis, special gratitude to William Douglas, Frances Richey, Trili Smith and Izona Warner. Thanks also to Tom Bonjour, Fannie Bunch, Sue Cooper, Marsha Foley, Dave Gish, Cheryl Guindon, Wilma Harry, Phyllis Imel, Rosena Johnson, Arlene Shoffner, Terry South, Susan Stiffey, Debbie Williams, Dodie Whitmer and Robert Zetzl.

In Helena, thanks and compliments to Marion Evenson and Jim Turner. I'm in debt to Alice Anderson, Greg Broadway, Gloria Gabaldon-Lesueur, Bernie Hartman, Ken Kohl, Rhonda McCarthy, Tom Miller, Brad Morris, Alice Morse, Bonnie Noble, Dave Pepin and Laurie Wiedmann. William Gibbons and Jerald Willbur of HOSTS were generous with their time. I enjoyed talking with Anne Adams, Kelly Burningham and Nicholas Gailushas.

At Roosevelt High School in the Bronx, special thanks to Ann Higgins and Al Sternberg. I am grateful to Michelle Birtz, Betsy Rulon, Susan Sedlmayer, Paul Shapiro and Marlene Warren. At Scarsdale High School, Tony Arenella and Susan Silva were generous and open with Farai Chideya. We learned a lot from students Keya Ambrose, Lisa Fairstein, Lee Gross, Sasha Kopelowitz, Arahm Lee, Joyce Matthew, Desi Morales, Ben Newman, Rigoberto Ocasio, Vanessa Rivera, Sarah Sagran, Atricia Stanley, Milagros Talentino, Ian Weston and Ian Worth. I have drawn on several papers by Ann Higgins, including a chapter called "The Just Community Educational Program: The Development of Moral Role-Taking as the Expression of Justice and Care," from the book *Who Cares?*, edited by Mary Brabeck (Praeger, New York, 1989); and a chapter, "Educating for Justice and Community: Lawrence Kohlberg's Vision of Moral Education," from the forthcoming book *Handbook of Moral Behavior and Development: Volume 3*, edited by W. M. Kurtines and J. L. Gewirtz (Lawrence Erlbaum Associates, Hillsdale, N.J.) I have also used *Lawrence Kohlberg's Approach to Moral Education*, by F. Clark Power, Ann Higgins and Lawrence Kohlberg (Columbia University Press, New York, 1989).

In Cleveland, I am particularly grateful to Tina Milano. Denise Roberts and Dorothy Valerian were helpful and generous. My thanks to Ethel Adrine, David Bergholz, Richard Boyd, Bob Coplan, Lily Drayton, Denise Duncan, Robert Ginn, Martin Gottlieb, Carol Keske, Vance Holt, George M. Humphrey II, Claudette McCraw, Paul Patton, Howard Steindler, Juanita Storey, Grace Weidenthal, Jim White and Mayor Mike White. I learned from students including Richard Bulgin, Kellie Edwards, Marc Graham, Anthony Hoges, Laquisha Jones, Cornell Jordan, Senetta Mays, Nichelle Porter, Anthony President, Gino Ranieri, Tomeka Robinson, Iptesam Saleh, Sonya Shakir, Melissa Snowden and Craig Wilson.

At Shoreham–Wading River, special thanks to Cary Bell and Ross Burkhardt. Dennis Littky and Joanne Urgese were generous and helpful. I am in debt to Allyson Adams, Bonne Sue Adams, Diane Burkhardt, Frank Caldorale, Matt Cavanaugh, Bob Coons, Carol Eriksen, Kathy Hild, Jennifer Hough, Pat Kearon, Winnie Pardo, April Pokarny, Jerry Silverstein and Diane Wikstrom.

No journalist is without debt to his colleagues. I have read and profited from stories in *The New York Times*, *The Washington Post*, *Newsweek*, *Time*, *Fortune*, *Forbes*, *The New Republic*, the *Phi Beta Kappan*, *Education Week*, *Teacher* magazine, *Teacher Education Quarterly*, *Educational Leadership*, *The NEA Today*, *The American School Board* and the *Harvard Educational Review*, among many others.

In a book on education, I particularly want to thank my own teachers. Among them, my high school principal, Dick Spiess, is a lasting model of care and integrity. At the University of Edinburgh, Tom Burns taught me how to see familiar things as if for the first time. I will be in their debt for life.

Index